Studies in the Philosophy of Paul Ricoeur

Studies in the Philosophy of Paul Ricoeur

Edited by Charles E. Reagan

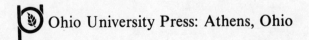Ohio University Press: Athens, Ohio

Printed in the United States of America by Oberlin Printing Co.
All rights reserved.

Library of Congress Cataloging in Publication Data
Main entry under title:

Studies in the philosophy of Paul Ricoeur.

    Bibliography: p.
    "Bibliography of Paul Ricoeur, Franz Vansina": p.
    1. Ricoeur, Paul—Addresses, essays, lectures.
I. Reagan, Charles E.
B2430.R554S78   194   79-10343
ISBN 0-8214-0223-4

To my wife Sharon

Contents

Abbreviations

CI: *The Conflict of Interpretations: Essays in Hermeneutics*, ed. D. Ihde (Evanston: Northwestern University Press, 1974).

FM: *Fallible Man*, trans. C. Kelbley (Chicago: Henry Regnery, 1965).

FN: *Freedom and Nature: The Voluntary and The Involuntary*, trans. E. Kohak (Evanston: Northwestern University Press, 1966).

FP: *Freud and Philosophy: An Essay on Interpretation*, trans. D. Savage (New Haven: Yale University Press, 1970).

H: *Husserl: An Analysis of His Phenomenology*, trans. E. Ballard and L. Embree (Evanston: Northwestern University Press, 1967).

HT: *History and Truth*, trans. C. Kelbley (Evanston: Northwestern University Press, 1965).

MV: *La Metaphore vive* (Paris: Editions du Seuil, 1975).
[Editor's note: When the essays in this volume were written, the English translation of this book was not yet published. Thus, all references to it are to the French version. It has recently been translated under the title: *The Rule of Metaphor: Multi-disciplinary Studies of the Creation of Meaning in Language*, trans. Robert Czerny (Toronto: Toronto University Press, 1977).]

PS: *Political and Social Essays*, ed. David Stewart and Joseph Bien (Athens: Ohio University Press, 1974).

SE: *The Symbolism of Evil*, trans. E. Buchanan (New York: Harper & Row, 1967).

PREFACE[1]

Paul Ricoeur

RESPONSE TO MY FRIENDS AND CRITICS

I thank Charles Reagan for giving me the chance to respond to the authors of the texts he has collected which deal with my work. I am indebted to the most critical of them because they did not limit themselves to showing the gaps and inconsistencies in my writings, indeed even exposing their mistaken orientations, but also they suggest corrections or reorientations that would be compatible with the main line of my work. With respect to those who are most favorable to my enterprise, I am indebted to them in another way: they do not limit themselves to giving a version—frequently clearer than my own—of analyses with which they agree, but they propose to the reader interpretations which go beyond the present state of my work, either by seeing a greater coherence in it than appears in the wide variety of titles and themes, or by sketching out lines of development which anticipate some future work, or by marking the gaps which could be filled by resources in my published work. To this extent the most favorable articles rejoin the most critical ones. This is why the order of my responses will not be determined by whether or not the articles are favorable, but by how radical their criticism, whether positive or negative. As a consequence, according to this ordering, I will address my first and my last comments to the articles which make the most incisive objections.

Robert Solomon finds odd the fact that "unlike Descartes" I have "never bothered to write anything like a 'treatise on the passions'." This is true. I have not written the previously planned "empiric of the passions." It is also true that in *Freedom and Nature* emotion figures only among the forms of the involuntary. This is why I am so attentive to the hermeneutic of the passions sketched in the fifth part of Solomon's essay and developed in his book, *The Passions.*[2]

Having admitted this much, I will take the liberty of making several remarks about my fragmentary contributions to this hermeneutic. With respect to the chapter on emotion in *Freedom and Nature,* I will underline only that its general aim is to rehabilitate emotion in opposition to the moralists and even to Sartre. Considered within the framework of a general theory of motivation, emotion is entirely that which arouses and moves, that is, incites to action. Replaced within this framework, emotion arises more from the complementary relation between the voluntary and the involuntary than from their dichotomic relation and would be put, like imagination, on the level of mediating factors. Furthermore its bodily component calls for the sort of synthesis between phenomenology and an objective approach that Solomon correctly demands.

I would like to add two more things. I would not want to classify emotion, as Solomon wants to do, as a species of the genus passion. The passions of which I speak in the *Symbolism of Evil,* following Kant—the passions of power, possession, and esteem—presuppose a will capable of embracing a totality of existence and capable of investing itself in a single thing. That is why the passivity of the passions is a completely different thing from that of the emotions. The passivity of the latter is simply bodily while the passivity of the passions is a complex form of the servile will. Beyond this heterogeneity between passion and emotion which is greater than Solomon admits, I would suggest that feeling is yet a third affective entity. I devoted the third part of *Fallible Man* to it under the title of "affective fragility." The characteristic of mediation between the voluntary and the involuntary that affectivity has is there strongly affirmed. But is feeling completely affectivity? Does it not have its own traits which distinguish it from emotion and from passion? To feel—to experience?—is a way of interiorizing any "object" that we have put at a distance and thus to assimilate to ourselves that which we have first objectified. Besides, feeling seems to have a specific relation with poetic imagination; poetic feeling, it seems to me, is a metaphorical transposition of emotion. Thus tragic Terror and Pity, described by Aristotle in the *Poetics,* are modes of fear and compassion, but "purified," according to the famous *Katharsis,* by the poetic word. But I readily admit that the domain of "affects" is far from having received from philosophers the same attention as that of knowledge or even that of action. I suspect that the concept of "passivity" covers highly heterogeneous phenomena which first ought to be distinguished from one another. We would not recover the profound unity of a being capable of feeling [*être-affecté*] except at the price of a laborious and ascetic ontological analysis such as that of Michel Henry. A Poetic of the Will cannot fail to take into account such an ontology of "passion" [*pâtir*].

I am grateful to David Stewart for having emphasized the mid-point of *Fallible Man* in my *Philosophy of the Will* for two reasons: first, the analysis of the structures of fallibility are at the "midpoint" [*milieu*] between the pure eidetic of the will and the symbolic of evil. Second, these structures of fallibility themselves constitute the mid-point, the fragile mediation, between the infinite pole and the finite pole in the trilogy of knowing, acting and feeling. In order to characterize the humanism which arises from this ontology of fragility and in order to oppose it to that of Sartre, David Stewart had the good idea to bring together *Fallible Man* and two other texts, "Negation and Primary Affirmation" and "What is Humanism?" The place of negation in this humanism is thus defined by its role with respect to the "fragile mediation" in the philosophical anthropology of *Fallible Man*. It is in the same way, in the sense of a limit, that I include it in the ultimate meaning of humanism: negation is an irreducible component of the anthropology of finite or bound freedom, which is another name for fragile mediation.

Mary Schaldenbrand, in an essay of rare insight, has placed my fragmentary contributions to the problem of imagination against the background of this problematic of fragile mediation. She is completely correct to tie the pivotal function of imagination to the theme of "kinship through conflict" which is the very meaning of the philosophical anthropology of *Fallible Man*. I learned a great deal from this study on three counts. First, she shows the continuity, not only of my interest in imagination from *Freedom and Nature* even to *The Rule of Metaphor,* but the continuity, from one book to the next, of the *theme* of "mediating imagination." In the successive contexts where the question of imagination is raised, it is always true to say that "imagining mediates opposition." In this respect, the change of viewpoint, from the phenomenological psychology of my first work to the hermeneutics of poetic function in my last work, has not entailed a change but rather a deeper investigation of the mediating function of imagination.

Second, I am grateful to Mary Schaldenbrand for having seen the inadequacies of the first analysis in the three volumes of *The Philosophy of the Will,* as well as their value in anticipating later analyses which take what she calls "a linguistic turn." Inadequacies: the danger of psychologism, the persistence of the perceptual model borrowed from Husserlian phenomenology, and finally, the affirmation without proof of the mediating role of the poetic image. Concerning the anticipations, she is right to emphasize that the analysis of the myths of evil already appeals to the mediation by texts which will be central in *The Rule of Metaphor.* In the same way, she is justified in saying that the resistance to any reduction of the imagination to fantasy, along psychoanalytic lines, and the recognition of a progressive-regressive dynamics of the image, proceeds from an interpretation of the symbolic function which already borders on metaphorical imagination.

Third, what most interested me in Mary Schaldenbrand's article is the way in which she ties metaphorical creativity to the constitution of the person and thus sketches out the ethical implications of the analyses of mediating imagination. Having done this, she boldly goes beyond these analyses and invites the reader as well as myself to think more thoroughly and to grasp better the idea that the freedom of imagination is also the imagination of freedom. To do this, we must go backwards, from *The Rule of Metaphor* to the problematic of *Fallible Man* and take up again the question left hanging about the mytho-poetic function and its relation to the constitution of the person. It is still an unaccomplished task for a Poetics of the Will, to link together imagination, ethics, and freedom.

If the philosophical anthropology of *Fallible Man* constitutes a good introduction to Mary Schaldenbrand's reflections on the mediating function of imagination, the latter constitutes an appropriate background for the reflections of Charles Reagan on "Psychoanalysis and Hermeneutics" and those of Patrick Bourgeois on the development which leads from "The Hermeneutics of Symbols to the Interpretation of Texts."

Charles Reagan has been willing to reconsider the whole discussion of the rather strange epistemological status of psychoanalysis in which a mixed discourse oscillates between, on the one hand, the language of natural science, mechanics, hydraulics, or neurology; and on the other hand, the language of intentions, motives, and purposes. He thus tests my thesis according to which this mixed language is well-founded to the extent that its object is itself mixed: the semantics of desire lies between desire and culture. Charles Reagan sees my thesis closer to the reformulations of the Freudian metapsychology in intentional terms of A. Flew, S. Toulmin, and R.S. Peters than to the reformulations in terms of an observational science of behavior. The weakness of intentional reformulations, according to him, is the usual failure to account for the right "to extend" intentional and motivational language outside of the sphere of consciousness. But this is precisely the problem of psychoanalysis. In order to give an account of my own position Charles Reagan has had the good idea to illuminate the theses of my book on Freud by my attempt to apply the model of the text to intentional action ("The Model of the Text: Meaningful Action Considered as a Text"). The semantic autonomy of the text with respect to the intentions of the author seems to hold the answer to the question left unresolved by the proponents of the intentionalist thesis, that is, how can the intentional model be extended beyond the control of consciousness. Moreover, by thus understanding psychoanalysis as an interpretation of semantically autonomous texts he thwarts the temptation to see it as an empirical science. Finally, he can account for psychoanalytic practice itself.

I am very appreciative to Charles Reagan for this rapprochement that I had overlooked. But he not only supports my thesis, he pushes much farther than I did in *Freud and Philosophy* the kinship between psychoanalytic explanation and historical understanding, emphasizing the narrative component included in analytic explanation. Since *Freud and Philosophy,* I myself have made some progress in the same direction, but at the cost of a considerable reworking of my overall interpretation of psychoanalysis. Instead of beginning with an account of the meta-psychology, I would begin now by examining the criteria of what counts as a fact in psychoanalysis, as a function of the therapeutic situation itself, and I would subordinate the evaluation of the metapsychology to this first inquiry at the level of case-histories. It is at precisely this level that we must recognize the claim of the narrative component of psychoanalysis (See my "The Question of Proof in Freud's Psychoanalytic Writings").[3]

The role attributed by Charles Reagan to the model of the text in the solution of the problems in Freudian epistemology leads to the commentary that Patrick Bourgeois devotes to the development running from "a hermeneutics of symbols to the interpretation of texts." I will first point out the parallelism between this evolution and the one analyzed by Mary Schaldenbrand. She has clearly shown that the development of the mediating imagination leads to a poetics of the imagination where metaphor is a text in miniature. Addressing himself directly to the epistemology of hermeneutics, Patrick Bourgeois describes quite well the three phases through which my definition of hermeneutics has passed. It was first centered on the interpretation of expressions with a double meaning which I called symbols. Then hermeneutics was defined by the interpretation of creations of meaning based on the polysemy of language. Lastly, hermeneutics received the same extension as the notion of a text to the extent that the text preserves at the level of its composition as a whole an intentional plurivocity. In giving an increasingly wider field of application to interpretation, these three definitions gave rise to a correlative enlargement of hermeneutics itself. Actually, it was not until *The Rule of Metaphor* that I came to understand the rule-following, systematic character of this enlargement. That is why Patrick Bourgeois is right to question the necessary character of a development which can appear to be dependent on the relatively contingent variety of fields of research: philosophical anthropology, psychoanalysis, linguistics, etc. Moreover, we can legitimately ask if the notion of a text contains in itself precise criteria of application and thus also a limit to its use.

David Pellauer responds to these questions in his remarkable essay. He begins by showing that the progressive enlargement of the hermeneutic field becomes apparent only after a certain number of problems have been solved. First, it was necessary to subordinate the semiological function (attached to the signs of the language [*la langue*]) to the semantic function (bearing on the original functioning of speech [*la parole*] in the framework of the sentence). Next, it was necessary to include the semantic function itself in a theory of discourse, understood as the work of speech, governed by generic laws such as those which control poetic or narrative composition. Based on this theory of discourse, it was still necessary to account for the transition from speech to writing by the fixation of the very meaning of the discourse in a medium external to the speaker. It is this phenomenon of *fixation* which makes possible the triple autonomy of the text with respect to the intention of the speaker, with respect to the first listener, and with respect to the original situation. Finally, once "textuality" itself has been identified, it is possible to correctly pose the problem of reference in the case of poetic discourse, where language appears closed on itself and "celebrates itself," to use an expression of Roland Barthes. David Pellauer completely accounts for the linking together of these problems.

In addition, he shows quite well how the question of distanciation, sharpened by reading and discussing Gadamer's main work *Truth and Method,* is grafted on that of the fixation of discourse through writing and on that of the autonomy of the text which results from it.

But in my view David Pellauer's contribution is most valuable in his discussion of the criteria for the extension of the concept of text. The question, in fact, cannot help but be troubling to the extent that the notion of text leads itself to applications of which a simple enumeration—from the dream to sacred texts, passing through every work exhibiting composition and style—does not seem to be able to limit. The enumeration does not even stop with works of discourse if it is true that we can analogically apply the notion of the text to human action, to the extent that it is not only meaningful but that it presents a kind of semantic autonomy by which it lends itself to a sort of "reading." In spite of this disturbing proliferation of applications, David Pellauer is right in looking for an internal principle of limitation of the concept of text first in the notion of discourse, then in that of fixation. The latter is implied in the notion discourse but is already contained in the gap which separates event and meaning, the saying and the said, in all discourse. But I willingly admit that it is not always easy to distinguish what is paradigmatic from what is only analogical in the use of the concept of text.

I will stop here a moment to compare the conclusions of Mary Schaldenbrand with those of David Pellauer. The first sees in mediating imagination the pivot of all of my analyses. The second also attaches the pivotal value to the achievement of the paradigm of the text for all of hermeneutics. I wonder if my two critics can both be right at once? To be honest, I am not well prepared to answer. First, because it is difficult for me to see my books and my articles as steps or stages in a single development. Each seems to be to be rather a response to a particular question determined by the questions left unanswered in the preceding work. Thus, *The Symbolism of Evil* is the result of a reflection on the limits of the pure eidetic employed in *Freedom and Nature.* In the same way, *Freud and Philosophy* attempts to answer the objection of a hermeneutics of suspicion which was ignored in *The Symbolism of Evil. The Conflict of Interpretations* tries to answer a greater challenge, the intersection of psychoanalysis and semiology. *The Rule of Metaphor* tries to give the semantic foundation which was lacking in my previous theory of symbol. In addition to my work looking discontinuous, I often feel uneasy that, after *The Symbolism of Evil,* all of my works are detours with respect to the interrupted line of *The Philosophy of the Will.* It is against this background that my friends draw two firm lines of development which correct my impression of my work as heterogeneous and displaced from its principal aim. But are these two general interpretations competitors? I will risk the following hypothesis: it is the mediating imagination which constitutes the guiding line of an underlying philosophical anthropology; thus it has ontological value. On the other hand, the text has a paradigmatic value for the epistemology of this ontology. Also, the two lines cross in many places: the one, mediating imagination, culminates in the tensive process of metaphor, which is a poem in miniature, thus a text. So the first general interpretation leads to the second. But, in turn, the text is only a segment of the hermeneutic arc; its hermeneutic function is to lay out a *world* in which I can understand myself. By appropriating the meaning of this world, the epistemology of the text is curved back towards ontology (and even towards ethics, if we follow the suggestion of Mary Schaldenbrand according to which mediating imagination and the constitution of the person are two interdependent processes). I willingly admit that it is one of the tasks of a Poetics of the Will to show that these intersections and exchanges between the problematics of epistemology and ontology (and even ethics) are not artificially postulated.

If this convergence of mediating imagination and the paradigm of the text has not yet been thought through for its own sake, it is at least at work in those of my essays devoted to the applications of philosophical hermeneutics to biblical exegesis. Beatriz Melano Couch concentrates on these essays in her perceptive article which I reinterpret in my own way in light of the two lines already developed. On the one hand, in effect, these essays can be placed in the extension of the line going from symbols to the text. From this point of view, biblical hermeneutics draws all the methodological consequences of the profound changes in philosophical hermeneutics coming after Heidegger and Gadamer: the role of writing with respect to speaking, the semantic autonomy of the text, the primacy of "the world of the text" over the intention of the author, finally, the subordination of self-understanding through the text to the explication of the new being projected by the text. In this sense, biblical exegesis is a particular field of application of a philosophical hermeneutics which moves from symbols to texts. But if we turn towards the specificity of the world of the text, thus towards the originality of the new being that it projects, biblical exegesis no longer appears as only a branch of hermeneutics, but as a singular task having as its stake the power of certain texts to "name God." This properly kerygmatic task thus transforms philosophical hermeneutics, which before encompassed biblical hermeneutics, into an *organon* included in biblical hermeneutics. But this reversal can be understood as an extension of the line marking the primacy of mediating imagination. Indeed, the new being announced by biblical texts can be interpreted as fundamentally imaginary. Before addressing themselves to a will from which they demand obedience, these texts appeal to an imagination which they open to new and radical possibilities. Religious symbols thus appear as the text of this fundamentally imaginary being.

To finish I would like to turn to the serious questions raised by Richard Zaner. If hermeneutics is without absolute knowledge, if it is always the arena of a conflict of interpretations, if, finally, it always involves a gamble—whether in the "pre-understanding" which begins the process, or in the appropriation that ends it—what is the status of the reflection of which hermeneutics is the development? Also, what sort of self emerges from this open process, this conflict, this gamble? Richard Zaner offers a strong objection. Philosophy, in its ultimate act of reflection, he says, cannot be itself a hermeneutics under pain of lacking the *phenomenological evidence* which alone can found the pretension to the truth of hermeneutic philosophy. The same objection can be formulated from the point of view of the self and no longer only of reflection. If we say with Freud that self-consciousness is just as deceitful as the consciousness of things is doubtful, then reflection on the self loses all certitude and remains forever an unfulfilled task, a simple idea in the Kantian sense. The "wager of reflection" thus doubles "the risks of the self," to use the terms of the title of Richard Zaner's essay.

This double objection, concerning the status of reflection and that of the self, leads the author to wonder if the phenomenological principle of ultimate evidence has not been sacrificed to the task of interpreting symbols. Furthermore, weren't the seeds of abandoning the central principle of evidence already sown in the decision to give up the eidetic of consciousness for the hermeneutic of symbols (then of texts)? But, continues the author, we cannot abandon this principle under the penalty of not being able to give any sense to the axiom that the symbol gives rise to *thought*, for thought is a judgment which appeals to some mode of evidence. Philosophy, therefore, cannot be at its very roots hermeneutics, but meta-hermeneutic. The systematic level of philosophy ought to be different from, and superior to, that of hermeneutics on which philosophy reflects: "the *statements about* the hermeneutical task, and the *practice of* hermeneutics," says Zaner, "are *not* at the same level."[4] It follows from this, in particular, that the Freudian adventures of consciousness and the self [*moi*]—from the disappropriation of an illusory meaning to the reappropriation of a symbolic meaning—do not attain the reflexive level where one finds Husserl in his egology and in his theory of transcendental intersubjectivity. Husserl asks a radically different question from that of every psychoanalysis: what are the conditions of possibility of being-as-self? The hermeneutic could not thus "go further" than the initial eidetic. If a dream or a text *must be* interpreted, it is still the principle of evidence which requires it to the extent that it leaves no other choice than "to interpret." In conclusion, philosophical discourse on equivocity must itself be univocal, if it wants to be philosophical. Thus philosophical reflection must not take part in the flow of symbols.

It is not possible to respond to this objection without taking up again the whole question of the relations between phenomenology and hermeneutics, as I began to do in an essay which bears this title.[5] I do not believe that hermeneutics replaces phenomenology. It is only opposed to the idealist interpretation of phenomenology, that is to say, to the claims that the ultimate foundation of all truth lies in the evidence of the Cogito. But hermeneutics presupposes phenomenology in at least three respects. First, it is phenomenology which by the reduction of natural evidence opens the question of meaning. Next, phenomenology makes interpretation a moment in the understanding of the self. Finally, it founds the understanding of the self in the self-evidence of the Cogito. Hermeneutics does not deny the self-evidence of the Cogito. It affirms only the purely formal character of this evidence. It is evident that consciousness is intentional; but what does it aim at concretely? It is evident that I am always in an historical situation: but in which situations? It is evident that I can always reflect, but what are the real obstacles to reflection? From paragraph nine on in the *Cartesian Meditations* Husserl suggests that the apodicticity of the evidence does not imply that it is adequate. We understand why. If the "I think" is an "I am," then the concreteness of experience is inseparable from the position of the "I think." The point of the criticism is thus marked, "regarding the possibilities of its fulfillment [i.e. that of the presumption implicit in the apodictic evidence] and their range (which may be apodictically determinable)." Husserl continues:

"How far can the transcendental ego be deceived about himself? And how far do those components extend that are absolutely indubitable, in spite of such possible deception? When making certain of the transcendental ego, we are standing at an altogether dangerous point, even if at first we leave out of consideration the difficult question of apodicticity."[6] That is why Husserl writes that "*adequacy and apodicticity* of evidence *need not go hand in hand.*"[7]

It is true that at this period Husserl does not yet give up the idea of an ultimate subject, of a "non-interested" mediating ego, not involved in the flow of his thoughts. This reflexive distance becomes problematic in *The Crisis,* where meditation *(Besinnung),* having become inseparable from the very history of the philosophical act, puts into play a "back-questioning" *(Rückfrage)* bearing on the "achievements" *(Leistungen)* of thought and aiming at finding again the ground of an ultimate foundation. The *mediating ego* is implied by the same stroke in the history on which it reflects.

Why is this so? Because transcendental reflection cannot extend beyond essential truths such as: consciousness is intentional, perception is presumptive, the understanding of the self is a process of interpretation, etc. These essential truths certainly constitute a very extensive network and are not limited to the empty formula *I* equals *I*. Moreover, these essential truths are, as Zaner requires, dependent on the phenomenological evidence. But it is this phenomenological evidence itself which discovers it is purely formal and which asks that pure reflection be carried out, become real in the very work of interpretation, which always finds itself caught in an historical situation and in a certain symbolic configuration. We ought not limit ourselves to making the movement from hermeneutic understanding towards a reflection which reflects on this hermeneutic understanding. We would be able to content ourselves with it if reflection bore on objects from which it would be able to effectively stand apart. But that on which it reflects is also reflection, in particular the understanding of the self through symbols and texts, and this hermeneutic understanding is what pure reflection needs in order to become real. In other words, the reflection on which the *ego meditans* reflects and from which it distinguishes itself by a secondary reflection is also that which can concretely carry it out. There is thus a double relation between abstract reflection and concrete reflection: a regressive relation of reduplication and distanciation of the second with respect to the first; and a progressive relation of making effective or carrying out of the first with respect to the second. This complex relation between two levels of reflection has the paradoxical character of a distance abstractly established and concretely abolished. This paradox has as a consequence an equally paradoxical status of the truth itself. The evidence of the *ego cogito cogitatum*, borne by the ultimate act of reflection, is enough to engender the *Idea* of univocal truth, as the limiting idea of philosophical discourse, and which is valid consequently for hermeneutic reflection also. But this evidence cannot be transferred to any of the contents of concrete reflection, which remains an open, conflictive process and which depends on some wager.

It is to this epistemological condition of hermeneutics that I attach, for my part, the necessity of humbly listening to the philosophers of the past. Michel Philibert suggests that this attitude, for which he generously gives me credit, is in accord with the instructions of the apostle Paul concerning the exercise of truth in charity. I would say, in turn, that these evangelical instructions express the recognition of the status of the truth in the hermeneutic order and consecrate that status by stamping on it the seal of charity.

Between the apodictic evidence of the ultimate reflection and the process of interpretation, there cannot be, therefore, anything other than a relation of endless *approximation*. Moreover, this relation of approximation is itself never known by absolute science. It too can only be presumed and stated in the modest and uncertain formula that I borrow from Gabriel Marcel: "*I hope* to be *in* the truth." The truth, not only formal and abstract, but actual and concrete, ceases to be asserted in a Promethean act of taking a position on the self by the self and of adequation of the self to the self. The truth is rather the lighted place in which it is possible to continue to live and to think. And to think *with* our very opponents themselves, without allowing the totality which contains us ever to become a knowledge about which we can overestimate ourselves and become arrogant.

Châtenay-Malabry

May, 1978

[1] Translated by Charles E. Reagan.

[2] Editor's note: Robert C. Solomon, *The Passions* (Garden City, N.Y., Anchor Press, 1977).

[3] Editor's Note: This article has been published in the *Journal of the American Psychoanalytic Association* 24 (No. 4, 1977). Also in C. Reagan and D. Stewart, editors, *The Philosophy of Paul Ricoeur: An Anthology of His Work* (Boston: Beacon Press, 1978) pp. 184-210.

[4] Editor's note: See below, p. 44.

[5] Editor's note. Ricoeur refers to his article "Phenomenology and Hermeneutics," *Nous*, XI, no. 1 (1975) pp. 85-102.

[6] Editor's note: E. Husserl, *Cartesian Meditations*, trans. D. Cairns. (The Hague: Martinus Nijhoff, 1960), p. 23.

[7] *Ibid.*, p. 22.

ACKNOWLEDGMENTS

I wish to acknowledge here my gratitude to all of the contributors to this volume and especially to David Stewart with whom I have had many hours of conversation on Ricoeur's work. I also thank Paul and Simone Ricoeur for the generosity and hospitality they have so graciously extended me and my family on many occasions during the past five years.

EDITOR'S INTRODUCTION

This collection of original essays on the work of Paul Ricoeur is aimed at readers who already have some acquaintance with his writings. These essays represent various approaches to his work: Some contain expositions of key concepts, such as "text," "symbol," "interpretation." In others we find the development of a theme, such as "imagination as mediator," traced across Ricoeur's writings, from the earliest to the most recent. Other contributors offer extensions of Ricoeur's themes and ideas, working out the details of his suggestions or applying them to new areas. Finally, some of the essays advance objections to certain of Ricoeur's methodological and substantive positions.

I do not intend to offer here a brief (and necessarily superficial) introduction to Ricoeur's work. There are already a number of such introductory overviews available, both book length and articles. François Lapointe has contributed to this collection (see Ch. 10) an updated bibliography of secondary sources. For an introduction to Ricoeur's own writings, I recommend the collections of articles compiled by him, *History and Truth* and *The Conflict of Interpretations*; or edited by others, *Social and Political Essays* and *The Philosophy of Paul Ricoeur: An Anthology of His Work*.

A second, and to my mind more persuasive, reason for not attempting a brief introduction here is that Ricoeur's work is so diverse and so vast. He has written on phenomenology, existentialism, symbolism, religion, language, psychoanalysis, politics, and metaphor. He has produced a phenomenological study of freedom, a long, detailed account of the symbols of evil, an extensive and profound study on Freud and psychoanalysis, and a virtual encyclopedia on metaphor. No modern philosopher, with the possible exception of Bertrand Russell, has written so much on so many different topics.

There is obviously no way that this collection could cover all of these topics. However, a wide and diverse range of topics is treated: Robert Solomon gives a very critical review of Ricoeur's remarks on emotion and passion. He claims that Ricoeur has never given a proper account of emotions for their own sake and that when he does speak of emotions he leans towards the view of emotions as forces rather than as acts. David Stewart has written a very engaging article on Ricoeur's 'humanism,' comparing him with Sartre and contradicting the common misconception that humanism must be atheistic and that Sartre is the sole representative of modern French humanism. Richard Zaner challenges Ricoeur's deviations from a more orthodox phenomenology, and Mary Schaldenbrand traces the importance of imagination as mediator in a number of Ricoeur's works.

Patrick Bourgeois discusses the progress of Ricoeur's philosophy of language from the rather limited concern with symbols to his more recent hermeneutics of texts. David Pellauer focuses on the importance of the text in Ricoeur's hermeneutical theory while Beatriz Melano Couch devotes her article to the interpretation of religious symbols in his work. Michel Philibert, a long-time friend of Ricoeur's, writes about his method, and more importantly, his attitude, his way of approaching philosophy. My contribution is an explanation of what Ricoeur means by psychoanalysis as hermeneutics. Finally, I am pleased that Francois Lapointe and Frans Vansina have given us revised and up-dated versions of their bibliographies, the first a bibliography of secondary sources and the second an abridged bibliography of Ricoeur's philosophical writings.

I

Robert C. Solomon

PAUL RICOEUR ON
PASSION AND EMOTION

This essay is a critical examination of what Ricoeur has to say about passion and emotion. While he has not given us a treatise on the passions he does give us a "sketch" in *Freedom and Nature*. Like so many other philosophers, Ricoeur treats passion and emotion as an addendum or a parenthetical aside, at best, to his more sweeping philosophical theories. What emerges from that brief sketch is a portrait of the passions so unappealing that it is no wonder that they play a minimal part in the rest of his philosophy. In short, he sees emotion on the side of the involuntary, less than wholly human, pathological. At best they are ambiguous or paradoxical. Throughout, Sartre and Ricoeur are compared and criticized. The author concludes with suggestions of what must be done to correct these sketches and to develop ultimately a proper theory of emotions.

Robert C. Solomon is Associate Professor of philosophy at the University of Texas at Austin. His principal publications are *From Rationalism to Existentialism, Phenomenology and Existentialism, Nietzsche, Existentialism*, and *On the Passions*.

Paul Ricoeur on Passion and Emotion

Robert C. Solomon

I. The Problem of Passion

Paul Ricoeur is a passionate philosopher. It is what first strikes the reader in his *Symbolism of Evil*. It is even apparent in his most austere study of Husserl. Beneath the elegant prose of serious scholarship, we are aware that this is a man *concerned*. His religious concern with the phenomena of sin, guilt, and defilement are only the most obvious examples. There is also rapture and ecstasy, and talk of Dionysus, desire and passion in general. And then too, love and fear. The difficult language, the learned references, the technicalities retained from traditional philosophy and theology, all of this makes Ricoeur's books and essays appear completely in the guise of academic philosophy, appropriate to the most distinguished post-Husserlian in France today. But in fact, he has far more of the passionate spirit of his teacher, Gabriel Marcel.

But what is odd about this is not the striking contrast between the difficult prose and the underlying passion—that is in the best French intellectual tradition. Reading Descartes, for example, Ricoeur immediately sees through the metaphysical distinctions that usually give rise to the most familiar bloodless controversies in modern philosophy and finds himself not so much persuaded as *moved:*

> The opposition of my being to the being of things, powerfully reinforced by my awareness of my own capacity for being, can very well move in the joyous mood which Descartes evokes in his *Treatise on the Passions* and his *Letters*. [FN, p. 65]

What is odd is rather the fact that Ricoeur, unlike Descartes, has never bothered to write anything like a "treatise on the passions," or to develop a theory of emotion, despite the fact that his entire philosophical enterprise is, in an important sense, supported by them. But the reason for this neglect, I suspect, is not hard to ascertain. In *Freedom and Nature* he does give us, not a theory, but a sketch of passion and emotion (much less, however, than Jean-Paul Sartre's "esquisse" of several years before). He tucks it away in the middle of that mammoth volume, and, like so many other philosophers, Ricoeur treats passion and emotion as an addendum or a parenthetical aside, at best, to his more sweeping philosophical theories.

But what emerges from that brief sketch is a portrait of the passions so unappealing that it is no wonder that they play a minimal part in the rest of his philosophy. At one point he says, "all passions make us unhappy." In general, and like his great predecessor Descartes, he finds emotions and passions to be less than wholly human, and he even quotes the distinctively Cartesian notion of "spirits" (that is, "animal spirits" in Descartes, also in Malebrance) in his characterization [FN, p. 256]. Consider the following passage, one of many:

> Emotion is a nascent disorder which constantly puts us on the way towards the pathological. [FN, p. 272]

and in *Symbolism of Evil;*

> . . . Henceforth included in the same existential category, which is called "flesh," "desires of the flesh," "care," "fear," "the sorrows of this world"; all of these words denote the opposite of liberty, [rather] slavery, bondage to the 'weak and beggarly elements.' [SE, p. 141]

Not a pleasant picture, particularly in the heart of a philosopher who is very much in the French rationalist tradition, however that tradition may be disguised under any number of more Romantic images.[1] In a philosophy devoted to intellect and will, the apparent "pathology" of the passions plays little positive part. This was true of Kant, and it is true of Ricoeur. But just as Kant ultimately finds the analysis of *feeling* to be the cornerstone of the third *Critique* which ties his *Critiques* of Reason and Will together, so I suspect that Ricoeur will find the same synthesizing element, precisely in this area he has so easily neglected.

II. PASSION AND EMOTION:
THE VOLUNTARY OR THE INVOLUNTARY?

Ricoeur's theory of passion and emotion is to be found almost entirely in the first volume of his *Freedom and Nature: the Voluntary and the Involuntary*. In fact, literally speaking, it is confined to a dozen or fewer pages in the middle of that book, although hints and supports can be found elsewhere. In *Symbolism of Evil,* passions and emotions are mentioned and invoked (possibly also evoked) and are the subject of analysis throughout; for example, there is defilement, sin and guilt (pp. 81, 161 and *passim*), despair (287), rapture *(ibid),* ecstasy *(ibid),* joy and frenzy (245) anger (299), scorn (48), anguish *(ibid),* dread (25), hope *(ibid),* fear *(ibid),* shame (40) and so on. The book is full of passions and emotions, but short on analysis. (What analysis there is fits in perfectly with the theses developed briefly in *Freedom and Nature,* as I shall soon show.) Ricoeur's admirable book on Husserl, as one would expect, tells us little about the passions. Although perhaps a passionate advocate of his own methodology, Husserl was hardly concerned with the less cognitive aspects of human existence. A few passing hints are the most we get; one must rather look to his followers, Heidegger and Scheler, for an attempt at phenomenological analysis. Heidegger, despite his famed mention of *mood* in *Being and Time*—hardly any analysis, given how little is dissected there—leaves the emotions in general and the structure of moods unresolved. Scheler, on the other hand, makes perhaps the best attempt to date to provide us with precisely such an account, and Ricoeur is evidently moved by it considerably:

> For my own part, I believe that there exists a certain emotional revelation of values in a given situation and that Max Scheler gave ethics a satisfactory orientation by his conception of the *emotional a priori.* [FN, p. 74]

Then too there is Ricoeur's book on Freud which would seem to promise a rich fund of theoretical concerns for the nature of passion and emotion. But the findings are disappointing, more because of Freud than Ricoeur. Freud never developed a theory of passion and emotion (or should we say, a theory of the *affects*), and he too can be seen to waver between a number of very different and sometimes inconsistent analyses.[2] Consequently, the argument centers on a topic parallel at least in form to Ricoeur's earlier work, the biological and the teleological, the mechanical versus the symbolic—in other words, the involuntary versus the voluntary. But where do passion and emotion fit into this long-established Aristotelean-Kantian—and now Ricoeurian dichotomy? It is surely not obvious in Freud (though he clearly tends to the involuntary). Neither was it clear in Aristotle, Kant, or Descartes, Malebranche, Hobbes, Hume, Nietzsche or Sartre, though all of them (excepting the last) also leaned to the involuntary. Ricoeur, more than most philosophers, has indicated (but scarcely argued) that the passions and emotions present a difficult intermediary position; or perhaps we should say, an *ambiguous* phenomenon. And to appreciate Ricoeur's insights and his troubles, we must turn to *Freedom and Nature* in particular.

Like his many predecessors, he easily gives way to the involuntaristic tradition:

> . . . the ambiguity of most emotions which bring together the truly corporeal involuntary of emotion strictly speaking and the intimate involuntary of the passions. [FN, p. 277]

But his position is qualified. For example, he comments that there is an intimate connection between emotions, passions and judgments, particularly "rapid, implicit value judgments." [FN, p. 256] This is complicated by the fact that these are *bodily* judgments, a general theme that remains as obscure in Ricoeur as it did in his friend, Maurice Merleau-

Ponty. "Obscure" because, in this instance in particular, it is never clear whether it is bodily *actions* that are in question (or that generalized form of intentionality that Merleau-Ponty called "motility") or rather bodily *reactions,* physiological impulses and their like. The latter alternative is surely supported by much that Ricoeur says, not least his talk of "physical stirring" and "organic paroxysm" [FN, p. 279] and his invocation of Descartes' "spirits". Ricoeur's view is finally confused by the links he suggests between passion and imagination [e.g., FN, p. 23], the view that "it is consciousness that *binds itself*" [e.g., FN, p. 280; italics mine] and, becoming "alienated," "provides an opportunity for mechanistic inter-pretation." [FN, p. 272] Like Sartre, he invokes the image of "the magic of consciousness" and "the acquiescence of will." [FN, p. 276] Not surprisingly, Ricoeur peppers his analysis with an emphasis on the "ambiguity" [FN, p. 277], the "paradoxes" [FN, p. 250], even the "mystery" of passion. In *Symbolism of Evil,* he comments:

> While it is indefinite, the *guilty* conscience is also a *conscience* that is shut in. . . . It "separates" itself in the very act by which it takes upon itself, and upon itself alone, the whole weight of evil. The guilty conscience is shut in even more secretly by an obscure acquiescence, in its evils by which it makes itself its own tormenter. It is in this sense that *the guilty conscience is a slave and not only consciousness of enslavement;* it is *the conscience without "promise".* [SE, p. 146; italics mine]

What are we to make of this? In a phrase, "voluntary or involuntary"? Sartre, employing similar metaphors in his "Esquisse d'une théorie des émotions"[3] of 1933, speaks of "consciousness degrading itself,"[4] of a voluntary "captivity,"[5] of a "trap in which we are caught"[6] and, most famously, of emotions as they "perform magical transformations of the world."[7] I mention these similarities, although Ricoeur does not mention them, because it seems clear to me that these two luminary French philosophers, although of markedly different temperaments and interests, were fighting the same struggle against the traditional view, and although both saw the means of overcoming it, neither succeeded in doing so. Ultimately, both philosophers were caught in the tradition, the view of the passions and emotions as *in*voluntary. Accordingly, I want to spend what may seem to many of Ricoeur's followers an inordinate amount of energy comparing them throughout this essay. (I shall do so most critically in section 4.) My intention, however, is ultimately to construct a theory that will do justice to both of them.[8]

Let us look more closely at the "ambiguities" that riddle Ricoeur's analysis of passion and emotion. First, however, it is necessary to separate those two terms, which we have so far been using in simple conjunction. In French, as in English, "passion" connotes a more violent and obsessive phenomenon; "emotion" less, (and "sentiment" still less). Théodule Ribot, for example, (the William James of French psychology) writes in his *Essai sur les Passions:* "A passion is an emotion prolonged and intellectualized: passions are *explosive."*[9] More recently, J.-A. Rony, in *Les passions,* distinguishes them similarly, "passions [are] violent emotions. . .incapable of adaption and obsessive."[10] The usage is similar in German, between *Leidenschaft* (passion, with obvious etymological connotations of "suffering," as in English "passion" and the French) and *Gefuhl* (emotion, more or less). Ricoeur, following this tradition, tells us that "emotion is the youth of our passions" [FN, p. 278], and "emotions. . . are the dawn of all passions" [FN, p. 278] and "emotion is nascent or renascent passion, because it is always its initial point." [FN, p. 278] The point is clear enough; emotion is the first stirring of feeling while passion is its full-grown and often violent development. Yet, even on this simple point, Ricoeur is not at ease. On the same page as the preceding illustrations, he comments; "There are always emotions which passion revives from a minor shock. In this sense all passion, which has the entire body to amplify it, takes on emotive form," [FN, p. 278] and, a bit before, "emotion is born of passion and passion of emotion." [FN, p. 277] And, "The majority of emotions, such as joy, sadness, fear or anger, arise from a ground in passion which introduces an involuntary factor other than wonder or shock. Here emotion appears as an ardent moment of passion." [FN, p. 277] This is not a serious confusion. On the one hand, Ricoeur wishes to bow to traditional usage and give "passion" a punch that "emotion" does not have. At the same time, he recognized the close interrelatedness of the two. More problematically, however, that interrelatedness has too much of the traditional theory embedded within it, as the previous quotations will show ("involuntary," "shock" and the stress on *body*). I myself would want to make the distinction in a more simple way; "passion" is the generic term and "emotion" refers to one of the species, in contrast to moods and desires, which are also passions but not emotions. The *intensity,* on this account, would not enter in at all; emotions may be as violent as passions, and passions might be calm and enduring, not at all obsessive (though surely concerned) and little involved with bodily rumblings of any obvious sort. But it is enough, for our purposes here, to point out the need to be cautious, to read into particular contexts for the distinction that Ricoeur is drawing, or not drawing, between passion and emotion. For the purposes of what more I have to say about him here, the distinction is not of crucial concern.

There are a number of recurrent themes in Ricoeur's analysis, decidedly distinct and not obviously compatible. There is a strong emphasis on "disorder" [FN, p. 272, 276, *et passim*] and "agitation". [FN, p. 277]. These terms are frequently found in the traditional literature, for example, in Descartes, Spinoza, Leibniz and Malebranche. More interestingly, they are frequent in Sartre and in Gilbert Ryle's *Concept of Mind*, in which "agitation" becomes the central term in the analysis of emotions proper. The terms are significant, because they indicate the inferior status that emotions and passions receive in philosophy generally, as confusions (as in Leibniz and Spinoza), as distorters of reason (as in Descartes and Malebranche), and as *breakdowns* in our normal patterns of behavior (as in Sartre and Ryle).

There is also continuous talk of the "involuntary," sometimes "involuntary factors" [e.g., FN, pp. 277, 279], sometimes as a rough equivalent of "unconscious actions" or "material events." [SE, p. 40] Most often, it is used in the usual contrast with *voluntary,* that which *we do* as opposed to what *happens to us.* Illuminating in this regard is the number of times that Ricoeur uses the notion of "shock" in regard to the emotions. [esp. FN, pp. 267-280] (Compare Sartre's analysis of "the face at the window.") The continuous emphasis on the body, particularly "physical stirrings" and "paroxysms" are clearly in line with a host of traditional theories, including the medieval physiological theories about bile, gall, spleen and phlegm, as well as the very sophisticated theories of James and Lange (and many others) in which the emotions are essentially nothing other than physiological disturbances of the viscera and central nervous system. At no point does Ricoeur defend any such thesis, although he discusses it at considerable length, with no special reference to emotions, in his book on Freud. [Cf. FP, pp. 71-86] But the ghost (an inapt metaphor) of such physicalistic theory hovers over his sketch throughout *Freedom and Nature.*

But there is a very different set of themes, all of which suggest that emotions and passions should rather be placed on the *voluntary* side of Ricoeur's central dichotomy. In *Symbolism of Evil,* for example, he tells us,

> If, then, man is essentially speech, the "passions" of speech are cardinal passions. Parmenides had already noted the bond connecting opinion, error, and confusion in naming. Now the "passions" of speech are *not passive passions,* so to speak. [SE, p. 340; italics mine]

And in the same passage quoted earlier in which he talks of "guilty conscience as a conscience that is shut in" [SE, p. 146], he adds that "it *'separates' itself* in the very act by which it *takes upon* itself . . . the whole weight of evil." [SE, p. 146; italics mine] The voluntaristic significance of this is evident, and it bears more than superficial resemblance to Sartre's thesis that "consciousness transforms itself" and "traps itself." In the key passage of his analysis, Ricoeur expresses this voluntaristic view explicitly:

> *Passion is consciousness which binds itself.* It is the *will making itself prisoner* of imaginary evils, a captive of Nothing, or better, of Vanity. Since its role is to rule over its body, *the will can only be its own slave.* Nourished by the wind and victim of the vertigo of fatality, *passion is in its essence wholly mental.* But it has very close dealings with emotion, which is most frequently its *physical stirring.* . . . Hence the ambiguity of most emotions which bring together the *truly corporeal involuntary emotion strictly speaking* and the *intimate involuntary of passions.* We can always find in fear and in rage the emotion of wonder, but also *a secret ruse of the will, an obscure complaisance to the vertigo.* This is why we could not approach these emotions directly. The *hidden purposiveness of fear* and rage which consciousness *adopts in order not to* follow a course of conduct of courage and mastery sums up the most *tortuous deceptions* of passion and far exceeds the context of bodily rebellion. But the *disorder* of the body which it amplifies gives to passion *the alibi it seeks* just at the right time. The *magic of consciousness* is not simple and many passions burn in it. It conceals a certain *acquiescence of the will of which emotion is never more than an intermittent corporeal flame.* [FN, p. 277, italics mine]

Despite the marked passivity of the final two sentences, the entire paragraph places passion clearly on the side of the voluntary. Passions may bind us, yes, but it is *consciousness that binds itself,* just as it is guilt that *takes on* its burden of evil. And insofar as passion is a "victim of vertigo," it is clearly a vertigo of its own imaginary design ("making itself a prisoner of imaginary evils. . ."), and even the insistence that emotion is "corporeal involuntary" and passions "intimate involuntary" is overpowered by the voluntaristic language that surrounds it. Passions and emotions are *willings.* But they are *deceptive* willings. (Again, compare Sartre, and in certain examples, Freud as well.) Fear and rage involve "a secret ruse of the will" and a "hidden purposiveness." And, again reminiscent of Sartre, Ricoeur makes it clear that emotions (or at least, certain emotions) are strategies of avoidance and escape, deceptions adopted by consciousness "in order not to follow a course of conduct of courage and mastery." Much earlier, he had made the same point:

> The bondage of passions is a bondage to *Nothing.* All passion is *vanity.* Reproach, suspicion. concupiscence, envy, hurt and grief are various names for chasing after the wind. This fiction, this lie, reveals the decisive role of imagination in the genesis of passion. [FN, p. 23]

"Fiction," "lie,"—hardly terms appropriate to physiological churnings or involuntary "shocks" and "distortions." The view emerges, therefore, of passions and emotions as purposive activities, laden with significance. And this view, in Ricoeur as in Sartre, brings the problem of passion clearly into that realm where philosophers reared in the phenomenological tradition can say things of great importance. Moreover, insofar as the key to passions and emotions is their *significance* (albeit a deceptive significance, which is why Ricoeur comments above that "we could not approach these emotions directly"), this brings them into that realm of symbolic analysis and hermeneutics in which Ricoeur has so distinguished himself. In fact, I would argue that such is precisely the account of emotions which recurs throughout *Symbolism of Evil* and his more recent work on interpretation and faith. But it is always hidden by the traditional involuntaristic model. Here is Professor Ricoeur, for example, doing a hermeneutics of the passions in spite of himself:

> In fact, the symbol, used as a means of detecting and deciphering human reality, will have been verified by its power to raise up, to illuminate, to give order to that region of human experience, that region of confession, which we were too ready to reduce to error, habit, *emotion, passivity*—in short, to one or another of the dimensions of finitude that have no need of the symbols of evil to open them up and discover them. [SE, p. 355, italics mine]

With the first part, we have a promising prolegomenon to an analysis of emotion and passion; but with the second, we have a flagrant return to the traditional view. But Professor Ricoeur betrays himself in his own analyses: we have already seen how his analysis of guilt (which pervades much of *Symbolism of Evil*) is interpreted neither in terms of passivity nor finitude. And consider his discussion, in the same work, of the passions of the tyrant; "that [unjust] desire is a creation of injustice and not vice versa. 'Injustice' then, and not the 'body' as such, makes desire a disease of the soul." [SE, p. 34] Now an adequate analysis of this move would go far beyond the scope of this paper, but let it suffice to note that the very idea of "injustice," from Plato and Aristotle through Hobbes, Rousseau, Marx and anyone else you like, is a *vice*, the contrary of a *virtue*, and thereby, as Aristotle tells us, *a state of character* and *an activity of the soul*, nothing *passive* at all (except, that is, insofar as we have to be brought up "correctly"—or in this case "wickedly"—as a necessary condition). In much more contemporary parlance, we might say that what is being discussed here is the *constitution* of the soul (and the world), and the matter at stake is of immense importance for any adequate understanding of the passions. That point (here with reference to desire rather than emotion or passion in general) is that *passion is a very sophisticated and highly developed system of constitutions*, and that *much of what is treated simply as the consequence or as the "stimulus" of our passions is in fact part and parcel of their symbolism*. There are more dramatic and well-developed examples throughout *Symbolism of Evil*, but the point is made, and I see no reason to pursue it further at this stage of the argument. Let's just say, what Ricoeur often *says* about the passions and what he sometimes *does* with them are strikingly different. And where what he *says* is a slip back to the traditional involuntaristic model and what he *does* with them sometimes provides us with the very best examples of his hermeneutical method, it is clearly the latter that is to be preferred.

III. THE ROLE OF METHODOLOGY

With respect to the problem of the passions, Ricoeur says virtually nothing about methodology. With respect to *Freedom and Nature*, as a whole, however, methodological considerations are evident throughout. In an obvious sense, the methodology is essentially *phenomenological*, but with as much evidence of the influence of Merleau-Ponty as of Husserl. (Many, of course, Merleau-Ponty foremost among them, would deny the severity of this difference.) Husserl's influence is evident, even when Ricoeur takes pains *not* to use Husserl's name to defend his own theories, the emphasis on "embodiment," of course, establishes a firm link with Merleau-Ponty and "existential phenomenology." Several recent inter-preters, notably Don Ihde, would rather say that Ricoeur's method has always been *hermeneutic*, even in *Freedom and Nature*.[12] Yet there need be no dispute on the matter, for there seems to be general agreement that there is continuity between the methods. I for one, find little reason even to distinguish them, except in some special cases. And what is so startling and possibly unique about Ricoeur's "methodology" is precisely the fact that he toys with them all—phenomenology, biology, psychoanalysis, linguistic analysis—and plays them off against one another. In *Freedom and Nature*, one might well say that the dominant methodology is Husserlian or Merleau-Pontian phenomenology: there is explicit use of the *epoché* and there is continuous emphasis on the *eidetic* reading of the Will to display "the fundamental possibilities of the Will." But there is always the appeal to other sources as well, as in Merleau-Ponty, and so the phenomenological reading is always balanced by clinical, traditional, theoretical, linguistic, or biological considerations.

Now all of this might seem to be a digression from our main concern, an understanding, critique and reconstruction of Ricoeur's sketch of the passions, but it is not. Let me state the connection as I see it, as simply as possible. Are passions "possibilities of the Will"? The heart of phenomenology, as I see it and as Ricoeur sees it, is its emphasis—at least as a methodological starting point—on *subjectivity*, or what one might call, "the first person standpoint." This, I take it, undercuts whatever momentous differences there may be between Husserl and Merleau-Ponty (and many other Phenomenologists) as well as including various key figures from the history of European philosophy, Descartes, Kant, and

Hegel in particular. In *Freedom and Nature*, Ricoeur uses this notion of "subjectivity" and its obvious contrast, "objectivity," to considerable advantage, playing them against each other and correcting the one-sided view each affords. Objective viewpoints (for example, empirical psychology) provide both a guide and a supplement to the phenomenological (subjective) method, but more than that, they help us to understand a certain obvious *internalization* of objective theories, when we provide allegedly subjective descriptions which in fact prove to be objective theories. (Much of Husserl's perpetual harping on "the pretheoretical" and "the things themselves" was an attempted curative for this subversion; more critically, it must be asked whether it is possible to have any phenomenological description without the infiltration of objective theories. The answer, and one of Ricoeur's most enduring contributions to phenomenology, would seem to indicate "no.")

With regard to the study of the passions, this use of phenomenology, combined with more objective viewpoints, has immediate benefits. By always keeping in mind Sartre's dictum that "it is *my* emotion that is under investigation," one avoids the traditional trap—the professional hazard of most psychologists—of paying attention only to the "publicly observable" aspects of emotion; their physiological components, their bodily manifestations and behavioral tendencies in actions, gestures and assorted "expressions." But keeping the objective parameters of emotion in mind, we can avoid the equally disastrous danger of assuming that our emotions are *only* certain modes of experience, independent of physiology, body and behavior. But even here, we can begin to see why Ricoeur's phenomenology of emotion is so "ambiguous": from the subjective side, it is apparent to him (as it was to Sartre), that emotions have a *significance*, a *meaning*, and therefore deserve to be analyzed as *projects*, as *symbols*, even as "lies" and "fictions." From the objective side, he appreciates the physiological and bodily components, the degree to which emotions can be *caused* and beyond our wills, and he adopts that mode of description which takes emotions (and passions in general) as phenomena that *happen* to one. The problem in Ricoeur is that these are never adequately tied together, at least in *Freedom and Nature*, and the discordant threads of each mode of description dangle loosely, as the fringes of a tapestry rather than as its fabric. (The problem in Sartre is quite different, though the result is the same; he opts for a wholly subjective stance, and loses much of what an objective corrective might offer him.)

It is at this point that Ricoeur's later methodology may be of some help to us, particularly in his treatment of Freud. Ricoeur himself sees *Freud and Philosophy* as a corrective to phenomenology as well as a corrective to the sometimes impossible theories of Freud himself. It is important to note that *Freud and Philosophy* is already explicitly hermeneutic in method as *Freedom and Nature* was not; he distinguishes the phenomenological hermeneutic as one of *belief*, the Freudian hermeneutic (and it *is*, he insists, a hermeneutic) as one of *suspicion*. The key point here is this: phenomenology begins with the Cartesian assumption that what one describes *in one's own case* has a certain privileged status. Phenomenological descriptions are, in an important sense, incorrigible. Freud argues just the opposite (as had Nietzsche before him), that what is "closest to us" might also be least known, and that it is not only possible but sometimes even likely that we shall misdescribe our own experiences. Where the emotions are at stake, it is hard to dispute this. (The question then, almost self-answering, is why phenomenologists and philosophers in general have so long avoided them.) Here Freud acts as a corrective for phenomenology. We can be *wrong* in our description of our own emotions. We can also be wrong in our phenomenological descriptions of the nature of emotions. *From one's own case*, one can't always tell. There is, of course, intersubjectivity, mutual reflection, and comparative reporting. But self-deception, as Freud and his followers are fond of pointing out, travels in groups as well as alone. Phenomenology provides the descriptions; Freudian analysis explodes the illusions. The one is a countermethodology to the other, and neither should be used alone.

This is methodology; but now for the substance. There is a series of "dialectics" in Freud which the Viennese master himself never resolved. In general, it is the dialectic between mechanism and teleology that disturbs him; he began as a scientist, became a quasi-phenomenologist, and never reconciled the two. But here we see again the dominant dichotomy (or should we now call it a "dialectic," too?) In Ricoeur's philosophy, the voluntary and the involuntary, the active, interpretive and the symbolic on the one hand; and the passive, the insignificant (in *this* sense), and the biological on the other. But in Ricoeur, there is the meeting of the Freudian and the phenomenological in "a third term," the *symbol*. [FP, p. 494] The language here is unfortunately obscure, "the symbol 'contains' the multiplicity. It remains to find the *concrete mixed texture*," that is "the symbol." [FP, P. 494] The ideal is a mixture of Freud's *archaeology* (or regressive, backward looking approach—to infancy, etc.) and Hegel's *teleology* (forward looking or progressive approach). I think that Ricoeur's interpretations of both Freud and Hegel can be seriously challenged, but I have no concern to do that here. What is vital is Ricoeur's belief in a synthesis that will serve both sides. And, in the case of the passions, this means that he believes that there is an analysis which will do justice both to the objective views and the subjective views of the passions, their involuntary and their voluntary aspects. The problem is, as far as I can see, that this is never done as such. What emerges from *Freud and Philosophy* is a giving up of the biological side of the matter virtually altogether, and turning Freud—or what emerges in the name of Freud—into hermeneutical and highly phenomenological product. Now this may be a way of resolving the central antinomy in Freud's theories. And it may well be the best way of analyzing the passions—whether within or without the phenomenological point of view. But it does not do what Ricoeur most wants it to do, and that is to preserve both moments in the "third term." There is no symbolism *in* biology, and when Freud even tries it in his early *Project*, he falls flat on his face. (That's why he never published it.) And so, at the end of his work, the ambiguities of Ricoeur's earlier account of emotions is still unresolved.

Perhaps one should at this point say something more of Ricoeur's work on methodology, the older analysis of Husserl and his more recent hermeneutics in general. In this later work, Ricoeur accuses phenomenology in a straightforward way of a certain naïveté, and again he brings in certain objective correlatives by way of correction. But what now becomes foremost among these objective correlatives is linguistics, and Ricoeur himself has described his most recent movement as "from existentialism to the philosophy of language."[13] It seems to me that there is indeed an answer to Ricoeur's dilemma in this work, though it would go far beyond our scope to discuss it here. Insofar as language is already, of necessity, a synthesis of objective considerations, mutual descriptions, and shared experiences, it serves extermely well, *in conjunction with phenomenology*, to provide the balanced perspective Ricoeur sought in *Freedom and Nature*. Ricoeur himself describes ordinary language as "a kind of conservatory for expressions which have preserved the highest descriptive power as regards human experience."[14] But conservatories sometimes build myths, and reference back to one's own experience is constantly necessary to test and, if necessary, to challenge the usually good authority of ordinary language. But neither alone can be the test. And both together solve Ricoeur's problem. But the resolution of his ambiguity between the voluntary and involuntary with regard to the passions seems to me to retain the ambiguity only at severe cost to the involuntary. Simply stated, it seems to me that, using Ricoeur's own methods of analysis, it can be argued convincingly that the passions lie wholly on the side of the voluntary, that they have a significance which lends them totally to analysis in a hermeneutical fashion, and that much of Ricoeur's best work has been aimed at a subject matter which he himself tried to ignore.

IV. RICOEUR AND SARTRE:
An Uncomfortable Duo

This essay is an analysis of Ricoeur's views, and lack of views, on the passions. An adequate analysis, however (which I do not pretend to be able to provide here) would certainly go back through those influences that have so heavily weighed on Ricoeur's own thinking, not just those two famous foreigners, Husserl and Freud (and Hegel, Scheler, etc.), but the French philosophers who were his earliest intellectual nourishment; Descartes, of course, Marcel, more personally, and a dozen others, who influenced the thinking of every French thinker in the past several decades or centuries. But the most revealing comparison and contrast, in my opinion, is between Ricoeur and a philosopher who would not count as such an "influence" at all, Jean-Paul Sartre. That *enfant terrible* of French letters developed the most single-minded and provocative account of the emotions in this century. He did what Ricoeur did not: to follow in the footsteps of Descartes in *explicitly* giving the passions their place in philosophy with a theory, or at least a "sketch" of a theory, in their own right. The comparison is apt and illuminating, despite the gross differences in the styles and temperaments of these two philosophers, because I believe that Sartre displays in an obvious way the conflict of interpretation of the passions that shows itself only implicitly in Ricoeur's work. (And given that Sartre's essay was published over a decade before Ricoeur's *Freedom and Nature*, the ascription of "influence" may not be wholly unreasonable.)

To begin with the obvious, Sartre, like Ricoeur, is writing about the emotions from an enthusiastically phenomenological point of view. (Sartre: "After all, phenomenology has scarcely been born."[15]) In both philosophers, the attempt is to find the "essential" or "indispensable structures of consciousness," the "fundamental possibilities of Will." [FN, *passim*][16] The approach, therefore, is self-consciously *subjective*; as Sartre insists, "the consciousness which must be interrogated . . . *is mine.*"[17] But a crucial difference emerges at this point: Sartre begins his essay with a brutal attack on psychology and all "objective" approaches. There is no quarter; he rejects the idea of emotion as a "corporeal phenomenon" and insists that emotions are strictly "structures of consciousness."[18] Ricoeur, on the other hand, allows psychology a full hearing, is wary—even in this early work—of giving absolute sovereignty to subjective description, and he insists, unlike Sartre, on the phenomenon of *embodiment* as essential to emotions. In other words, emotions are *essentially* "corporeal." [FN, p. 277]

Sartre's attack on psychology and traditional theories of emotion (particularly those of James, Janet, and Freud) is aimed at replacing them with a very different *kind* of theory, a *voluntaristic* theory, a view of emotions as *activities*, as *doings*, as *acts* of consciousness. Looking forward to *Being and Nothingness*, one can see why this move will be so important to him, in terms of the all-important ascription of responsibility. But it is the voluntaristic thesis in its own right that concerns us here. Why does he accept it? Because, he insists, emotions have a *significance*, a *meaning*, and this is possible only if they are, in Husserl's sense (which Sartre expands considerably) *acts of consciousness*. But here we can see how Ricoeur, although he does not adopt the voluntaristic model explicitly—in fact, he explicitly rejects it—follows Sartre in a very important way. He does not use the "act" terminology, which would make the emotions too obviously connected to the Will, but he continuously uses the language of significance and meaning. This emerges, as I have argued, not only in his theory but even more so in his actual analyses. And on this basis, one can argue that, in the sense that emotions have significance, or, we might now say, are *intentional*, they must be *acts* as well, at least in Husserl's sense. This is not yet voluntarism, of course, for Sartre explicitly adds an ingredient that goes beyond mere intentionality. He calls it *finalité*, in other words, *purposiveness*; he claims that emotions are *acts with a purpose*. This would seem, at first glance, to be precisely the opposite of Ricoeur's thesis, for it would seem that, in *Freedom and Nature* in particular, the emotions are precisely distinguished from purposiveness and willing. But let us look again. Returning to the passage quoted from *Symbolism of Evil* concerning guilt, is it not there clear that my guilt is just this, a purposive willing? Now we may well disagree with the *rationality* of that purpose. And one might even agree (though I would not; Sartre would) that such purposes tend to make us unhappy. But the point is this: emotions, in Ricoeur's own terms, are clearly "possibilities of Will." That is, they are actual willings, which he himself shows us with considerable detail.

But are the emotions purposive, according to Ricoeur? Do they have *finalité*? Consider the following paragraph, discussing "emotive forms of conduct," he argues:

> The moment of emotion . . . places the will at the mercy of the body in revolt. Herein lies all the ambiguity of emotion. It is because it is *not a reflex* but an embryonic passion that it is *partly subject to wisdom;* though it always *takes us* by surprise and *renders* ineffective the very weapons which seek to defeat it on its own ground, that of the body, . . . *I do not cure myself of anger* without curing myself of excessive self-esteem and of susceptibility to injury deriving from it: these are the *bad imaginations, oppressors of the will* which constitute the combustible matter of emotion. If anger did not contain all that, if it were a simple reflex, how could we understand why the moralists have devoted so many maxims and often veritable tomes to it? [FN, p. 278]

The "ambiguity" remains, of course; but I am asking the reader not to ignore the involuntaristic language, which is obvious enough, but to look through it at the voluntaristic and purposive descriptions, which are equally obvious, if only one looks for them. The descriptions deceive because, every time Ricoeur attributes some voluntaristic aspect to the emotion, he switches grammatical subjects, and moves to "the moment of emotion" (rather than "the emotion"), "I do not cure myself" (when the point implicit is precisely that it is *the anger itself* that is part and parcel of the clearly voluntaristic act of thinking too highly of oneself) "bad imaginations" (when it is the emotion itself that, as he earlier insists, is inseparable from imagination). And the final comment quoted is most revealing: why have so many moralists dwelt on the emotions? Not just because, as in Kant (and as occasionally hinted at in Ricoeur, [e.g. FN, p. 272] they are "pathological" and disrupters of morality, but rather because, as Hume and Rousseau and long before them Plato and Aristotle saw so clearly, the emotions are *essential* to morality. But why is this? Consider the following; moralists (and all of us) often condemn certain emotions (resentment, envy, jealousy), praise others (love, *righteous* indignation, faith); and they (and we) say of particular emotions in particular situations that they are "unreasonable" or "reasonable," "warranted" or "un-warranted" (cf. "righteous" above as applied to indignation), and even "stupid," "embarrassing" (note the emotion ascribed to an emotion here) and "foolish" (as in "foolish love"). This is not a point that escapes Ricoeur in the least, *when he is discussing subject matter of morality rather than when he is theorizing about emotions.* Like Marcel before him, and like Kierkegaard before Marcel, Ricoeur's understanding of the passions is most admirable when he isn't theorizing about them. Kierkegaard, for example, makes passion sound like so much Danish beer bubbling about and threatening to spill over inside the psyche. But when he gets down to a description of dread, or Divine love, or resentment, he is marvelous. They would all have been better to follow Pascal (who was not entirely clear on the matter either) when he insisted that "le coeur a ses *raisons*, que la raison ne connait point." I would put the matter more forcefully (if much less elegantly); passions *are* reasons (or as Nietzsche put it, "as if every passion did not have its quantum of reason"). And Ricoeur, though he denies it in his theorizing, accepts this view demonstrably in his analyses. The emotions, he hints, are intentional and purposive acts of consciousness. The purposes here are tied to self-esteem, although this is left unexplained except for a brief appeal to Descartes, who left the matter unresolved also. (Elsewhere the purpose is said to be deception and avoidance. But these can be easily synthesized in particular cases.)

Ricoeur, like Sartre, sees the voluntaristic side of the emotions. But is there another side? On the face of it, Sartre would say "no," Ricoeur "yes" (and there lies the "ambiguity" of emotion). But further reading makes both answers debatable. We have already shown how Ricoeur, despite his emphasis on the involuntary, uses the voluntary at crucial junctures in his analyses. Sartre is a case for the converse: he begins with a very heavy-handed voluntaristic thesis, and lets it degenerate as he proceeds into the heart of his own theory. For example, he too begins to talk about the body as essential to emotion (e.g. "using the body as a means of incantation")[19] and talks as Ricoeur talks about the *entrapment* of consciousness ("consciousness that binds itself") and the *degradation* of consciousness. Notice in Sartre as in Ricoeur, however, that this entrapment and degradation is imposed upon consciousness *by itself,* and trapped or not, it is still therefore an act, and a purposive act at that. But Sartre calls the emotions, which he has hitherto been defending, "inferior modes of behavior" and "ineffective." We can see the "ambiguity" thus entering Sartre's essay as well, and here is the comparative moral I wish to draw: in the problematic abyss between the voluntary and the involuntary, the emotions (and the passions in general) seem to be suspended. They are neither straightforward bodily disturbances (gallstones or dyspepsia, for example); nor are they willings in an obvious sense (intentional actions, creative imaginings). They seem to stand between, neither freedom nor nature. And this ambiguous status has led generations of philosophers, Descartes and Kant, for example, to say some rather absurd things about them. But the "ambiguity" can be resolved, and Ricoeur, following Sartre, seems to have most of the ingredients for doing it.

V. PROLEGOMENA TO A HERMENEUTICS OF THE PASSIONS

What must be elaborated are the significances and purposiveness of the emotions; what are the *structures* of emotion? How do different emotions differ? What do they *mean?* What role do they play in our lives? Mere disruptions? (Surely not.) Avoidance and deception? (Not always, at least.) What is the connection with *self-esteem?* What is the connection with *commitment?*, with *faith?*, with meaningful work and relationships? These are the goals of a hermeneutics of the passions, just of the sort that Professor Ricoeur has so forcefully given us regarding that grim triad of sin, guilt, and defilement. But what is needed is a general *theory,* and make no mistake, it is a theory of *interpretation:* not just interpretation *of* the passions, rather, every passion *is* an interpretation, a way of constituting the world, the creation of a mythology and a dramatic-moral *structure* of our world.[20] There need be no hard split, however, between these passionate structures and "more rational" or "logical" structures; to talk about "mythology" here is not to assume for a moment that, as Ernst Cassirer used to argue, the "pre-logic" of the emotions is significantly different from the articulate logic of our "more rational" pursuits. I don't intend to defend any of this here. All I claim is that these are projects which are implicit in Ricoeur's own work, and that the basis of his own continuous efforts to understand human nature through a study of action, language, will, and psychology can best be turned to this area he has demeaned and neglected in theory. Or perhaps we can say, not only are the passions "possibilities of will," they are *fundamental* possibilities of will, the basic symbolic structures imposed on our world in our every experience.

But if the voluntary side of Ricoeur's "ambiguity" is to be so elaborated, the involuntary side must be explained. Where arises the seeming passivity of passion, which has been so obsessive for virtually every author on the subject? Can the seeming involuntary nature of the emotions be accounted for in terms of the purely voluntary?

The first move is to understand the phenomenon of embodiment: this does not mean that we must examine the very complex doctrines of Ricoeur (and Merleau-Ponty), but it does mean that we must distinguish two very different senses of "corporeal" when we say, along with Ricoeur (and ultimately Sartre, too) that the emotions are *bodily*. First, there is that sense of corporeality that means simply, *physiological*: palpitations, adrenaline-flowing, pulse-racing, muscles-locking, nerves-jangling, bowels-loosening, capillaries-dilating. Second, there is the very sophisticated phenomenon of *embodiment* that appears in these philosophical authors, which is not physiological but *behavioral,* which is essentially tied to *action*. But this second sense is common to all forms of perception as well as emotions, desires, and passions in general. We can accept, therefore, that the emotions are "corporeal" in this second sense without any danger to a voluntaristic model whatsoever. Just as *looking* is surely voluntary, so might be *getting angry,* despite the fact (or because of the fact) that both of them are dependent upon embodiment, properly described.

But the first sense of corporeal, as physiological, is, we may say, simply tangential to emotion, not its essence. Of course, it is very likely the case that, in any intense emotion, all of the appropriate physiological goings-on will occur, but as a *causal consequence,* not as the essence, of emotion. You can insist if you like that such causation is itself *necessary,* if we are to speak of emotion. But a necessary effect is not yet an essence, and so that aspect of emotion which so many authors have taken to be the essence of involuntariness turns out not to be part of the essense of emotion at all.

The same may be said of the *feeling* of emotion, which simply follows (as James said that it did), the physiological consequences of emotion. But the feeling isn't the emotion (as James thought); it too is merely a causal consequence (even if, perhaps, a necessary one). And even if it were true that the feelings, like the physiological flushings, are not plausibly said to be voluntary, this says little about the essence of emotion.

The second step is more interesting. Both Ricoeur and Sartre speak of the emotions as being self-entrapments ("binding itself"); and here is an obvious answer to the "ambiguity" in question. One "traps oneself" or "deceives oneself" and one is, in an obvious sense, "one's own victim," both perpetrator and victim. Seen as victim, one seems passive; as perpetrator, one is active. But, where Victim and perpetrator are the same, a certain *acquiescence* on the part of the victim is required. (Ricoeur uses this word several times). The apparent passivity, in other words, is a voluntary passivity, a *willing*ness to play a certain role or take a certain part.

But this isn't sufficient; if the passivity of passion were simply acquiescence, then why should it be so difficult to change our passions, or initiate them in ourselves, or "cure" them, as Ricoeur (following Descartes) points out? The answer, I believe, lies in the very significance and purposiveness of the passions. A truism: passions are passionate. Their symbols are not randomly chosen or of passing interest; they are vital to us. Religious symbols, which Ricoeur attends to, are but a single example of these very basic and vital *investments* we make in our chosen mythologies and world views. Having chosen to see oneself as "naturally superior" to other people, certain emotions necessarily follow in particular circumstances. (Here is the connection between emotions and self-esteem pointed out by Descartes and Ricoeur.) One has invested in that self-image, and one cannot, except at great personal cost, give it up. So, as a form of protection (and not necessarily avoidance nor even "deception"), one becomes righteously indignant at casual insults, resentful of the smallest slight, prideful at the least chance. It may be *extremely difficult* to give up a self-image, and, consequently, to be able to give up any number of passions which support that image. But to say that it is "extremely difficult" is not to say that one *cannot* do so, nor is it to indicate in the slightest that those passions are caused and passive rather than intended and active. The project for a hermeneutics of the passions, therefore, is to uncover these symbolic investments, to see how they tie together and mutually support one another, to understand how it is that we invest in such degrading passions as resentment, envy, self-contempt and self-pity, as well as the religious-leaning passions of sin, guilt and defilement.

For too long, the passions have been mere footnotes in philosophy, tailing along at the bottom of some weighty treatise on epistemology, phenomenology, ontology, or morals. They do not deserve this degraded status, and, particularly in the work of those philosophers who have proven appreciation for the importance of the passions in our lives, they would seem to deserve proper treatment of their own. Paul Ricoeur has not yet attempted any such treatment. This essay ends in the hope that he will.

NOTES

1. One would say the same of Sartre, for example, whose treatment of the passions is remarkably similar in its essential aspects. (*See* Section 4, "Ricoeur and Sartre: An Uncomfortable Duo.") Iris Murdoch once called Sartre a "Romantic Rationalist"; I would

not hesitate to do so for Ricoeur, thus underscoring his mixed allegiances to the rigors of the philosophical intellect and his almost medieval commitment to personal concerns writ large ("the human condition," some have called it).

2.   *See*, for example, David Sachs, "Freud and Emotions": in R. Wollheim, ed., *Freud* (New York: Doubleday-Anchor, 1974) and my essay "Freud's Neurological Theory of Mind" in the same volume.

3.   J.-P. Sartre, "Esquisse d'une théorie des emotions," in *Actualité* scientifiques et industielles, series no. 838 (Paris: Hermann. 1939), [copyright dated Feb. 23, 1940]— Translated into English as *The Emotions: Outline of a Theory*, B. Frechtman, trans. (New York: Philosophical Library, 1948) and by P. Mairet, trans. (London: Methuen, 1962). All translations here are based on the 2nd edition, Hermann, 1948.

4.   *Ibid.*, pp. 42, 45; (75) * *et passim.*

5.   *Ibid.*, p. 43; (79).

6.   *Ibid.*, p. 46; (78).

7.   *Ibid.*, p. 33; (58) *et passim.*

8.   *See also* my "Sartre on Emotions" in P. Schilpp, ed., *Sartre.* (La Salle, Illinois: Open Court Press, 1977) and my *The Passions* (New York: Doubleday-Anchor, 1976) for my own theory.

9.   Théodule Ribot, *Essai sur les passions* (Paris: Alcan, 1912).

10.   J.-A. Rony, *Les Passions* (Paris: Presses Universitaires de France, 1961).

11.   Sartre, p. 45.

12.   Don Ihde, *Hermeneutic Phenomenology: The Philosophy of Paul Ricoeur* (Evanston: Northwestern University Press, 1971).

13.   *See* Paul Ricoeur, "From Existentialism to the Philosophy of Language," *Philosophy Today*, Vol. XVII, Summer 1973, pp. 88-96.

14.   *Ibid.*, p. 95.

15.   Sartre, p. 12; (19).

16.   *Ibid.*, p. 10; (15).

17.   *Ibid.*, p. 8; (11).

18.   *Ibid.*, p. 12; (19).

19.   *Ibid.*, p. 39; (70).

20.   I have argued these theses at length in my book, *The Passions.*

* Note: the first page numbers refer to the original French version. The numbers in parenthesis refer to B. Frechtman's English translation of the same.

I want to thank Daniel Doss and Terry Boswell for their research assistance and Charles Reagan for his encouragement.

II

David Stewart

EXISTENTIAL HUMANISM

Ever since Jean-Paul Sartre's identification of his own existentialism as a humanism, the presumption has been strong that any humanism worthy of the name is not only atheistic but is derived from a philosophy of freedom as originating in the nothingness of human consciousness. Indeed, Sartre himself has encouraged such an interpretation by identifying his own view as the only viable form of humanism, an identification made possible by his reinterpretation of the meaning of humanism and by a somewhat one-sided application of existentialist themes. One of the undercurrents in the work of Paul Ricoeur is a subtle dialogue with these Sartrean principles and a search for a humanism that would be neither atheistic nor based on the dichotomy between being and nothingness. Although not completely explicit in any one of Ricoeur's works, the shape of his humanistic alternative can easily be grasped by taking his work as a whole.

David Stewart is Professor of philosophy at Ohio University, Athens, Ohio. His principal publications are *Exploring Phenomenology* (with A. Mickunas); *Political and Social Essays* by Paul Ricoeur (edited with J. Bien); and *The Philosophy of Paul Ricoeur: An Anthology of his Work* (edited with Charles Reagan).

Existential Humanism

David Stewart

Ever since Jean-Paul Sartre's identification of his own existentialism as a humanism, the presumption has been strong that any humanism worthy of the name is not only atheistic but is derived from a philosophy of freedom as originating in the nothingness of human consciousness. Indeed, Sartre himself has encouraged such an interpretation by identifying his own view as the only viable form of humanism, an identification made possible by his reinterpretation of the meaning of humanism and by a somewhat one-sided application of existentialist themes. One of the undercurrents in the work of Paul Ricoeur is a subtle dialogue with these Sartrean principles and a search for a humanism that would be neither atheistic nor based on the dichotomy between being and nothingness. Although not completely explicit in any one of Ricoeur's works, the shape of his humanistic alternative can easily be grasped by taking Ricoeur's work as a whole.

Any attempt to distill a humanism from Ricoeur's work would have to begin with *Fallible Man,* but it is important to remember that *Fallible Man* is the midpoint in Ricoeur's *Philosophie de la volonté,* the initial volume of which offers a phenomenological analysis of the will in its dialectic between the voluntary and the involuntary. Temporarily set aside or bracketed in this study were both transcendence and the fault. Transcendence was put out of question until a way could be found in which it could be reintegrated in a dialectic with freedom, a task reserved for the as-yet-unpublished third volume provisionally entitled *Poetics of the Will.* The reality of evil, which appears as a gap or "fault" in man's nature (in the geological sense of a rift or rupture), was likewise bracketed so the eidetic analysis of the will could proceed unhindered by the existential reality of evil and also because evil can only be approached philosophically through the indirect route of the language of symbols and myths. Even a brief summary of the analysis of *Fallible Man* is neither possible nor desirable at this point, but a few general statements about the direction of this work will set the stage for our further analysis.

One of the purposes of *Fallible Man* is to initiate the process of removing the brackets from the fault. When one turns to the appearance of evil in human reality—the only place it can make its appearance—one discovers that the existential fact of the fault is always expressed at its most basic level in the language of symbols and myths. As Ricoeur shows in his *Symbolism of Evil,* this language of avowal or confession shows a remarkable consistency among various cultures in that the symbolic avowal of the fault testifies that it is experienced as an irrational element in, as a deviation from, man's essential possibilities. And to understand this symbolic discourse, one must examine the nature of human reality to discover man who not only is capable of error but—as the myths tell us—has already fallen. But if man's most basic experience of his faulted nature is expressed in symbols and myths, rigorous philosophical speculation requires a hermeneutic if it is to take these myths seriously. Such a principle of interpretation can provide the bridge between the language of symbolic discourse and rigorous philosophical reflection only if one first shows how the possibility of evil is inscribed in the very situation of man. The analyses of *Fallible Man* are thus the prelude to letting the symbols and myths of evil "give rise to thought."

In his eidetic analysis of the will in *Freedom and Nature* Ricoeur stressed that both the finite and infinite poles of acting must be understood in their dialectic interplay if we are to understand man, and he continues this same dialectic in *Fallible Man*: perspective and truth, character and the good, pleasure and happiness are the finite and infinite poles of a dialectical tension which cannot be eliminated.

In the background of this dialectical tension, however, is man's desire for totality which, as Kant reminds us, is reason's continual but unfulfilled demand. Taking a clue from Kant, Ricoeur analyzes three modalities of consciousness using a Kantian triadic model as guide. The three modalities are knowing, acting, feeling—or reason, will, and appetite. The grand division in Kant is between the theoretical and practical, with the theoretical providing the basic outline of Ricoeur's approach; that is, the "objectivity" of the object is the synthesis between sensibility and understanding. Accordingly Ricoeur seeks a synthesis of these dialectical poles, but as his analysis shows, the tension is never relaxed but only revealed as a "fragility," which is the occasion for the fault.

Ricoeur's approach also has phenomenological roots, although Ricoeur's phenomenology is hardly "orthodox." Rejected by Ricoeur is not only the eidetic reduction but the notions of transcendental subjectivity which, Ricoeur believes, led Husserl to an absolutizing of the *cogito* and to the idealism of the *Cartesian Meditations.* Ricoeur also accuses Husserl of not clearly distinguishing between intention and intuition, and here Ricoeur appeals to Kant. An empty intention is unfulfilled unless it is given an intuition, a content. Change the terms and you have Ricoeur's two poles of the finite and the infinite: the finite intuition in tension with the infinite intention, with the constant dialectic between them that is both the genius of our humanity but also the possibility of the fault.

What is important for Ricoeur's humanism is his appropriation of the Kantian model on the affective level. Just as, on the theoretical level, the "objectivity" supplied by pure imagination is the synthesis of the finite perspective and the infinite word, so on the practical level respect (in the Kantian sense) is the synthesis of character and happiness. The fragility of this synthesis is clearly seen in the affective order in the conflict between the principle of pleasure and the principle of happiness. Man's humanity is projected in the feeling of possession, power, and worth, which are seen most vividly in their distorted forms of greed, unrestrained power, and vainglory. But through the fallen, one can glimpse the primordial—those essential possibilities in man which appear distorted and confused in their perverted manifestations. What all this is pointing to are the levels of conflict within man which were only dimly seen heretofore on the margins of philosophy. Man is precisely that which mediates between the finite and the infinite, the limited and the desire for totality. This conflict signals man's disproportion with himself.

I.   RICOEUR AND SARTRE

There is still another dimension to Ricoeur's analysis of the human situation, and this is provided by his correction of Sartre's ontology, which is based in the dialectic between being and nothingness. Sartre's approach constantly risks becoming a voluntarism; Ricoeur provides an alternative in his analysis of the dialectic not between being and nothingness but between the voluntary and involuntary aspects of human volition. For Ricoeur, the finite pole of this dialectic is not nothing; perspective is a partial truth, character is a necessary part of man's quest for happiness. In short, man is not nothing; he is a being continually surpassing itself in a constant quest for totality. To be sure, Ricoeur recognizes the importance of negation in his account of the limits placed on man's quest for totality. The negation in the order of knowing, for example, is the limitation of the infinite word by finite perspective. But the function of negation is not to lead to a philosophy of nothingness, as Sartre would have it. Negation, for Ricoeur, leads to a philosophy of limits, not to an attempt of man to pull free from the *en soi* accumulated by his own past.

In short, Ricoeur demurs against Sartre for having an inadequate philosophy of being. Sartre bases his entire philosophy of freedom on the metaphysics of negation and nothingness and constitutes freedom as nothingness. But nothingness, Ricoeur insists, is not non-being. Failure to make this distinction can lead to an ethical and ontological nihilism, and

Ricoeur observes that Sartre's "whole theory of value is encumbered with this flimsy conception of being."[1] In contrast, Ricoeur wants to follow negation not to a philosophy of nothingness but to a negation of negation in a new kind of affirmation. As Ricoeur puts it, "the benefit of a meditation on negation is . . . to carry our idea of being beyond a phenomenology of the thing or a metaphysics of essence up to this act of existing of which it may be equally said that it is without essence or that all its essence is to exist."[2] But the question of ontology can only be approached on the basis of a prior reflection that Ricoeur, again taking Kant as guide, terms transcendental. Such a reflection would be reflection "from the inside," as he puts it, and would attempt to understand "the ontological conditions of reflection" themselves.[3]

In his perceptive article "Negativity and Primary Affirmation," Ricoeur pushes this type of transcendental reflection to its limits. The question to be answered by this inquiry is: does being have priority over the nothingness within the very core of human consciousness? The answer to this question is significant not only because it provides an alternative to a Sartrean ontology of being and nothingness but also because it governs a style of philosophy, "a style of 'yes' and not a style of 'no,' and perhaps even a style characterized by joy and not by anguish."[4] In seeking this new philosophical style, Ricoeur returns to the philosophical anthropology developed in *Fallible Man*. As has already been mentioned, Ricoeur's phenomenological analysis of fallibility uncovered the fact that knowing and acting have an infinite as well as finite pole. The conflict between the finite and infinite poles of knowing, between perspective and the verb, is synthesized in Pure Imagination (to follow Kant) with the correlative concepts of "objectivity" and universal truth. In acting, the finite pole of character, with its affective and practical perspective, is transcended by a reaching out toward happiness. The synthesis of these finite and infinite aspects of acting is "respect," in the Kantian sense, wherein the other person is accepted and treated as a person.

This act of transcending perspective and character is a kind of negation, but it is not a negation leading to an ontology of nothingness as the ground and possibility of free action. Ricoeur observes that "I cannot *express* my transcendence over my perspective without expressing myself negatively: as transcendence, I am not what I am as point of view."[5] The same is also true of the act of transcending character in the constitution of the other, for the "positing of another's existence involves the same mark of negativity as the movement of transcendence by which I transgress my perspective: another is the not-I *par excellence,* just as the universal is the not-this *par excellence.*"[6] But reflection on this transcendence of the finitude of perspective and character reveals it as being more than a simple negation. Prior to the negation of finitude is an already constituted language of otherness which expresses the finitude of perspective as this . . . not that, or posits the Other as the not-I. It is impossible, Ricoeur insists, to "express the distinct without recourse to negation: this is not that."[7] The very experience of finitude itself is expressed by the language of negation: want is expressed as an "I don't have," the past by "no longer," the future by "not yet."

It is one thing to recognize the irreducible function of negation in raising the finite to the level of expression, but it is quite different to follow negation to a philosophy of non-being, as does Sartre. Ricoeur argues that the experience of finitude actually points the way toward a negation prior to the negating act resulting from transcending the finitude of perspective. For this reason, the act of transcending perspective and character actually constitutes a double negation—a negation of negation—or a denegation, to use Ricoeur's term.

> Denegation is negation of negation. More exactly, the thought which aims at meaning beyond finite perspective, the taking up of a position which aims at validity beyond the point of view of the will itself, is, in comparison with the negation of finitude, in a specific relation which is stated rather well in an expression such as this: I think, I want, *in spite of* my finitude. *In spite of* . . . , such seems to me to be the most concrete relation between negation as transcendence and negation as finitude, between denegation and annihilation.[8]

This "in spite of," Ricoeur reminds us elsewhere, is a veritable category of hope.[9] The upshot of Ricoeur's analysis is to see more in the dialectic and ambiguity between the finite and infinite in human reality than despair and anguish by following negation to a double negation that points the way to a primary affirmation.

To recapitulate, Ricoeur's analysis of knowing and acting reveals a negation inherent in the finitude of perspective and character. Needs are expressed as a lack; the past as no longer, and the future as the not-yet. Finite existence itself gives rise to feelings of contingency, the non-necessity of existing. The recognition of the Other emphasizes the other as the not-I. But this first level of negation is itself negated by the transcendence of perspective and character: one's point of view is transcended by universal truths; one's character is surmounted by "respect," which, in its most extreme form, sublimates even vital needs to the welfare of the Other who is thereby constituted as a person. This transcendence of perspective and finite character is a negation of the prior negation, i.e., a *de*negation. This denegation is best expressed by the category "in spite of," which can be read as a truly human category of hope. The question remains whether this negation of negation is the final word. Ricoeur says that it is not. One can discover an affirmation within the very heart of negation, but this raises reflection from an existential level to an ontological level.

As was previously mentioned, Ricoeur's quarrel with Sartre is over an inadequate ontology. Sartre's *Being and Nothingness* posits nothingness as the source of freedom. Every authentically human act, Sartre says, is a nihilating act. Human freedom springs from the nothingness that "lies coiled in the heart of being—like a worm."[10] But what is this nothingness in the very heart of human being? The basic disagreement between Ricoeur and Sartre is over the answer to this question. According to Sartre, nothingness is essential to freedom; Ricoeur argues, in contrast, that a recognition of the significance of nihilating acts does not lead to an ontology of being and nothingness. Ricoeur observes that "the whole of Sartre's philosophy rests on the right to call 'nothingness' what our previous analysis only allowed us to name 'nihilating acts'."[11] Although Sartre's ontology requires the identification of nihilating acts with the nothingness of human freedom, Ricoeur argues that such a confusion is not only unnecessary but unjustified. Why does Sartre confuse nihilating acts with nothingness? Ricoeur argues it is because of Sartre's failure adequately to distinguish causes from motives. Ricoeur's analysis of the will in *Freedom and Nature* explored with considerable thoroughness the distinctions between motives and causes, a distinction Sartre blurs. As Ricoeur puts it, "when I insist on the negative aspect of freedom, I simply mean that self-determination is a determination by motives and *not* by causes. . . . Negation is only in the definition, not in the act."[12] Not only does Ricoeur deny that nihilating acts lead to an ontology of nothingness, he insists that every negation presupposes a prior valuation, which implies an affirmation of being is included."[13] To rebel, Ricoeur observes, is not only to say no, it is also to affirm a value.

II. The Meaning of Humanism

Not only do Ricoeur and Sartre proceed on the basis of different ontologies, they also differ in their understanding of the meaning of humanism. For Sartre, humanism can only be legitimate when man is made the center not only of freedom but of the creation of values. Coupled with this emphasis on man as the creator of values is Sartre's rejection of any human nature, for he sees such a view as inalterably linked with the notion of a creator-God who fashions man in terms of a pre-established model of humanness. In a well-known passage Sartre says that "the concept of man in the mind of God is comparable to the concept of a papercutter in the mind of the manufacturer, and, following certain techniques and a conception, God produces man. . . . Thus, the individual man is the realisation of a certain concept in the divine intelligence."[14] It can be argued that such a view of man was never seriously defended, even though Sartre attributes it to such diverse thinkers as Descartes, Leibniz, Diderot, Voltaire, and Kant. It is beyond dispute, however, that this view of man was not reflected in the humanism of the Renaissance. The fifteenth-century Italian humanist Pico della Mirandola, in his *Oration on the Dignity of Man,* puts the following speech in the mouth of God in his address to Adam, a speech that sounds as though it could have been written by a card-carrying existentialist.

> I have given you, Adam, neither a predetermined place nor a particular aspect nor any special prerogatives in order that you may take and possess these through your own decision and choice. . . . You shall determine your own nature without constraint from any barrier, by means of the freedom to whose power I have entrusted you. I have placed you at the center of the world so that . . . like a free and sovereign artificer, you might mold and fashion yourself into that form you yourself have chosen.[15]

To be sure, Ricoeur's humanism is closer to that of the humanists of the Italian Renaissance than to Sartre's form of humanism, although like Sartre Ricoeur's philosophical roots are in the phenomenological tradition. Crucial for Ricoeur's view of man, however, is the work of Gabriel Marcel, for whom phenomenology becomes existential while simultaneously preserving the mystery of incarnate existence. Referring to Marcel's well-known distinction between problem and mystery, Ricoeur notes that there are two senses for Marcel in which man's being is not a problem but a mystery: on the one hand, the "mystery" of being designates man's rootedness in being or in the sacred; on the other hand, incarnate existence itself gives an "irreducible opacity" to man's being which resists all attempts to schematize it.[16] This dual direction in Marcel toward mystery as well as the concreteness of the "personal body" *(corps propre)* serves as a "break with the idolatry of the anonymous epistomological subject" and offers a "restoration of an experience at once personal and integral which extends between the two poles of the carnal and the mysterious."[17]

Ricoeur's adaptation of these Marcelian themes is seen clearly in *Fallible Man,* but in an article written in 1960, "*L'Homme et son mystère,*" which encapsulates the themes of *L'Homme faillible* (published in the same year), Ricoeur explicitly interprets the "mystery" of man as consisting in his disproportion with himself, a disproportion made possible by the affective fragility so painstakingly analyzed in *Fallible Man.* "If there is a mystery of man," Ricoeur observes, "it is because man, disproportionate in himself, exists as an *intermediary* being, as a *mixture,* forever obscure to himself."[18] In short, man appears to himself as ambiguous, forever caught in the dialectic between the finite and infinite, the voluntary and the involuntary, freedom and nature. There are good grounds for Charles Kelbley's assessment that Ricoeur's analysis of man, whether from theological, political, or philosophical perspectives, "elucidates the ambiguous status of mankind which no logic of philosophy or of history can coordinate short of imposing a violent synthesis of the truth."[19]

Although labels are misleading, Sartre explicitly adopts the rubric "existentialist humanism" for his position, a somewhat unfair appropriation both of the terms existentialism and humanism. If a label were appropriate for Ricoeur's humanism, it would be "Christian humanism," although such a designation would mask Ricoeur's own adaptation of Husserlian phenomenology and would conjur up images of a simplistic grafting of Christian dogma onto a philosophy in which man plays a pivotal role. In an article written in 1951, Ricoeur rejects any such facile meaning of "Christian" humanism. There are, he notes, two naïve views of the meaning of Christian humanism, both of which he rejects. The first would see Christianity as added to a neutral and secular view of humanism; the second views Christian doctrine as making good on a humanistic expectation which remains unfulfilled in its purely secular manifestation. No humanism can be worthy of the name "Christian" unless it sees man engaged in a struggle "in situation" (cultural, political, technological, philosophical, and so forth), a struggle that will remain ambiguous and can express its meaning only eschatologically.[20] I will return to the eschatological theme later, but it is first necessary to disengage the term "humanism" from its identification with Christianity in order to see what constitutes a viable humanism today.

In his perceptive article "What Does *Humanism* Mean?" Ricoeur suggests several levels of meaning inherent in the notion. At its first level, echoing the humanism of the Renaissance, humanism is a recovery of man's cultural past, a "resistance to forgetfulness."[21] Although this is humanism only in its narrow sense, the role of the intellectual in preserving man's intellectual heritage is crucially important in a technological society in view of the fact that technology has no past. At a second level, however, humanism is a response to the tendency of technology to objectify man in his work and in his consumption of the products of his work. One of the functions of the humanistic disciplines is to revivify man's sense of efficaciousness in his work and by doing so to resist the objectification of man in his products. This sense of the humanities—focused on the cultural and artistic accomplishments of man—is implicit in humanism, but it also points to a third meaning of humanism as the élan of humanity, a phrase used by Ricoeur to underscore a theme to which he repeatedly returns.

As the élan of humanity, humanism takes on the function of renewing society through the rational belief in the efficaciousness of human action. This efficaciousness, however, is never assured; it can only be approached as a risk and as a wager, a wager that the man of culture can be efficacious in society even without attempting to do so and without knowing precisely how his action will effect renewal. The risk for the man of culture is that he will try to force this efficaciousness by saying "only expected things." Clearly with a reference to *littérature engagée*, Ricoeur observes that the "engaged" intellectual runs the risk of only repeating the "banality" of the current epoch's "vision of the world."[22] Ricoeur's point is that the artist can be efficacious not by attempting to accomplish some ulterior purpose but by remaining true to the creative impulses of his own discipline. "An artist who chooses to be useful or edifying will immediately cease to be a creator. Artists, writers, and thinkers serve society best when they serve without knowing or intending to, that is, by remaining faithful to the internal problems of their art and their meditation, and with the most demanding impulse issuing from themselves."[23] As a movement toward the renewal of the meaning of man in society, and as a rational conviction in the efficaciousness of the actions of the intellectual, humanism is the élan of humanity only in the sense of a wager or, as Ricoeur puts it, a postulate of practical reason in the Kantian sense.

There is also a Kantian echo in the final meaning of humanism, that is humanism as a philosophy of limits. A philosophy of limits, Ricoeur insists, is both Kantian and Christian—Christian in the sense that the *eschaton* signals that all our projects are provisional; Kantian in the sense of a limit idea, "I think everything and I demand everything, but I am never able to know it."[24] The Nietzschean formula "human, all too human" still reflects what Ricoeur calls "the intoxication of absolute knowledge." The "sobriety of humanism," he insists, is protected by changing the formula to human, *only* human. "Man is man when he knows that he is *only* man."[25] It is here that one can see in what sense Ricoeur's humanism deserves to be called Christian, for the eschatological proclamation in the gospels of the Kingdom of God adds, in the language of scripture, limits not unlike those Kant imposed upon the pretensions of reason. Reflectively, philosophy can capture from the eschatological language of the gospels the sense of limit that must be imposed upon all human projects. All solutions are temporary, all human projects incomplete, all political constructions provisional. Eschatology, Ricoeur observes, announces the "*delay* of all syntheses, in the *postponement* of the solution to all dialectics."[26]

The contrast between Ricoeur and Sartre on this point is vivid. Sartre speaks of man's essential project as the desire to be God, but this desire is only a vain attempt of consciousness to provide the ground of its own being, to escape the nothingness of the for-itself in its own being in-itself.[27] This Sartre rejects, finding that "the initial project of being God, which 'defines' man, comes close to being the same as a human 'nature' or an 'essence'."[28] For Ricoeur, God provides a limit in a vastly different sense; God signifies not only the limitation to all human attempts to ground its own existence but also adds a limiting concept to all the pretensions of reason to achieve totality. In short, the idea of God is a limit concept both ontologically and epistemologically, which is only another way of underscoring the irreducible mystery of incarnate existence. Ricoeur's humanism is more modest than Sartre's. The analyses of *Freedom and Nature*, as well as those of *Fallible Man*, emphasize the significance of limiting ideas. Man is free but not totally free; his freedom is a "bound freedom." Man's disproportion within himself arises from the limitation upon man's unlimited desire for happiness and the infinite reach of speech imposed by the finitude of character and perspective. Even the man of culture acts without absolute knowledge of his own effectiveness, for confidence in the efficaciousness of such action is of the order of belief and not knowledge.[29] Man himself is both limited and limiting, but such is the condition of our humanity. If all human action reflects the sense of "wager" and "risk" that Ricoeur constantly alludes to, then the very notion of humanism itself will be permeated through and through with the view of man himself as a wager. Or as Ricoeur sums it up, "Perhaps it is necessary for us to believe that God Himself, wishing to be known and loved freely, ran this risk which is named Man."[30]

NOTES

1. Paul Ricoeur, "Negativity and Primary Affirmation," in HT, p. 324.

2. *Ibid.*, p. 325.

3. *Ibid.*, p. 306.

4. *Ibid.*, p. 305.

5. *Ibid.*, p. 311.

6. *Ibid.*, p. 313.

7. *Ibid.*, p. 316.

8. *Ibid.*, p. 318.

9. Paul Ricoeur, "The Hermeneutics of Symbols and Philosophical Reflection," *International Philosophical Quarterly* 2, no. 2 (May, 1962), p. 218.

10. Jean-Paul Sartre, *Being and Nothingness*, trans. Hazel E. Barnes (New York: Philosophical Library, 1950), p. 21.

11. Paul Ricoeur, "Negativity and Primary Affirmation," p. 319.

12. *Ibid.*, p. 321.

13. *Ibid.*, p. 322.

14. Jean-Paul Sartre, *Existentialism*, trans. Bernard Frechtman (New York: Philosophical Library, 1947), p. 17.

15. *Encyclopedia of Philosophy*, s.v. "Humanism," vol. 4, p. 70.

16. Paul Ricoeur, "L'Homme et son mystère," in *Le Mystère* (Paris: Horay, 1960), p. 119.

17. Paul Ricoeur, "Existential Phenomenology," in *Husserl: An Analysis of His Phenomenology*, trans. Edward G. Ballard and Lester E. Embree (Evanston: Northwestern University Press, 1967), p. 208.

18. "L'Homme et son mystère," p. 125.

19. "Introduction", HT, p. xxi.

20. Paul Ricoeur, "La Question de l' 'humanisme chrétien,' " *Foi et Vie* 49 (1951), p. 330.

21. Paul Ricoeur, "What Does *Humanism* Mean?" in *Political and Social Essays*, ed. David Stewart and Joseph Bien (Athens: Ohio University Press, 1974), p. 70.

22. *Ibid.*, p. 84.

23. *Ibid.*

24. *Ibid.*, p. 86.

25. *Ibid.*

26. Paul Ricoeur, "Preface to the First Edition," HT, p. 12.

27. *Being and Nothingness*, p. 566.

28. *Ibid.*

29. "What Does Humanism Mean?" p. 86.

30. "The Image of God and the Epoch of Man," HT, p. 128.

III

Richard M. Zaner

THE ADVENTURE OF INTERPRETATION:
THE REFLECTIVE WAGER AND THE
HAZARDS OF THE SELF

In this wide-ranging discussion of philosophy, reflection, interpretation and the self, the author reviews Ricoeur's positions and criticizes him on a number of points. For example, when Ricoeur says philosophy itself is hermeneutics and must have recourse to symbols, he objects that if philosophy is hermeneutics, what is the logical status of that "meta" claim? He argues that hermeneutics is not and cannot be a move away from or beyond the phenomenological principle of evidence. Also, while a study of Freud has advanced our understanding of the self, it is not a repudiation of an eidetics of the self. In short, the author tries to defend a more orthodox phenomenology against Ricoeur's "revisions" concerning the nature of philosophical reflection on the self.

Richard Zaner is Easterwood Professor of philosophy at Southern Methodist University, Dallas, Texas. His numerous publications include *The Problem of Embodiment, The Way of Phenomenology*, editor of Alfred Schutz *Reflections on the Problems of Relevance*, editor of *Phenomenology and Existentialism* (with D. Ihde), and *Selected Studies in Phenomenology and Existential Philosophy* (with D. Ihde) and *The Essential Writings of E. Husserl* (with T. Engelhardt).

The Adventure of Interpretation:
The Reflective Wager and the
Hazards of Self

RICHARD M. ZANER

Few ideas are so distinctive of Paul Ricoeur's later writings as the "enchanting" aphorism, "The symbol gives rise to thought." [SE, p. 348] The overarching theme of his career, securing a genuinely reflective philosophy, indeed, eventually led straight to symbols, myths, and thence to Freud. The connection between symbols and thinking is thus at the center.

This "thinking," he came to believe, being essentially tied to, bound by, and provoked by, symbols, can no longer be taken as phenomenological eidetics; rather, it is hermeneutics. [FP, p. 31] It is "bound" in just the way symbols are "bound": *to* their literal, sensible meanings ("opacity") and *by* the second meaning contained within these ("revealing power"). Symbols are "overdetermined" [FP, p. 19], and this excess is what puts interpretation in motion: the *logos* of *mythos* is hermeneutical. Symbols demand interpretative thinking; but so, too, he contends does *philosophy* (as hermeneutical) *demand symbols*. This, he recognizes, seems quite scandalous.

(1) On the one hand, the very plurality of the languages within which symbols alone have their place seems to introduce a radical contingency into philosophy which, for its part, seems contrariwise committed to universality. And, while rigorous philosophy seems to require univocal significations, symbols are essentially opaque, equivocal. Here, two points:

(a) Ricoeur not only recognizes, but insists, that the philosopher is "unavoidably oriented"; he "does not speak from nowhere," [SE, pp. 20-21; FP, p. 48] but is always situated within a particular "cultural memory." This alone, however, is what gives rise to philosophy's questions in the first place; and, it is only "in the midst of contingency that rational sequences [can] be detected." [SE, pp. 23-24] Philosophy, to be concrete, is unavoidably in the midst of contingency; as such, its "detective work" is a work of interpretation.

(b) More formidable, however, is this: how can philosophy attend rigorously to symbols, when these are nested within natural languages and thus subject to their notorious infelicities: verbal equivocacy and syntactical *amphiboly*? The "logic" of thought seems to demand strict *univocity*; thus, the "intolerance of symbolic logic" to equivocity and amphiboly, which would be necessary to a philosophy *qua* hermeneutics (thinking which demands symbols), "forces hermeneutics to radically justify its own language." [FP, p. 50] For him, the *only* way to do this is by a "transcendental logic of double meanings," a logic that is not simply "alongside" symbolic logic, but that alone can "ground" the hermeneutical adventure: the focus must be on "the conditions of possibility of a domain of objectivity in general." [FP, pp. 48, 52] Thus, not being at the same level as traditional logical calculus, it is not bound by the requirement of univocity. The case for interpretation rests entirely on the reflective function of interpretative thought; "the indirect, symbolic language of reflection *can* be valid, not *because* it is equivocal, but *in spite* of its being equivocal." [FP, pp. 53-54]

(2)   Even if that is correct, a perplexing embarrassment still crops up, necessarily. "Wherever a man dreams or raves, another man rises to give an interpretation." [SE, p. 350] But this does not say *which* interpretation must be given; indeed, it is *essential* that *other* interpretations be possible. The central paradox of symbols, and for philosophy, beyond the question of truth/falsity, beyond the question of honesty/lying, is that of *illusion*. The bond between symbols and interpretation "furnishes a new motive for suspicion. Any interpretation can be revoked; no myths without exegesis, but no exegesis without contesting." [FP, pp. 41-42] More acutely, not only are there always a variety of interpretations available for any symbol, but there is an internal polarity, a double solicitation, here: symbols may be taken either as cunning deceits, illusions, distortions requiring an equally cunning suspicion and concerted effort at unmasking (Freud, Marx, Nietzsche); or, they may be taken as revelations, hierophantic disclosures of the "sacred," to be "heard" concernfully as one "addressed" by a primal word. This "conflict of interpretations" within hermeneutics is central and inevitable. But, as with the first issue, the key to the paradox here is in the problematic of reflection. The reflecting philosopher confronts a veritable *task* to be taken up: the overcoming of the "war" lies, "in the strong and philosophical sense of the term, [in] an adventure of the *Cogito* and the reflective philosophy that proceeds therefrom." [FM, p. 37] Whether symbols "disguise" or "reveal" can be learned only from actual reflective "work," a work which tackles the "school of suspicion" (mainly, Freud) head-on in the form of a discipline of thinking. This is no mere sportive exercise; it is an actual undergoing by the reflective self seeking its own authentic being—hence, the encounter with Freud is necessary.

(3)   A final piece of the scandal philosophy faces: the "immensity of the wager of this hermeneutics" [SE, p. 350] is not only that it is at war within itself, but that it is, after all, a kind of *wager,* whose outcome is by no means known from the outset. The bet is that Ricoeur's "third way," a kind of

transcendental deduction in the manner of Kant, will in its own way demonstrate that the fullness (boundedness) of language and of the human world embodied and expressed therein *are made possible* by the semantics, the mythics, and the poetics of symbols.

The "pay-off" lies in this, that in its "power to raise up, to illuminate, to give order to . . . human experience," [SE, p. 355] philosophy, following up the inner movements of symbols, "has for its task of qualitative transformation of reflexive consciousness. Every symbol is finally a hierophant, a manifestation of the bond between man and the sacred." [SE, p. 356] But this will become manifest only if philosophy actually confronts the polar opposite—the "unmasking" and "double guile" of Freudian psychoanalysis—and "appropriates" it to itself as "stages" of its own reflective journey of self-disclosure.

Clearly, the central issues of this problematic are *the self* and the nature of *reflection.* [FP, pp. xii, 42-43, 420] For this, it is necessary to prepare the ground by considering the nature of symbols themselves, then to confront Freud and the problematic of "unmasking" and "suspicion." Only then will it be possible to appreciate the exact issues of self and reflection.

In what sense do "symbols give rise to thought"? Briefly, symbols (e.g. "stain") reveal a double intentionality: a literal meaning ("stain" = "unclean") which, however, is itself a conventional sign within language that intentively points to a second meaning *like* the first ("stained," and "unclean," man is taken symbolically "like" this, i.e., as "impure" and morally "defiled"). The second meaning is *not given otherwise* than through the first: this is the "opacity." But, the second *is* "given": there is thus a "donative" movement to the second through, and *only* through, the first. [SE, pp. 15-18] Symbols are thus essentially *bound-to* (literal, conventional meanings) and *bound-by* (the analogically donative meaning). Consequently, though there is obviously much more to this, symbols are not quite the same as myths, even while deeply tied to them. Symbols, as spontaneously created meanings enigmatically evoking "likenesses" of another level, make possible the narrative elaboration of myths (e.g., "exile" and "defilement" make possible the mythical history of the expulsion of Adam and Eve).

This "double meaning" structure—the "semantic structure"—is not sufficient to make the intrinsic need for reflective thought clear and demanding. It is rather "the second trait of symbols," says the *Freud* book—their *mythical* function—which shows new traits of symbols, specifically that symbols are the "dawn of reflection." [FP, pp. 38-40] First, myths introduce exemplary personages which (a) *generalize* human experience in the form of universal paradigms functioning to enable individual persons to "read" their own condition and destiny, (b) through the narratives involving them in events happening "once upon a time," human experience receives *temporal orientation,* a beginning and an end, and (c) these myths recount, transhistorically, the "irrational break" which generates the two primitive "ways" of hermeneutics: the innocence of coming-to-be, and the guilt of history.

Beyond the semantic and mythic functions, every narratively nested symbol intrinsically refers to still other myths: e.g. the myths of evil are the obverse of that of salvation. Thus, every symbol shows not only *semantic opacity* and *mythic structuring,* but also *systemic references:* "each symbol belongs to a meaningful totality which furnishes the first scheme of the system." [FP, p. 40]

Symbols, then as semantically "doubled" meanings, mythical revelations of the human estate, and systemically located within a totality, inherently demand a reflective hermeneutics, an "architectonic task" of interpretation.

But is the reverse also true? Does philosophy itself demand symbols, myths, equivocacy? Is it the case that "the philosophic act, in its innermost nature, not only does not exclude, but requires something like an interpretation"? [FP, p. 41] The problem Ricoeur here faces, in his effort to show that philosophy itself is hermeneutics, is that if philosophy is to be hermeneutical, it must "have recourse" to symbols. But this means that philosophy must be rooted in an act which is intrinsically divisive: for interpretation yields internally conflicting "ways." Symbols at once "disguise" and "reveal." Hence, the task for Ricoeur is to "test" whether these radical alternatives can be "reconciled," "mediated," "surmounted." This is the task of the *Freud* book, and on its completion hangs the very possibility of making sense of self, reflection, philosophy.

II

This is truly slippery terrain, especially in the context of Freud's work, which is surely an exceptional exhibition of the guises and disguises, the cunning and dread of being a subject. To understand Freud's work as "about the subject" is to find that "the subject is never the subject one thinks it is." [FP, p. 420] That fact itself forces a change in our notions of self and of reflection. Here, three points are crucial.

(1) We think we are "closest" to, most "immediate" with, ourselves. Philosophers, too, have made much of this "immediacy of self-consciousness." But even modest reflection shows a striking internal cacophony of voices, deceptions, wishes, images, ruses, feelings, cultural fronts, fantasies, all of which bubble up from unsuspected depths and surprise, embarrass, delight, even terrorize.

Indeed, if anything is "immediately present" in self-consciousness, it is at best an empty feeling. What is incontestable in the Cartesian doubt is "but a certitude devoid of truth . . . that I exist and that I think," and this is hardly self-knowledge. [FP, p. 44] This "immediacy" is in fact an illusion; even transcendental phenomenological reflection, Husserl recognized, must face this possibility of deception.[1] Reflection, thus, cannot be a form of intuition; rather, reflection captures, or re-captures the "Ego of the Ego Cogito in the mirror of its objects, its works, its acts . . . The first truth—*I am, I think*—remains as abstract and empty as it is invincible; it has to be 'mediated' by the ideas, actions, works, institutions, and monuments that objectify it." [FP, p. 43] In this sense, reflection is a reappropriation of the self I am, but which has become "lost" to me through the myriad of distractions, diversions, and employments of daily life, as also through the clutter of "works" and other outer displays which self projects. This "diaspora . . . signifies that I do not at first possess what I am." [FP, p. 45] Hence, reflection on self is a task *(Aufgabe)*; self is not *gegeben* but *aufgegeben*.

But Freud's work—especially the data gleaned in clinical settings (dreams most of all)—compels us to recognize "thoughts" *(Gedanken)* which are excluded from consciousness by forces barring conscious notice. [FP, p. 118] Hints, signs, of psychical activities and "ideas" which are in no way conscious abound in human life. Indeed, consciousness here becomes what is *least* known to itself; there has thus occurred in Freud's work a kind of "reduction," but it is not the Husserlian reduction *to* consciousness. In a sort of "epoché in reverse," Ricoeur argues, Freud's discoveries are in effect a reduction *of* consciousness itself. "Henceforward there is a question . . . of the process of becoming-conscious *(Bewusstwerden)*, in place of the so-called evidence of being-conscious *(Bewusstsein)*." [FP, p. 424] The immediacy of consciousness has been *dispossessed,* displaced as a pretension, an illusion.

(2) Nor is this all, for with the dispossession of consciousness *(Bewusstsein)*, there must as well be a dispossession of the *object* of consciousness. And, just this occurs in Freud's work. Precisely inasmuch as one is here dealing with psychical matters which are *barred* from "becoming conscious," the notion of the "Unconscious" lies totally outside of phenomenology—indeed, is a veritable "antiphenomenology." [FP, pp. 117-22, 424-25, 428, 443] Hence, consciousness is a "text" which is truncated, requiring interpolation in order to establish meaning and connection. [FP, pp. 119-20]

Especially with the introduction of the concepts of "instinct" *(Trieb)* and their "vicissitudes," the "object" can no longer have the primacy of being a "phenomenological clue," precisely because it is *displaced*: it is that at which instincts "aim," as something wished-for, hated, desired, feared, etc.

(3)   For the same reasons, the topography and economics which Freud constructs to "read" the lacunary text of consciousness requires the dispossession of the *ego*. Like the "object," it is similarly an "aim" of an instinct *(Ichtrieb)*, a "variable in an economic function." [FP, p. 126] Precisely here is the place of *narcissism*: the generic notion of self-love (conceived as "instinct") effectively dispossesses the ego. It is "no longer the subject of the Cogito but the object of desire . . . which exchanges itself for object values on the market of libidinal investments or cathexes." [FP, p. 425]

This "dispossessed" ego, like the dispossessed consciousness and object, must be taken up into reflection: the most intimate of all, myself, cannot escape radical questioning. Narcissism leads to the reflective discovery:

> that as soon as the apodictic truth *I think, I am* is uttered, it is blocked by a pseudo-evidence: an abortive Cogito has already taken the place of the first truth of reflection, *I think, I am*. At the very heart of the Ego Cogito I discover an instinct all of whose derived forms point toward something altogether primitive and primordial, which Freud calls primary narcissism. [FP, p. 425]

Center of resistance to truth though it is, narcissism has received three profound blows in the history of science, says Freud. On the one hand, the Copernican revolution forced man to give up his view of himself as center and lord of the cosmos; then, Darwin's and others' work forced him to give up his view of himself as lord over animals and as distinctively different from them. Now, with Freud, we are forced to a still deeper humiliation: the ego is not even master in its own house, the mind. [FP, pp. 182-83, 426-27]

Hence, the tripartite dispossession inextricably requires that the "first truth" (*I think, I am*) must be a "forgetfulness," a "wounding," a constant "vacillation." Man is a being who is essentially "threatened": from the outside, the world; from conscience (source of guilt), and most powerfully from within (the menace of the instincts).

III

Ricoeur insists that Freud's topography and economics, even though "perfectly adapted to a struggle against illusion," never come to grips with the primary "positing of the self [as] a truth which posits itself." [FP, pp. 428; 43] What is the "I" of the "I think"? On this, Freud's work is "very disappointing," but it is a lack having its source in the humiliation and wounding which psychoanalysis inflicts on narcissism. The "disappointment," that is, is not a definitive *conclusion* about Freud's work, but one of the necessary *stages* which reflection must suffer in order to disabuse itself of the multiple, beguiling disguises with which the self masks itself.

Reflection thus is obliged to become equally as cunning in unmasking the self, as the self is in constructing itself as a fugitive. This task, though, is anchored in Freud's work despite its silence on the vital issue. The root of the metapsychology, its fundamental hypothesis [FP, p. 137], is the notion of "psychical representatives of instincts." [FP, pp. 115-16, 135-50] Unknowable in their biological being, instincts are always designated, or "represented," in the psychism by ideas and by affects. Indeed, this it the *only* way instincts can enter into the psychism and thus have efficacy. The unconscious and the conscious, thus, are not "absolute," but only "relative" others; they show a profound affinity. [FP, p. 430]

There are thus grounds for "restoring" what was "dispossessed": the ideational and affective representatives, the latter being the more crucial, as will be seen. The adventure thus far has yielded "a wounded Cogito . . . a Cogito that posits itself but does not possess itself: a Cogito that sees its original truth only in and through the avowal of the inadequacy, illusion, and lying of actual consciousness." [FP, p. 439] The "positing of self" in the "first truth," i.e., turns out to be the emergence of self as posited in its own fundamental "desire-to-be." It is in *effort* that one finds the core sense of self, not in the cool, refractory rays of perceptual awareness.

Pursuing the Freudian "regression" (understood philosophically as "archaeology"), one continually comes up against this efforting—which, if at all "sayable," is so only via *metaphors* of force or potency. Surely true in Freud's work, which is fundamentally a "revelation of the archaic," [FP, p. 440] it must also be true for its philosophical appropriation. The plumbing of the "ever prior" reveals the core of psychical depth: the system, "Unconscious," consists of instinctual representatives which constantly "discharge their cathexis," and yet remain "timeless," exempt from any sense of contradiction, heedless of (external) reality. The same is later attributed (by Freud) to the *id* (*das Es*), but what is crucial is that the "primordial"[2] is "the impersonal and the neuter . . . a neuter that, never being an *I think*, is something like an *It speaks*, which expresses itself in laconisms, displacements of emphasis of meaning, and the rhetoric of dreams and jokes." [FP, p. 443]

This "archaic" is expressive of the essentially hidden darkness of self, its neuter sea of tumultuous, instinctual impulses. The vital point is the unsurpassable character of desire: [FP, p. 445] "that which, in the unconscious, is capable of speaking, that which is able to be represented, refers back to a substrate that cannot be symbolized: desire as desire." [FP, pp. 453-54] Here is the *sum* of the *Cogito, ergo sum*.

Utilizing Leibniz's notions of "expression" and "appetition," [FP, pp. 455-56] Ricoeur thinks that critical insight into this archaic phenomenon is possible because it opens up understanding of the "double law of representation: as standing for objects or things, representation is pretension of truth; but it is also the expression of life, expression of effort or appetite." [FP, p. 456] Freud's stress on the *barrier* between these is, while his true originality, also productive of a crucial paradox: for there can be no direct conscious awareness of these roots, no direct reflection. For the *psychoanalyst* the only mode of access is the battery of "techniques" [FP, pp. 408-18] with all the struggle inherent to them.

For the *philosopher*, who has no psychoanalytic praxis or technique, the sole wedge into this rudimentary primordial is the "homogeneity" between the unconscious and the conscious—i.e., the "psychical representatives." Reflection, however, shows that however "unnameable . . . [desire] is turned from the very outset toward language; . . . [it] is both the non-spoken and the wish-to-speak." [FP, p. 457] Thus, the twofold law of expressivity reveals two modes of inquiry: either a gnosiology which takes up the representation in respect of its intentiveness to objects; or an "exegesis" which explores the desires that lie "hidden" within that intentionality. "Intentiveness" to objects is thus severely *opposed* to "manifestation" of desire, of life; the latter lies "hidden within," and even "interferes" with, the former. [FP, p. 458]

Reflection must thereby be a reappropriation, a grasping of the "Ego in its effort to exist, in its desire to be . . . Effort and desire are the two sides of this positing of the self in the first truth: *I am*." [FP, p. 46] It is only through its works, often unclear and revocable, that reflection can grasp this self, for they alone truly bear witness to that effort and desire. This means that philosophy must perforce be hermeneutical, for the act of existing cannot be grasped "except in signs scattered in the world." [FP, p. 46]

IV

The archaeology discovers a great deal more: the essentially teleological character of self (the articulation of which requires Hegel's dialectics); the significant modes of human feeling (detected already by Kant), in having, power, and valuing; and the core place of creativity and the awesome encounter with the sacred. The self is not only this desiring; it is as well, *as desire*, a "demand"—i.e. a desire for an avowal from another's desire; a recognition, an attesttation, a proof that the self is autonomous. Thus, in the unending *mutuality of recognition* (as found in Hegel's dialectics of master and slave) the self is seen to be essentially with-other-selves, in the work of mutual reduplication of self-consciousness. [cf. FP, pp. 467-72] And, through encounters with ever richer strata of objectivities (having, power, valuing) incorporated into thereby ever richer strata of selfhood, the self comes to greater maturity (comes to it-*self*). Finally, in the hierophantic and creative reach of symbols and myths, the self is mediated to its final, truly "spiritual" stage, its fuller tapestries interwoven with the patterns of other persons, world, ultimately, the sacred.

The central features of Ricoeur's conception of self—its core moments— are sufficiently at hand, however, without having to detail these later stages. What is necessary is a reflection with Ricoeur on the underlying, the archaic.

V

By virtue of their semantic, mythic, and systemic structures, symbols demand interpretative understanding. So far as self ciphers, it calls for deciphering.

Another way of expressing part of the point here: "methods" of inquiry must take their guides, be grounded in, the "things themselves" which are to be investigated. The principle underlying this canon of method is a *principle of evidence (Evidenz)*. For every objectivity (every thematized or thematizable state-of-affairs), there is an originary mode of evidence pertaining to it, by or through which alone it is "presented *originaliter*," or by means of which one is at all aware of it as such. Such evidences, encounters, of necessity *vary* according as the objectivity itself varies.[3] Disclosing the most originary mode of evidential encounter (*"Evidenz est ein Erfahrung,"* as Husserl stresses) is thus equivalent to the disclosure of the "thing itself."[4] In Ricoeur's own terms, ". . . we must stop dissociating method and doctrine, stop taking the method without the doctrine. Here, the doctrine is the method." [FP, p. 433]

Yet, though alluded to in several places, and figuring importantly in others, the phenomenological principle is found to be wanting, and in fact is dropped, in the face of the task of interpreting symbols. Their "revealing power" is grounded in their "donative character," and this is to have "already broken the phenomenological neutrality." For here, I am not a subject studying some object; I find myself, rather, a being who is "spoken to." The symbol "draws me," "makes me participate in what is announced to me." This is not phenomenology, but "an existential assimilation, according to the movement of analogy, of my being to being." [FP, p. 31] Remarking on his earlier work he makes the break quite plain: "A hermeneutic method, coupled with reflection, goes much farther than an eidetic method I was then practicing." [FP, p. 458] So far as I can see, with this step, Ricoeur has in effect given up the central principle of evidence which otherwise seems essential to his own work.

Now, though, two critical issues arise. On the one hand, the claim that "symbols give rise to thought" *is itself a judgment which inherently appeals to some mode of evidence*, on the sole basis of which one could at all understand the claim and, ultimately, come to either agreement or disagreement with it. It matters not in the least whether *this* evidence turns out to be "interpretative" or not—the principle of evidence must still hold, if this is indeed the way by means of which we are at all cognizant of and eventually knowledgeable of symbols. Hence, it cannot be the case that "hermeneutics" stands opposed to "phenomenology" and the principle of evidence.

On the other hand, the claim that philosophy itself demands symbols [FP, p. 41] is quite a different claim, as Ricoeur recognizes. But, if philosophy is hermeneutics, we are left with a profound enigma. What is the status of the *claim that* "the philosophical act, in its innermost nature, is hermeneutical"? Either it is *itself* hermeneutical, or it is not. If it is, it can only be called (with an awkward stretching of the tongue) *meta*-hermeneutical (a "circle" which, so far as I can see, is not at all the "hermeneutical circle"). If it is not hermeneutical, then philosophy is not and cannot be hermeneutical at its root. However, even if it is itself a hermeneutical claim, its "meta" status must itself be accounted for, and the *difference in systematic levels or status is unavoidably admitted.*

This is no small issue, for on it hangs the problem of how we are to understand the very project Ricoeur embarks upon, not to mention its "results." Ricoeur seems aware of the problem in the early pages of the *Freud* book: hermeneutics stands in need of being radically justified, and only a *"transcendental logic"* concerning the "conditions for the very possibility of . . ." can accomplish this crucial task. The difficulty here is that, on the one hand, while calling for a "radical justification *of* hermeneutics, he promptly goes on in the next sentence to assert that this logic *"is proper to"* hermeneutics. The text seems clear that this ambiguous phrase is taken to mean that hermeneutics *is itself coextensive with* this logic—a "logic of double meanings." But, again, the "of" is quite ambiguous: it might mean "is proper to" in the sense of "properly falls within" or "belongs to," in which case one could hardly call it "transcendental." Or, it might be "establishes the condition for the possibility of" double meanings, in which case it can hardly itself be *at the same level* as what it thereby establishes.

Beyond the ambiguities, however, is the difference in systematic level inherent to Ricoeur's "talk-about" symbols, hermeneutics, interpretation. This "talk-about" can only be transcendental, and cannot therefore be confused with what it is supposed to justify radically—viz., hermeneutics. It may well be that one must "live in the *aura* of meaning" of the symbols in order to understand them; but this claim as such is not at the same level as that inquiry, since it speaks to what is transcendentally necessary in order to conduct such an inquiry. To confuse these, as I think Ricoeur does, is to *vitiate the very sense of inquiry at both levels.*

VI

These remarks bear directly on the focal issues of self and of reflection. What is the "question of self"? Ricoeur's early study of *The Voluntary and the Involuntary* puts it this way, following a deliberately Husserlian phenomenology.[5] Taking up the "reflexive direction of decision," and agreeing (as does the *Freud* book) with the Cartesian "Cogito," he contends that "a certain presence to myself must covertly accompany all intentional consciousness." Yet "such an immediate self-presence clinging to the very thrust of consciousness" is not found in such explicit judgments as "It is I who. . . ." *This* self-affirmation is a kind of "prereflexive imputation of myself . . . a self-reference which is not yet self-observation. . . ." Now, the question here is, "How is this possible?" The quest, in turn, must be a working back "to the conditions which make it possible." That is, *this* problematic is manifestly a transcendentally eidetic one.

But just this kind of inquiry, while on the one hand being asserted as necessary to justify hermeneutics itself, is precisely what is found wanting in the *Freud* book. Hermeneutics goes "much farther." At most, what was then called "self-presence" is now to be understood merely as a "first tendency [of reflection] to identify itself with immediate consciousness." [FP, p. 54]

Not surprisingly, the *question* asked in the *Freud* book has also shifted: "What new self-understanding comes out of this interpretation, and what self is it which thus comes to self-understanding?" [FP, p. xii] The question, in short, has become two-pronged. On the one hand, it concerns, the *"meaning"* of self and reflection: "What does Reflection signify? What does the Self of self-reflection signify? [FP, pp. 42-43] On the other hand, the question concerns what *The Symbolism of Evil* called "a qualitative transformation of reflexive consciousness," a "participation" in the "revealing power of symbols." [SE, p. 356] The *Freud* book, too, exhibits both lines, expressly advancing the idea that authentic reflection "itself undergoes change by incorporating into itself the discourse of its own archaeology; instead of abstract reflection, it starts to become concrete reflection." [FP, p. 342] The polar opposite of this is not merely "abstract" reflection, but rather the *pretension* to reflect "neutrally," which is "to speak from nowhere." It is thus no surprise that Ricoeur "breaks" with his former "phenomenology": *the very questions he poses are no longer the same, they are not transcendental but rather the hermeneutical questions of interpreting "meaning."* This fact renders the very sense of his appeal to "transcendental conditions for the possibility of . . ." highly dubious at the least. To repeat: the *statements about* the hermeneutical task, and the *practice of* hermeneutics, are *not* at the same level.

Yet, the appeal to the transcendental, as I understand it, can only be perfectly right. And, in fact, there are haunting reminders sprinkled throughout the *Freud* book that give one pause. In one curious passage (curious, because the point is not reverted to again), writing about the dispossession of the object, Ricoeur points out that the true genesis of the notion of the object, within Freud's work, is merely an "ostensible antiphenomenology."[6] It is "merely the long detour at the end of which the object will again become the transcendental guide, but for a highly mediated reflection. . . ." Husserl's passive genesis indicates the area of research here, but Freud remains original in his linking of this genesis with that of love and hate—the desires. [FP, p. 425]

Earlier, too, Ricoeur suggests that "what is economically reconstructed at the end of this process [narcissism] is precisely 'the object' in the phenomenological sense." [FP, p. 126] Thus, the history of the object is the history of the object-function, and this is the history of desire. The so-called "antiphenomenology" is "ostensible" just because, as I see it, the "object-function" in psychoanalysis is indeed *not* incommensurate with "the object" in the phenomenological sense, which, like that in Freud, is a "sedimentation" resulting from the complex functions of *Passivität*. While Freud has stressed desire far more than did Husserl, this difference surely makes no difference *in principle*. Indeed, in many ways, Ricoeur's own philosophical reflection on desire seems quite capable of being understood as an *eidetics of desire*, using (here) Freud's work as a clue.

More important is the notion of "dispossession." Consider that of "the object." To what does this refer? If (as Ricoeur has suggested) "the object function" is really the "object" in the phenomenological sense, then this can hardly be what is "dispossessed" (i.e. the machinery of the primary process and of narcissism can hardly be said to be dispossessed). And phenomenologically, when one engages the epoché and reduction at all seriously, one's thematization can hardly be said to "dispossess" the object as it is taken (intended) by the natural consciousness whose "object" it is. What, then, does this "dispossession" signify? I can only skim a few surfaces here, but these are important indices, suggestive of a deeply troubling matter. As Ricoeur nicely shows, [FP, pp. 375-390] there are some alluring similarities between Husserl and Freud. Notwithstanding these, phenomenology is not only not psychoanalysis, but can give only an approximate understanding of it. The first is certainly true; the latter is problematical. In any case, the point here is that *the entire issue of "dispossession" falls within the clinical discipline of psychoanalysis*.

Nor could it be otherwise, as Ricoeur shows. "Psychoanalysis is not a reflexive discipline; the off-centering it brings about is fundamentally different from the 'reduction' in that *it is very strictly constituted by* what

Freud calls the 'analytic technique' . . ." (*My emphasis*). [FP, p. 390]
Here, two things. First, this being so, it seems most gratuitous to interpret
Freud's "dispossession" as a "reduction *of* " consciousness in contrast to
Husserl's "reduction *to*" consciousness; to write of an "epoché in reverse";
and to characterize psychoanalysis as an "antiphenomenology." The stress
must be on the "fundamental difference": we have here a *non*-phenom-
enology, not an *anti*-phenomenology; nor is there a "reduction" in
Husserl's sense. Thus, the second point: the "technique" simply has no
counterpart in a "reflexive discipline" *of any kind*. The terms of that technique, similarly, have their sense strictly within their appropriate clinical
context: object, intersubjectivity, ego, unconscious, conscious, transference, resistance, etc., have no "conceivable phenomenological equiva-
lents." [FP, p. 414]

Nor could that be otherwise—not only for phenomenology, but for any
reflexive discipline, *hermeneutics included*. The problematic of "dispossess-
sion" has its place solely within that psychoanalytic praxis. Thus, the effort
to "reappropriate" Freud's work within hermeneutics seems suspect to
begin with. But, more, what could such "reappropriation" actually signify?
That is, in what ways can reflexive philosophy "relate" to Freudian
analysis?

So far as I can see, philosophical discourse with analysis (or other clinical
disciplines) is possible on two counts (realizing that this is itself an immense
topic). First, one must be able to explore the "conditions for the very
possibility of" that analysis itself. Where Freud, e.g., treats intersubjectivity within his notion of "technique," Husserl explores the conditions for the
possibility of "relating to another person" as such (however well or badly
this may be done). Where Freud takes his work as science, phenomenology
explores the conditions for the possibility of science as such.

Second, philosophical engagement with analysis is possible wherever
Freud's claims exceed the limits of his own praxis. Thus, when he maintains
not only that the neurotic is not master in his own house, but "above all the
man of morality, the ethical man," [FP, p. 183] then surely this claim is
properly philosophical and assessable *only* as such. On both counts,
furthermore, there is certainly no way—*beyond actual demonstration*—to
say that only hermeneutics can properly "relate" to analysis. That
demonstration is not forthcoming; and, what reasons Ricoeur gives are
quite inadequate (indeed, seem to me to involve him necessarily in
phenomenological "evidencing"), and where relevant apply no less to a
hermeneutics than to phenomenology: they apply to *any* reflexive
discipline.

But Ricoeur formulates the question of self in *quite another way*:

First, it must be made clear that it is in reflection and for reflection that psychoanalysis is an archeology; it is an archeology *of the subject*. But of what subject? What must the subject of reflection be if it is likewise to be the subject of psychoanalysis? [FP, p. 420]

The first point here clearly concerns the project of philosophically *assessing the status of psychoanalysis itself*: its claims, sources, evidences, etc., which show that it is an "archeology." This is "Freudianism" taken, if you will, as an "acceptance-phenomenon."[7] As such, *this* issue must be kept rigorously distinct (however closely related) from the very *different* issue concerning the self (and, reflection).

That other issue is the concern of the second part of the passage. But, here it is necessary to notice that there is at once a mixing of different issues, and a posing of the proper question. To ask, "of what subject?" is to *remain within* the problematic pertaining to the explication of the sense of "Freudianism" itself. But to ask, "What must the subject of reflection be if it is likewise to be the subject of psychoanalysis?" is *to pose a radically different question*, for this concerns *the trancendental conditions for the possibility of being-as-self* (subject), such that to be this is likewise to be-able-to-be both reflectively apprehended ("of reflection") and neurotic ("of psychoanalysis"). What this question sets out as problematical is not at all "Freudianism"-qua-acceptance-phenomenon, but the "self"-qua-phenomenon.

This transcendental question, however, does not seem to be the one Ricoeur explicitly pursues. What concerns him, to the contrary, is the effort to take "Freudianism" as a "stage of reflection," as a necessary "way" for transforming the self, to work through the metapsychology, reflectively attempting to find in it (to reappropriate) the "subject *of*" the "archeology," and *not the conditions for the possibility of being-as-subject* within that archeology.

Clarifying these questions helps in another way. Namely, it seems to me that the force and epistemic status of Freud's vaunted "antiphenomenology" is hardly that. In one sense, as we already saw, so long as it remains within the particular clinical settings of therapy, it is "*non*," or better, "*a*-phenomenological"—for the very reasons Ricoeur states. But to the extent that analysis either does, or can be shown to, engage in speculation which exceeds that context, then it is unabashedly philosophical. Here, however, there is a subtlety: whether explicitly or implicitly philosophical (maintaining, e.g., that human subjectivity *as such and without exception* reveals the sort of archaism Freud has postulated and claimed to find clinically), does not the very possibility of clinically encountered phenomena—hysteria, autism, dreams, etc.—however they may be specifically and therapeutically interpreted, point to the transcendental? I mean: independently, e.g., of whether dreams are taken as the disguised discourse of desire, revelations of occult phenomena beyond the ken of normal awareness, or whatever, there is a significant transcendental problematic concerning the "conditions" without which that occurrence would not be possible; i.e., what dreaming signifies for "being-a-self." It is the same as regards "illusion," "deception," and the like: how is it possible for me to be deceived (or is it to "deceive myself"?), to mask myself to myself . . . ? This kind of issue is, it seems to me, not at all the one Ricoeur engages in, even though he raises the question.

VII

These considerations bring me almost full circle. Many of Ricoeur's results about the self—effort, desire, mutuality, feeling, and the like—seem *either to suppose the truth* of Freud's analytic (as an "archaism"); *or,* they must be understood as *phenomenologically "verifying"* the properly philosophical content of Freudian analysis. Judging from the text, it would seem that the latter is closer to the case. For if one asks of Freud's analytics, what is the rationale, the ground, for at all introducing such notions as the "unconscious," it seems clear that it is done as a way of making sense of, accounting for, what must otherwise remain utterly incomprehensible though plainly there in experience—the clinically discovered phenomena such as hysteria, autism, etc. Ricoeur points the way here:

> the justification of the unconscious takes on an aspect of scientific necessity: the text of consciousness is a lacunary, truncated text; the assumption of the unconscious is equivalent to a work of interpolation that introduces meaning and connection into the text. [FP, pp. 119-20]

The rationale is found in what is regarded by Freud as an assumption necessary to be able to account for the critical phenomena. The "interpolation" seems little short of a *transcendental* supposition: the facts of the "dream-work" are not possible, not accountable for, *except on condition that* the one-who-dreams continually undergoes processes of imagining, feigning, fantasying—of which, however, he must be continually *unaware* in any explicit manner. And this is eventually said to be so *for us all, and not simply for the patients actually encountered.* In order to be able to be the dreamer (at least, so far as Freud is concerned), it is *essential,* thus, that there be the system, Unconscious. But this, as Ricoeur reminds us, is not merely a supposition: the "realism" of the Unconscious is a positing of the Unconscious as "real," efficacious. As such, it must somehow *be accessible,* make itself felt, give signs, for otherwise it would be on a par with the instincts in their biological character: utterly unknowable, and thereby would collapse the edifice of *psycho*analysis.

The "instinctual representatives," in the end, Ricoeur points out, are on the side of the psychical. Hence, there is indeed *a mode of access to, and therefore a mode of evidence for* (these are strictly correlative) the unconscious. This mode of access is available to the patient only by way of difficult, tortuous "work"; and, it is available (almost beforehand, one might even say) to the psychoanalyst, but again, with "work." Thus, numerous, clinically encountered and now reflectively considered examples of these "representatives" show rather ample grounds for the "interpolation." To the extent, of course, that these examples come from *actual* encounters, all the "evidence" here can warrant is a conclusion pertaining to the region of actuality *(Wirklichkeit)*. To make out grounds for the ostensibly transcendental status of the interpolation, evidence concerning the "possibility" (any possible subject whatever) must be found—namely, by way of reflective philosophical inquiry of the kind Ricoeur himself often practices, or which, by attempting to "appropriate" the "work" of Freud, seems to be yielded by that mode of reflection. Ricoeur's conclusions, after all, *concern any possible "self"*; hence, it seems not unreasonable to understand them as transcendental. Being-a-self is *essentially* (among other things) to exhibit oneself as a desire-to-be.

That is, in the course of being guided by Freud's analysis, Ricoeur comes up with what must be called the *eidetic core of being-a-self:* the effort-to-be, an effort which, as profound desire to be acknowledged as such by others, would (if further delineated) show how it is even possible for a "self" to be deluded or genuine, masked or open, split or whole, terrorized or acknowledged. This self-positing as desire-to-be, however, seems to be precisely what *The Voluntary and the Involuntary* had already begun to uncover under the name of the prereflective "imputation of myself" located and implicitly affirmed in my actions, deeds, and works. Thus, although the *Freud* book has surely *advanced* this considerably, it can hardly be seen as a *repudiation*; the "much farther" which Ricoeur has now gone is not at all due to a dropping of his earlier "eidetics." Just the opposite.

I thus see no reason whatever for a supposed move "from" phenomenology "to" hermeneutics, even in the case of studying a "text" in the usual sense. After all, the principle of evidence, taken rigorously, *requires* that one's "method" have its source and grounds in the "things themselves," in the modes of evidence strictly proper to them (and thus, in his terms, inseparable from "doctrine"). *If these "things"* ("texts") *are such as must be "interpreted"*—that being the originary mode of evidence through which alone they are accessible to us, and on the basis of which judgments about them can alone be made—*then surely the phenomenological principle of evidence leaves one no choice but to "interpret."* Hence, "interpretation" can only be understood as at once the mode of evidence for, the way by which we come to experience, and the method for phenomenological inquiry into, these "texts."

Ricoeur *need* not differ on that point. Nor need he be at odds with the real demand for grounding hermeneutics in transcendental logic. In this sense and to this extent, there can hardly be a question of a choice between methods, or between supposedly "less" adequate and "more" adequate methods: the very thing demanded by Ricoeur is inherent to the principle of evidence, hence is phenomenological.

But, on the questions of self and reflection, it seems to me Ricoeur would sharply diverge from my suggestions. For, he holds that his inquiry into "self" has discovered a being that is at root a "being-hidden," a "being-in-disguise": "As a man of desire I go forth in disguise—*larvatus prodeo.*" [FP, p. 7] While the self is rooted within the intentionality of consciousness (the one side of the law of expressivity), it is also, and more fundamentally, rooted in "life, desire and effort" (the other side of that law). And, this more basic status of self is not only the discovery of the "unsurpassable nature of life, but the interference of desire with intentionality, upon which desire inflicts an invincible obscurity, an ineluctable partiality." [FP, p. 458]

But here matters grow very elusive. I agree with Ricoeur: reflection and self are critical issues, closely intertwined and contextured by desire, effort. We both agree with Husserl: "I, the meditating phenomenologist, set myself the all-embracing task of *uncovering myself,* in my full concreteness—that is, with all the intentional correlates that are included therein."[8] But Ricoeur would insist that "desire" *interferes* with, inflicts an "invincible obscurity" on, intentionality. This is quite questionable.

Desire itself is surely "intentive" just as much as other psychical processes *(Erlebnisse).* And, indeed, *it must be so even for Ricoeur:* desire does, after all, 'tend to," "wish for," speech, utterance, manifestation. Whatever the mode of expression, the "desire-to-be" is intentive *in its own way* (but, then, so is every process, in its own way). Though it *may* well be "hidden," "distorted," and the like, still this *does not in the least belie but precisely reveals its manifestly intentive character.* But even though some modes of desiring are disguised, surely not all are; some, indeed, are strikingly clear and unmistakable, even very subtle desirings—whether or not some particular persons are capable of recognizing the gestures of desire. Even so, however, these too are no less intentive in their own manner than are the disguised desirings. Hence, it is most improper to *oppose* desire to intentionality; this succeeds only in obfuscating their nature.

On the other hand, pointing this out helps us to see that the real opposition Ricoeur is urging is not that, but rather the opposition between what Husserl had called the "doxic" and "non-doxic," between what Ricoeur wishes to call "acts of knowing" and the desire-to-be. [cf. FP, p. 458] Here, several further issues crop up.

To speak of acts of knowing at the level of question here (the ground sense of "self") is not at all proper. Just prior to this, though, Ricoeur draws the opposition more clearly: between the *"intentionality"* which is "ruled by the objects that manifest themselves in that intentionality," and the *"manifestation"* of effort and desire "hidden in that intentionality." [FP, pp. 457, 458] Now, as was already emphasized, what is wrong here is that even if true, the latter claim simply fails to grasp the very sense of desire Ricoeur himself claims it has: that it is "turned toward language." But here there is subtlety Ricoeur seems to me to have overlooked. To adopt Ricoeur's mode of expression, desire not only "wishes" to be spoken; rather, it seeks to be located in *"speech-about"* and in two crucial senses. There is the efforting to *manifest self*, to express self (speech "about" myself); but this speech is, as Ricoeur knows well, speech desiring the other. The speech-about is "about" myself as ineluctably *in the world with others,* hence it is "about" my circum-stances: what stands around me and helps to constitute in some way what I am. We must recall the prime feature of desire for Ricoeur: that it is "desire of *another* desire," i.e., a "demand," and is thus essentially set within the world of others, and this being-set-within can only be the peculiar mode of intentiveness characteristic of "desire."

That such "speaking-as-manifesting-myself and "-as-about-the-world" is multivalently signifying, thus, is not only not surprising in light of this complex intentiveness, but probably quite essential. We must ask, though, why does the effort-to-be manifest itself in enigmas? Why is it that being-self is, among other things, able-to-be deceived, able-to-be neurotic, able-to-be even blanketly obscured to itself (as in autism)? If truth is a task, and I agree, then surely so also is deception, illusion, fraud, feigning. These latter are no less than the former always a "having-to-be-maintained," they are "tasks" or "projects." And these'tasks, no less than that of "truth," are *intentive.* Hence, even desire and effort "relate" to the circumstances of life, quite as much as "believings," "perceivings," "knowings"; they relate to the environing world, and intentively shape it as well as manifest a particular "self" expressing itself. The distinguishable but inseparable complexus of intentive life is matched by its strict correlate, the surrounding milieu, and that milieu, however distinguishable, is strictly inseparable from that life. The dualism of intentionality and manifestation of desire turns out, then, to be a kind of "false consciousness."

Furthermore, however a particular self may particularly express itself, whatever it may "strive to be," it is clear, on the one hand, that this "striving" cannot be opposed to "believing" (in Husserl's broad sense), for the latter itself is a "striving-to-believe," a "striving-to-know," what and who to reckon with things, how to orient oneself within the milieu, and ultimately, I suppose, a wanting to know what is "real." For the self, the "real" is precisely what it must, or believes it must, "reckon with," with respect to which the self "needs to know" what to hold by. This "needing to know," which is a telling exhibiting of one's "effort-to-be," is thus not so much "hidden disguisedly" in the intentiveness-to-objects as *it is* that intentiveness in its core form.[9]

But, on the other hand, given this, it then is necessary to ask what the notion of "indirect discourse" amounts to. "Indirect" in relation to what? "Direct" discourse? But what might that be? Surely not logical calculus, for Ricoeur has already shown that its urge to univocity is severely limited, and appropriate only for highly specific purposes and problems. It represents, if you will, an abstraction (indeed, a complex of abstractions) *away* from natural language, so far away that while it may be written it can in no way be "spoken": Hence, it cannot be "discourse" at all. Then what is "indirect" discourse?

It may be, as Ricoeur suggests, that the "disguised," "laconic," or "fantasy" discourses—the fabric of the speech of dreams, hysterics, neurotics, and in a clear way the rest of us—may well be the *only discourse* of self in its eidetic core: the discourses of desire. Metaphor, metonomy, laconism, as well as analogy, allegory, myth, symbol, story and even colloquialism, joke, irony, satire—all these may well be the only, or at least the primary, discourses for that being whose *eidos* is striving, efforting, needing, desiring . . . *at once* to make itself known or present to others *and* to disclose or know that self-same world of others.[10] The self's "talk," that is, is not so much "indirect" as opposed to some so-called "direct" discourse; it is rather that this "talk" is what it is—self-revealing/other-encountering—precisely because the self which strives is what it is.

What thus becomes prominent is not some sort of contrast between that mode of discourse and, say, symbolic logic—which is not even a discourse. Rather, what is at issue is the discourse of self, its modalities of utterance (at once intentive-to, and intentive-manifestations-of), and their *philosophical articulation*. The issue concerns the marked contrast between the upsurge of self and the language of reflective philosophical inquiry seeking to understand the (and "its") self in the fairest and most rigorous way possible.

VIII

I thus complete the circle of this inquiry: the problematic of reflection on self cannot signify the collapse of this reflection into what is reflected-upon; nor can its language be literally (or, uncritically) the language of the reflected-upon. Philosophy must obviously reflect upon the self, its manifestations, discourses, and the like. But, whether these be "symbolic" or not, philosophy loses itself if it is taken to be *also* symbolic in the same sense. To the "equivocity" of symbols, it is necessary to contrast, not the "univocity" of formal calculus, but the *univocity of philosophical discourse*.

To this point, there is no better witness than Ricoeur. It is *perfectly clear*, indeed *univocally* clear, what Ricoeur means by, e.g., "symbol," "speech," "language," "hermeneutics," and the like. Whether he is explicating Freud's texts or the textures of self, he is again clear, or at a minimum is *striving to be univocally clear*—however difficult and complex a task that surely is. If, then, he means by "reappropriation" of self a strict effort to *repeat* philosophically what the self as reflected-upon shows itself to be, then this is just wrong. His philosophical discourse *is not itself* equivocal, ambiguous, cunning, disguised, a repetition of the laconisms of the subterranean self. Philosophical language is not that of logical calculus; but *neither is it that of the self reflected-upon*.

Husserl put this point exactly:

> Owing to the instability and ambiguity of common language and its much too great complacency about completeness of expression, *we require, even when we use its means of expression, a new legitimation of significations* by orienting them according to accrued insights, and a fixing of words as expressing the significations thus legitimated. *That too we count as part of our normative principle of evidence . . . .*[11] *(My emphasis)*

Just this Ricoeur in fact tries to *practice,* but his professed *aim* seems sometimes quite different. What he does not recognize is that this effort to "fix" expressions, when and only as legitimated by "accrued insights," is part of the normative principle of evidence already emphasized above. Thus, although he believes that reflective philosophy must "have recourse to symbols," it is quite evident that this "recourse" is not itself a "doing again" of what is "done" in the discourses of self, nor is it a collapse of that reflection into that discourse. Where the self "metaphors," philosophy reflectively apprehends and then expresses in judgments which are *about* these metaphors. Or, at the very least, philosophy has an intrinsic requirement to reach the clarity proper to the "things themselves" being studied, and proper to its own nature and tasks as philosophy—guided at every step by the full principle of evidence.[12]

The claim that reflection is a "reappropriation" of self is thus in one clear sense false. But there is a sense in which, even though misleading, it might well be true. Insofar as reflection is itself a *mode of "experiencing"*—experiencing, precisely, what is reflected-upon in its own integrity and context—insofar as reflection *thematizes* the self, then I suppose one might take this as an "appropriation." And, since what is now reflectively thematized was not before thematized, there is a sense in which something is "altered": from being hitherto not reflected-upon to being reflected-upon. But this alteration in modality surely does not alter the "thing" thus apprehended: it could hardly be part of Ricoeur's claim that *his own reflection on desire of itself indelibly changes desires* in its own proper character. Thus, if "appropriation" means a "transformation of reflexive consciousness" in this sense, it strikes me as plainly false in Ricoeur's own terms; either that, or else a confusion of the tasks of philosophy with those of therapy.

Such considerations, however, make it much clearer just where Ricoeur seems radically to diverge. Distinguishing between "straight-forward" awareness of something, and "reflective" awareness of that straightforward awareness, Husserl points out:

> The proper task of reflection, however, is not to repeat the original process, but to consider it and explicate what can be found in it. . . . Precisely thereby an experiential knowing (which at first is descriptive) becomes possible, that experiential knowing *(erfahrungswissen)* to which we owe all conceivable cognizance *(Kenntnis)* and cognition *(Erkenntnis)* of our intentional living . . . The reflecting Ego's non-participation in the "positing" (believing, taking a position as to being) that is part of the straightforward house-perception in no wise alters the fact that his *reflecting* experiencing is precisely an *experiencing* of the house-perception with all its moments, which belonged to it before and are continuing to take shape. . . . The non-participating, the abstaining, of the Ego who has the phenomenological attitude is *his* affair, not that of the perceiving [desiring, etc.] he considers reflectively, nor that of the naturally perceiving [desiring, etc.] Ego. We may add that it is itself accessible to an appropriate reflection; and only by means of this do we know anything about it.[13]

Because of what he takes to be the "overdetermination of meaning" of symbols, Ricoeur contends that *reflection must be precisely a "participation"* in the movements of symbols themselves; reflection on self must be an "existential assimilation" of the reflecting self with the self reflected-upon, and thereby a "qualitative transformation" of both. Still, it is solely because of that stance on reflection's task that his effort to take Freud's analytics as "stages of reflection" makes any sense; only thereby, too, is the turn to Hegelian dialectics even possible; only thereby is the urge to "mediate" sensible.

But this stance is fateful for Ricoeur's own enterprise: its consequence is that it vitiates the sense of it. Reflection in its philosophical guise is a "reappropriation" in the sense of a doing for the "self" of the reflecting philosopher what Freud's analytics at least purports to do for the "self" of the afflicted patient: *the philosopher turns out to be his own therapist.* And, so far as the philosopher talks and writes, his "texts" must, one must suppose, become therapeutic for his readers and auditors—those who authentically "hear" his "speech."

That I am on the other side of this gulf should be clear. Unquestionably, at one level Ricoeur is right: the self confronted with authentic symbols (myths even more) cannot hope to understand them except by going whither they lead, and how; the overdetermination of symbols determines the definite path of that inquiry. Still, it must be recognized that *conducting that inquiry,* and *stating what is necessary in order for that inquiry to be possible* are evidently different matters. To study the symbol of exile, and to study what is requisite for the study of the symbol of exile: these cannot be collapsed, any more than can reflection be collapsed into what is reflected-upon. Whether in doing the former I am led to the *apprehension of myself as exiled,* is one thing (and about this there are different opinions); but that this would be utterly senseless to propose as regards the philosophical/transcendental study of the structures of symbols as such, seems to me unambiguously clear—even in Ricoeur's study.

Philosophical *reflection* is thus to be rigorously distinguished from straightforward consciousness of whatever objectivity; just so, philosophical discourse must be kept rigorously distinct from the discourses of self, precisely in order to be able to study them and the self they exhibit. It has seemed to me that Ricoeur violates both, even while the actual content of his study does not.

Thus, it may be that the task of the emerging self is hermeneutical, having all of its pitfalls and guile to contend with along that way. But when the self becomes reflective upon itself, seeking to unravel the "that by virtue of which *it is at all,*" it takes on for itself another kind of task, the task of understanding itself in its own *eidos.* This task can hardly denigrate the hermeneutics of emergence, since that is precisely what it must now come to understand; yet neither can it collapse the tasks, since that serves neither, and disserves both.

NOTES

1. Cf. Edmund Husserl, *Cartesian Meditations,* tr. Dorion Cairns (The Hague: Martinus Nijhoff, 1960), p. 23; cited by Ricoeur, FP, pp. 377-78, 421. Ricoeur does not seem to appreciate, though, that this "possibility of deception" is itself quite "evident," adequately and apodictically.

2. Ricoeur points out, though, that what is "primordial" in psychoanalysis ("what takes precedence in the order of distortion or disguise") is not at all what is primary in transcendental terms. [FP, p. 154]

3. Cf. Edmund Husserl, *Formal and Transcendental Logic,* tr. Dorion Cairns (The Hague: Martinus Nijhoff, 1969), Part II, Chaps. 4 and 6. Also, my "Reflections on Evidence and Criticism in the Theory of Consciousness," in L.E. Embree (ed.), *Life-World and Consciousness. Essays for Aron Gurwitsch* (Evanston: Northwestern University Press, 1972), pp. 209-30.

4. Cf. *Cartesian Meditations, op cit.,* Med. 1.

5. FN, pp. 55-59; *see also* pp. 6-17.

6.   Nowhere else is the "antiphenomenology" so characterized. It is rather asserted either by itself, or qualified by "totally," [FP, p. 119] called an "inverted phenomenology," [FP, p. 443] or a "pseudo" or "quasi" phenomenology. [FP, pp. 133, 134]

7.   There is a perfect parallel between the study of "Freudianism" and Husserl's study of "science" as an "acceptance-phenomenon." As Husserl disclosed, e.g., that "evidence," "judgment," "grounding," and so on are essential to "science," Ricoeur finds psychoanalysis unintelligible except as a discourse on the "subject." It is surprising that Ricoeur seems never to appreciate this precise parallel. *See* Husserl, *Cartesian Meditations, op. cit.,* Med. 1.

8.   *Ibid.,* p. 38.

9.   I should note that here it seems necessary to modify Husserl's position, that the doxic found the non-doxic. But it is not that one must take the reverse of Husserl, and claim that the latter founds the former. Rather, at their roots, the doxic and the non-doxic are *indistinguishably bound* up in the single "potent," *urge-to-be* hinted at by Ricoeur in his usage of "effort-to-be." Only subsequent experience, phenomenologically, brings about the effective distinguishing and differentiating of these modalities.

10.   Precisely what Merleau-Ponty had analyzed, following Husserl, as the *"Urpräsenz"* a definitive of human being: that the "presence-to-self" is also a *"déprésentation"* and "me jette hors de moi." See *Phenomenology of Perception*, tr. Colin Smith (London/New York: Routledge and Kegan Paul/Humanities Press, 1962), p. 363.

11.   *Cartesian Meditations, op cit.,* p. 14.

12.   Cf. Dorion Cairns, "An Approach to Husserlian Phenomenology," in F. Kersten and R. Zaner (eds.), *Phenomenology: Continuation and Criticism* (The Hague: Martinus Nijhoff, 1973), pp. 223-38, esp. 224-27, where the principle is stated with precision.

13.   *Cartesian Meditations, op cit.,* pp. 34-35.

IV

Mary Schaldenbrand

METAPHORIC IMAGINATION:
KINSHIP THROUGH CONFLICT

This essay proceeds from a paradoxic awareness: Remarking the need for a philosophy of imagination, Ricoeur implies its present absence. And yet, when we return to his major works, we find that all of them assign to imagining the pivot-function. Admittedly, taken as they stand, these major works by no means compose a systematic philosophy of imagining. But, when recovered and reinterpreted within the linguistic context of recent studies in metaphor, they confirm the judgment: from its beginning until now, the work of Ricoeur consistently develops the philosophic sense of imagination as "mediating function." This essay critically examines the role of imagination in Ricoeur's major works, especially in *La Metaphore vive*.

Mary Schaldenbrand is Professor of philosophy at Loyola University, Chicago, Illinois. Among her published articles are "Gabriel Marcel: Philosopher of Intersubjectivity" and "Time, the Self and Hope."

Metaphoric Imagination:
Kinship Through Conflict

MARY SCHALDENBRAND

Whereas the image was lately condemned as inferior to fact, it is now increasingly preferred to fact. How do we explain this reversal? It might be said: today the positivist temper is yielding to one more pragmatic. If the pragmatic mind prizes efficacity above all else, the image is bound to be preferred. For it demonstrates power of a type especially dear to market societies. It sells things. Indeed, it not only sells merchandise; it sells candidates for public office, the ideologies that divide our world, even war and "peace."[1] Small cause for wonder, then, if image-making is currently a thriving and expanding industry.

But this explanation attains only the use and abuse of image power. Left unclarified is the power itself. Psychologists border on the essential when they underline the decisive importance of self-images. By implication, they corroborate what Ricoeur early proposed in an arresting formula: we live only what we imagine. [SE, p. 278]

If the formula holds, a task both urgent and formidable confronts philosophers today. What calls for thinking is the image, its productivity and fateful bearing upon human affairs. Even as the closing eighteenth century provoked a critique of reason, so the closing twentieth century provokes a critique of imagination. Ricoeur, in any case, was lately moved to mark the problem. In 1972 he wrote: "To my mind, a philosophy of imagination is badly needed."[2]

This essay proceeds from a paradoxic awareness. Remarking the need for a philosophy of imagination, Ricoeur implies its present absence. And yet, when I return to his major works, I find that all of them assign to imagining the pivot-function. Though represented as stages in a "Philosophy of Willing," they could as well be taken as stages in a developing philosophy of imagination. In effect, what Ricoeur calls for is already underway in his own work.

Admittedly, taken as they stand, these major works by no means compose a systematic philosophy of imagining. But, when recovered and reinterpreted within the linguistic context of recent studies in metaphor, they confirm the judgment: from its beginning until now, the work of Ricoeur consistently develops the philosophic sense of imagination as "mediating function." His work, while not yet achieving an explicit and systematic critique of imagination, puts us well on the way toward doing so.

Supporting this claim is here the major task. In addition, however, I think it useful to indicate more precisely what is at stake. As presented by Ricoeur, imaginal mediation bears importantly upon: (a) constitution of the person, (b) philosophic method, (c) notions of reality and truth.[3]

This study develops its argument in four steps: 1. A brief introduction considers difficulties attending the project itself, for "imagination" hardly names a well-defined problem. 2. Then, from the precise viewpoint of imaginal mediation, the first four major works are examined. 3. With the fifth major work, *La Métaphore vive*, mediating imagination takes a decisive turn; as pivot of the metaphoric process, its power to make kinship emerge through conflict becomes accessible to reflection in new depth and amplitude. 4. Finally, by way of concluding, a small beginning is made toward critical appropriation.

I. INTRODUCTION

When, late in 1973, Ricoeur directed a seminar on imagination, he began by noting the "quasi-eclipse" of this problem in contemporary philosophy. The subject has acquired, deservedly it would seem, a bad reputation. How explain it? A principal reason is an abusive use made of the image by a certain empiricist tradition which, equating it with "idea," reduced the concept to psychology. From Descartes to Husserl, the battle against psychologism has been essentially a battle against gnosiological pretensions of the image.[4]

A difficulty more radical than reputation, however, disquiets the phenomenologist: does "imagination" name a unified, identifiable phenomenon? So diverse is its vocabulary, not only from one language to another but within one and the same language, that it seems to lack the unity of object prerequisite to any systematic research. Even the single word "fantasy" ranges between extremes of sense apparently irreducible. For, among other things, it includes: a. randomly evoking absent things, b. evoking absent things through existing things (e.g., paintings), c. evoking absent and non-existent things (e.g., dreams, stories), d. mistaking absent and non-existing things for present and existing things (e.g., hallucinations, misinterpreted perceptions). Where is the concept that unifies a series whose members slide between not perceiving and perceiving what is not, between qualified belief and unqualified belief, between consciousness of absence and consciousness of presence?

If imagination lacks unity of content, it may yet claim unity of function. Since Aristotle in fact, philosophy has identified it less by content than by functional "level." Not that independent unity is thereby assured. Placed midway between two strong polar functions, sensation and conceptual thought, imagination undergoes the pull of powerful and opposing attractive forces.

Deleterious indeed is this instable position of intermediary. Ricoeur marks it well: drawn under the sway of sensation, imagination is defined on its terms. Thus, it becomes a function of absence rather than presence, an impression "weak" rather than "strong," an impression "quasi" or "pseudo" rather than "true" or "authentic." Conversely, in approaching the level of conceptual thought, imagination becomes only "preconceptual" or "figurative." Oddly enough, despite the radical opposition of these reference points, the result is the same. Whether compared to sensation or conceptual thought, both functions "true in themselves," imagination appears as lacking truth. From here it is but a short step to familiar reductions: the "function of absence" reduces to "function of deception"; the "realm of fictions" reduces to "régime of illusion."

With Kant, however, the source of these reductions is itself shown to be illusory. For neither sensation nor intellection is an independent function. To apprehend them is always to apprehend them as already fused. Or, more exactly, it is to understand them as co-constituting the objectivity of objects. What makes possible their fusion is a synthetic act. This act can no longer be thought as the intermediacy of "level." On the contrary, it must be thought as mediating function.

Approached from the Kantian turning-point, major works of Ricoeur exhibit a remarkable development of imagination theory. Common to all of them is this theme: imagining mediates oppositions. But, even as it perdures, the sense of "mediating imagination" shifts, transposes, combines with other themes, assumes new modalities. At the end, early senses reappear as, at once, completed and transformed. Inversely, what appears at last is prefigured from the beginning.

II. MEDIATING IMAGINATION

In *Freedom and Nature,* first of the major works, imagining mediates a three-fold opposition of voluntary and involuntary functions within willing. Of these three mediations, the first two cohere with phenomenological psychology: thus, willing as decision is neither pure spontaneity nor blind causality. Thanks to the "image" which anticipates fulfillment, extremes of arbitrariness and determinism are reconciled.[5] For, as "light" of motive, the image gives *reasons* for deciding which in no way reduce to *causes.* [FN, p. 96] Similarly, when the voluntary movement which completes decision is blocked by organic extremes of too much or too little stimulation, the "image" again mediates. This time, however, its *emotive* function overcomes opposites.[6] By producing an image whose bodily orchestration falls between a "spectator image" too faintly resonated and a "hallucinating image" too strongly resonated, imagination reconciles the paralysing extremes of inertia and shock.

Faced with the final opposition of voluntary and involuntary functions, mediating imagination shifts dramatically from phenomenological psychology to poetry. For now the sense of "involuntary" becomes "invincible necessity." No longer cut to the measure of subjectivity, necessity has become coextensive with life. Its triple limit is inscribed at birth: existing as perspective, destined to death, submitted to evil. Confronted by fatedness, "willing" is prey to deadly extremes: at one end, sterile and futile refusal; at the other, capitulation to "the spell of objectivity." If these extremes can be reconciled, it is through "consent to the Whole."[7] But only the poetic work can so evoke the Whole that hard necessity transforms to the power of metamorphosis.[8] Thus transformed, the Whole evokes consent freely given, the consent of admiration. Still, admiration is not enough. How *can* we admire evil or consent to it? Rooted in hope, imagination engenders the myth of deliverance. Nor does the myth born of hope function as "lofty evasion" of willing. To hope means to resist evil even in consenting to it. [FN, pp. 479-81]

Not only is the mediating function of imagination affirmed and closely examined in this earliest of major works. At least four important anticipations of later theory emerge: 1. Then, as now, the poetic work as a whole mediates oppositions. 2. It is "figuring" a whole that effects mediations. 3. As rooted in hope, the mytho-poetic function imagines freedom. 4. In effecting mediations, pictorial and affective-emotive aspects of the image come into play.

To emphasize "anticipations" is to underline the achievements of *Freedom and Nature*. What of its shortcomings? More than likely, the "image" that mediates decision and voluntary movement is here vulnerable to charges of psychologism.[9] Further, the mediating poetic image is here less thought than lyrically affirmed. And, as everyone knows, lyricism cannot count as theory. Finally, this work appears to assume a dual dependence of imagination incompatible with taking it seriously on its own terms: first, it seems not to question the perceptual model typical of Husserlian phenomenology; second, in rejecting a Sartrean imagination which completely negates the real, it makes aesthetic imagination depend for its "elsewhere" upon the "inner-wordly concern of need." [FN, pp. 97-98]

To deny these difficulties would be pointless. Yet acknowledging them seems hardly less so. For, in claiming a development of imagination theory in the work of Ricoeur, it is already acknowledged that unsatisfactory early positions yield to better ones in due course. At all events, vulnerability to psychologism is later overcome when the image is interpreted linguistically. What is first asserted lyrically is then able to be thought. Nor is there any doubt that, upon encountering Freud, Ricoeur learns the limits of Husserlian phenomenology and renounces any tendency to privilege a perceptual model.

Fallible Man, by its turn from Husserl to Kant, sets in motion these corrective developments. Not that this second work is simply discontinuous with the first. Clearly, it continues the dominant theme of *Freedom and Nature.* Here, too, imagining mediates oppositions. Nor are the oppositions here mediated discontinuous with voluntary and involuntary functions. Rather, these latter now reach a point of utmost radicality as extremes of finitude and infinitude. But, even as *Fallible Man* builds on *Freedom and Nature,* it breaks new ground. Four breakthroughs are of critical importance to imagination theory:

1. Imagining is now understood as productively present within perception. Far from being merely "heir of the perceived," it presides at the birth of perceptual objects. Thanks to this Kantian turn, mediating imagination shifts to the transcendental dimension of object-constitutions. [FM, pp. 27-28, 57-71]

2. As making objects possible, transcendental imagination "sketches" the unity of their two sides: finite perspective and infinite sense. [FM, pp. 61-63] The turn to Kant thereby effects a liberation of the image: negatively, it can no longer be reduced merely to reproductive "picturing." Positively, it can now be understood through the *schema,* i.e., a moving figuration, an organizing and "wholing" movement.

3. Ricoeur, moreover, gives the Kantian schema a linguistic turn. In naming, nouns "sketch in the void" a total sense which takes "flesh" in the never completed interplay of perspectives. Though the verb also names, it adds the awesome "is" and "is not" of affirming and denying. Taken together, these analyses conjoin schematizing imagination to linguistic functions constitutive of discourse as "saying something of something." [FM, pp. 41-52]

4. If the schematizing function is present in all naming and all affirming or denying, the sense of "object" cannot be confined to epistemology. Still, the object of knowledge is never left behind; as included in objects of praxis and culture, it is rather brought to concreteness. Implied here is a decided turn away from anything like a "faculty" theory. Imagination is a synthetic function operative in all object-constitution.[10]

The Symbolism of Evil, as following upon *Fallible Man,* might appear retrogressive. It retreats from transcendental imagination which mediates all naming, all affirming and denying, to consider only one type of discourse: namely, the language of symbol and myth. Further, it considers this type only from the viewpoint of evil and fault.

But a particular viewpoint need not hamper thought. Indeed, with *The Symbolism of Evil* comes the astonishing discovery whose formula is by now familiar: "The symbol gives rise to thought." But how understand this "giving"? Ricoeur describes it as essentially a tripartite process:

1. an "assimilation" to symbolic-mythic meanings
2. through their "re-enactment"
3. in "sympathetic imagination." [SE, p. 3]

Considered as an event, it becomes "symmorphosis." [SE, p. 275] In becoming symmorphosis, mediating imagination both recapitulates earlier phases of development and begins a new adventure.

"Assimilation to" intends a reversal: whereas "assimilation of" indicates a meaning-movement initiated and controlled by subjectivity, "assimilation to" indicates a meaning-movement whose beginning and end elude this domination. Thus, *The Symbolism of Evil* here continues that de-centering of subjectivity begun in *Freedom and Nature* as "consent to the Whole." Here, too, de-centering is mediated by the mytho-poetic function.

Repetition, however, is not without an important difference. Mediation now intends a subject infected by evil, an evil irreducible to its willing because "always already there." Further, what mediates is not the poetic word simply, but the great cosmic symbols of evil as these are embedded and dramatized in myth. Finally, as condition of its possibility, mediating requires entry into their meaning-movement. Only as drawn and conducted by them is the subject of evil and fault able to span the extremes. For the extremes that now require spanning are no longer those of refusal and fascination; rather, they are the extremes of evil from its utmost point of exteriority to its inmost point of interiority.

In turn, traversing the "between" of external evil and internal fault requires the mediation of types. For, as providing a "numbered multiplicity," they counter the vagueness of "making one too quickly" and the confusion of "making many too quickly." [SE, pp. 171-74] Ricoeur therefore constructs a progressive series of type-stages. Precisely as serving, not classification but mediation, they signal a shift of consequence: invoked now is a phenomenology less Husserlian than Hegelian.

If types mediate, they must be continuous; but, as *types*, they must be discontinuous. Working within types, the image allows both continuity and discontinuity. Because "root images" figure situations basic and common, e.g., being infected, making a journey, going astray, they carry meaning from stage to stage. What effects discontinuity is the diversity of intentions inhabiting root images. Discovery of diverse intentions, however, requires yet another mediation: namely, texts. Apart from context, image-intention can be neither discerned nor verified.

To acknowledge the critical function of texts in type mediation is to understand why *The Symbolism of Evil* includes so impressive an array of textual sources. They are truly astonishing in number and variety. In supporting his interpretations, Ricoeur draws upon ethnological studies, literary and historical works, works of philosphical and theological speculation.

This appeal to texts, multiple and diverse, makes plain also why "sympathetic imagination" must function as "milieu" of mediating types. By "sympathetic" Ricoeur here intends an "as if" belief, that is, a provisional or neutralized belief. But provisional belief is not disinterested; paradoxic though it seems, it depends on "interest in the whole." If "interest in the whole" recalls "consent to the Whole," it must quickly be said: here the "whole" mediates, not consent, but refusal to close off the horizon by "making one too quickly."

Like both earlier works, *The Symbolism of Evil* affirms imagining as mediation. But it makes new and important gains. Now the mediating schematism includes, in addition to a transcendental function, the poetic function. Now, too, the linguistic schema extends beyond noun and verb to text. Nor is the image any longer acknowledged with reluctance.[11] Instead, Ricoeur dares to say: "Life is a symbol, an image, before being experienced and lived." For, indeed, "One lives only what one imagines, . . ." [SE, p. 278]

It is triply fortunate that Ricoeur encountered Freud in depth after *The Symbolism of Evil*. First, having found the image luminous, he cannot accept its reduction to illusion. Second, having joined the image firmly to linguistic productivity, he is prepared to counter a method which confines it to pictorial and reproductive functions. Finally, the reality implications of symmorphosis enable him to question more effectively a positivist "reality principle." In sum, the stage is set for his "debate" with Freud, a debate that entails long and close scrutiny of Freudian texts. What is at stake is clearly momentous: it is the fate of productive imagining, precisely, its "mytho-poetic core." [FP, pp. 35-36]

Of course, Ricoeur does not deny an illusive image function. Rather, in the manner of Kant, he wants both to legitimize and limit it. What justifies it is Freudian "economics." Insofar as the image is a magical substitute, a technique of instant satisfaction, it lends itself admirably to "pleasure-principle" strategems. But the economics which legitimates also limits. Insofar as Freud is faithful to his method, he can know of images, not meaning itself but how their meanings bear on levels of psychic tension.

How images affect the rise and fall of psychic costs, how they figure on the balance sheet of pleasure-pain investments and withdrawals, this only is caught in the net of psychic economics. Not that its "catch" is unimportant. Experience increasingly counsels systematic study of a regressive and illusive image function.

But regressive movement is defined through an opposing progressive movement. Ricoeur here looks again to Hegelian phenomenology. Unlike Freud, Hegel unfolds the sense of immediate consciousness "forwards." Thus, the truth "figured" in master-slave consciousness comes to light only in the figure that follows it: stoical consciousness. In turn, stoical consciousness reveals its truth only through the "skeptical consciousness" which follows it. In sum, meaning-movement in the *Phenomenology of Spirit* proceeds from "end to beginning" since "the truth of one moment resides in the subsequent moment."

Taught by Hegel, Ricoeur proposes a progressive-regressive dynamic of image functions. How this dynamic works can be seen through an example especially favored by Freud: the *Oedipus Rex* of Sophocles. Ricoeur first develops oppositions between classical and Freudian interpretations. Psychoanalysis understands *Oedipus Rex* as return to the enigma of birth, undying origin of perverse desires; its core problem is sexual; thus, its key figure is the sphinx, image of the unconscious. Conversely, classical interpretation looks toward self-recognition, a recognition that never comes at first but only at last; its core problem is not sex but light; thus, its key figure is Tiresias, blind seer: image of truth that shines through darkness. But, thanks to the dramatic symbolism of Sophocles, these antitheses are overcome. Dramas of birth and truth interlace. Discovery of self-truth is inscribed in discovery of origins. "Origins," however, is here over-determined. For the self-blinding that follows recognition of parental origins is more than punishment for crimes of sex. It becomes the "dark night of sense" wherein Oedipus learns the final truth of his blinding: not punishment of crime but crime of punishment that originates in arrogant anger of non-truth. [FP, pp. 514-19]

In its progressive-regressive reading of the Sophoclean Oedipus symbol, *Freud and Philosophy* borders on metaphoric imagination. First, what here carries the dual image function is an entire dramatic work. Second, if this work is understood as at once symbolizing the truth of birth and the birth of truth, opposing movements of disguise and disclosure descend and ascend on one and the same vector of sense. Third, these opposing movements of disguise and disclosure, of regression and progression, comport opposing relations to tensivity: whereas regression reduces it, progression maintains and builds it. From the standpoint of tensivity, then, the progressive image function works against the elimination of tension. But all three ways of "bordering" must appear opaque until metaphoric imagination is set out.

III. METAPHORIC IMAGINATION

From fear of "making one too quickly," a side-step approach is taken. First, the context is established as "metaphoric process." How the image functions within this process is shown at a second stage: "the image and metaphoric process." Lastly, "metaphoric imagination and reference" examines the claim of metaphoric imagination to disclose the truth of "what is."

1. *Metaphoric process*

Understood through its Greek root, *metapherein*, metaphor indicates a process. Meaning is "carried over" from one thing to which it ordinarily belongs to another somehow like it. But common usage, reflecting a rhetoric in decline, has all but eliminated even this dynamism. Or, rather, it has reduced it to the mere substitution of one word for another. Of the *sub*stituted word, all that can be said is: it is more colorful, more pleasing. No new information is given by it. Thus, restitution of the ordinary or "proper" word makes no meaningful difference. In effect, metaphor has become a stylistic device, an ornament, a "figure of speech."[12]

What Ricoeur proposes is the antithesis of ornament theory. To "metaphorize" is to accomplish a metamorphosis, not of language only, but of the real as well. World-shattering and world-creating, the metaphoric process is hardly reducible to replacing common words with more colorful counterparts. And yet Ricoeur does not simply dismiss a "substitutional" theory of metaphor. Oppositions, after all, invite mediations.

Oddly enough, the ornamental notion of metaphor hails from a rhetoric long dead. Ricoeur wonders why it died. For, before it died of futility, rhetoric was dangerous. Technique of persuasion, it gave its masters awesome power: power to dispose of words without things, power to dispose of persons in disposing of words. [MV, p. 15] That, indeed, is why Plato condemned it and Aristotle domesticated it. How, then, explain its demise?

Certain neo-rhetoricians explain it through a series of amputations. First, two of the three major parts were cut away: argument and composition. Then, its remaining "theory of style" was cut down to "classification of figures." Of its figures, only two escaped the knife: "metonymy" and "metaphor." Finally, even these were respectively reduced to "contiguity" and "resemblance." While not denying these facts, Ricoeur finds them not decisive. What is decisive is the fact of an early infection: the dictatorship of the word and, in particular, the preeminence of the noun.

In Aristotelian theory of metaphor, preeminence of the noun is explicit at two critical points: 1. Metaphor is defined in the *Poetics* as "giving the thing a *name* that belongs to something else; . . ."[13] Though the function of metaphor differs in passing from *Poetics* to *Rhetoric*, its definition remains the same. 2. Aristotelian "lexis," the locus of metaphoric function in both *Poetics* and *Rhetoric*, accords to the noun a pivot function. Noun privilege at the level of "lexis" easily translates to noun privilege at the level of metaphor. Not surprisingly, then, the Aristotelian theory of metaphor abounds in allusions supportive of substitution theory postulates: opposition of (a) strange and (b) ordinary noun meanings; "deviance" of (a) from (b); borrowing of (a) from (b); substitution of (a) for (b); possibility of replacing (a) with (b); the ornamental and pleasing effect of substituting (a) for (b).

Following upon Aristotle, classical rhetoric ends where ancient rhetoric begins. For, as Ricoeur shows of Fontanier, whose work is among the last, noun primacy continues to hold sway and, by implication, the postulates of substitution theory. [MV, pp. 68-86]

But, if classical rhetoric died in the nineteenth century, the "new rhetoric" of French structuralism was born in the twentieth. Referred to a theory of metaphor, its project would seem radical: whereas classical rhetoric was content to register "deviance," structuralist rhetoric aims to explain it. [MV, pp. 173-76]. Not stopping at the word, it looks to nuclear components: "sèmes." How word meanings change through addition and subtraction of these infra-linguistic elements is the question it wants precisely to answer. "Precisely" here means determining the number of additions and subtractions required to produce and reduce "deviance."

Admittedly, this approach is novel. The irony is: novel metaphors elude it. Like classical rhetoric, the "new rhetoric" of French structuralism works only with well-worn metaphors. It fails to reach the point of metaphoric invention. Might not the reason lie in another irony? Despite its high degree of technicity, this new rhetoric fails to challenge an old assumption, namely: metaphor is the work of a single word whose "strange" sense is put in place of a "proper" sense. [MV, pp. 129-30, 215-16]

And yet, by contemporary English authors especially, the postulate of substitution theory is not only challenged but rejected. In a pioneer work, *Philosophy of Rhetoric*, I. A. Richards attacks the "superstition" that words have proper or primary meanings. In and of themselves, words have no meaning. Of course, words "stand for" something. What they stand for, however, is neither atomic ideas nor atomic things. Rather, words abbreviate "missing parts of context."

Applied to metaphor, this contextual theory of meaning has major consequences: 1. Because context is established first through the sentence, metaphoric meaning is displaced from naming to the predicative function. 2. Referred to the sentence, metaphor becomes the intersecting point of interacting contexts. Through interplay of differing contextual levels, something is presented "under the sign" of something else. 3. As presenting something through something else, metaphor includes *both* a concrete image which "presents" and an underlying meaning evoked by the presenting image. [MV, pp. 100-07] If, with Richards, we call the first "vehicle" and the second "tenor," metaphoric process means the tensive and mutal "passing into" of tenor and vehicle.

Through the work of Max Black, Ricoeur clarifies and develops further the dialectic of metaphoric process. Logician and epistemologist, Black replaces the "vehicle-tenor" pair with one less psychological, more exact: "focus-frame." Between the metaphoric word which focalises interaction and the "frame" where words function non-metaphorically, contrast is patent; thus, the tensivity of this process and its semantic quality are more aptly indicated. Besides, by relating metaphor to scientific "models," Black underscores its contribution to a logic of invention. Here again, however, Ricoeur finds irony: concerned with invention, this analysis skirts the enigma of semantic innovation. For, though metaphoric-focus works on metaphoric-frame by filtering meanings not based on common usage, these meanings finally reduce to "systems of associated commonplaces." [MV, pp. 109-16] Not unexpectedly, then, Black exhibits metaphoric process only through commonplace examples.

To Monroe Beardsley, who comes to metaphor through literary criticism, Ricoeur gives credit for "partly" resolving the problem of metaphoric inventivity. First, Beardsley insists upon logical absurdity as a pivot of metaphoric strategy. In metaphoric attribution, what is predicated of the principal subject is "logically empty," that is, incompatible or contradictory. Thus, the poet speaks of "metaphysical" streets. But contradiction alone does not make a metaphor. In proceeding to a second point, Beardsley takes a step of decisive import: a metaphor occurs only when the reader, goaded by contradiction, sets out to overcome it. Confronted by an enigma, a "metaphorical twist," the reader unravels it by constructing new meaning. For, from the entire spread of connotations evoked by absurd attribution, selection is made of those which, beneath apparent incongruity, uncover hidden kinship. [MV, pp. 123-24]

Still, it is one thing to stress the constructive side of the metaphoric process; it is quite another to account for it. Why the explication of Beardsley falls short is of prime interest to this study: the "metaphorical twist" which elicits meaning construction is but the reverse side of a process where the image function presides. [MV, pp. 238-42] Neither the "spread of connotations" invoked by Beardsley nor the "systems of associated commonplaces" invoked by Black involves any necessary reference to image deployment. Indeed, Ricoeur notes a progressive eclipse of the image function in Anglo-Saxon interaction theory.

In bypassing the image, theorists of interaction not only lose the key to metaphoric invention; they abandon their metaphoric logic. For the "image" has long been solidary with "resemblance" which, in turn, has long been solidary with a substitutional theory of metaphor. Now if, as interactionists contend, these theories oppose each other, their opposition invites the search for hidden kinship. Is not metaphor, tensively understood, a matter of mediating oppositions?

Ricoeur, in any case, refuses a simple rejection of "image" and "resemblance." With characteristic concern for mediating opposites, he examines works whose substitutional cast is evident. In each of them, he uncovers implicit recognition of tensivity and the contextual interaction productive of it. Thus, they point beyond metaphor-word to metaphor-predicate. But mediation works both ways. Especially to the point here is an implicit recognition on the side of interaction theory: "image" and "resemblance" are ingredient to metaphoric process.[14] How explicate their operative presence if not by uncovering the truth, admittedly partial, of the substition theory?

2. *The image and metaphoric process*

Uncovering the truth of substitution theory entails reinterpreting its key notions, "image" and "resemblance," through its opposite: a contextual theory of metaphor. This reinterpretation begins as a "plea for resemblance." In pleading its case, Ricoeur makes four points. [MV, pp. 245-54]

First, resemblance is even more necessary to tensive than to substitutive theory. Far from making it superfluous, notions of "tensive interaction" and "logical contradiction" strictly require it. For the work of rapprochement is essential to metaphor precisely as reduction of tension, mutation of meaning whereby what initially appears estranged and distant exhibits kinship and draws near. Clearly, this "work of resemblance" cannot be contained within a semiotics. As working between terms put in tension through predication, it is itself a work of predication.

But resemblance is not only produced through predication; it constructs predication as well. In making his second point, Ricoeur grants its paradoxic quality. To justify it, he invokes the paradox of metaphor itself: it is both "epiphoric" and "diaphoric," intuitive and constructive. As "epiphor" or "transfer" of meaning, metaphor rests on insight. Hence, Aristotle holds it unteachable. Having an "eye for likeness" is the gift of genius. [MV, p. 39] And yet, "epiphor" envelops the discursive moment of "diaphor." Aristotle is again instructive: in matters of proportional analogy, resemblance is less seen than construed. To see the "like" of proportion calls into play the constructive reason of the skilled geometer. [MV, p. 248] Between the gift of genius that sees the "like" and the geometer's skill that calculates it, there need be no contradiction.

All the same, this appeal to intuition may well appear suspect. Is a semantic theory of metaphor here reverting to psychology? Ricoeur counters: despite its psychological look, the metaphoric paradox of insight and construction is in fact purely semantic. Located in discourse, it has always to do with an odd allocation of predicates. For metaphor, as Nelson Goodman metaphorically remarks, is "an affair between a predicate with a past and an object which yields in protesting." To paraphrase: "protesting" is what remains of the old marriage, literal predication, even as contradiction unmakes it; "yielding" is what comes about, thanks to this new rapprochement.

Seeing the "like" beyond divorce, paradoxic "diaphor of epiphor," gives the key to a third point in defense of metaphoric resemblance, namely, its claim to logical status. Ricoeur here considers the charge that metaphor is mere equivocation: "anything resembles anything—or almost!" This objection would hold if, in metaphoric resemblance, sameness and difference were confused, commingled. In fact, however, they remain opposed. Within metaphoric statements, literal contradiction maintains difference, sameness is perceived *despite* difference. Neither univocal or equivocal, metaphor effects a polemical unity, a place of encounter where "same" and "different" confront each other.

In light of this conflictual structure, types of metaphoric transfer distinguished by Aristotle indicate a logic hitherto hidden. To transport meaning from "genus to species" and "species to genus" is doubtless to transgress logical boundaries. In modern terms, it is to make a "category mistake." But here "mistake" is calculated, strategic. Transgressing conceptual frontiers enables emergence of meaning through connecting what these very boundaries have blocked. Upon the ruins of old categories become too confining, new and larger configurations are built. An instrument of discovery, metaphoric resemblance is hardly illogical. Indeed, Ricoeur dares to hypothesize: might not the metaphoric strategy that ruins logical categories be one with the process that builds them?

Finally, at stage four of his "plea for resemblance," Ricoeur arrives at the pivot function of metaphoric process: the "image" which puts likeness "under our eyes." [MV. p. 253] All three preceding stages were needed for this arrival. If metaphoric resemblance is a paradoxic union of discursivity and insight, of saying and seeing, its pivot-image unites both. It is at once verbal and pictural. But here everything depends on inserting the image-picture within an image movement properly semantic. Failing this, creative imagination loses its chance: reduced to the "faded impression" of Humean psychology, its image is reproductive only. Then the sheepfold of metaphor is exposed to the wolf of psychologism. What remains of the image, now the "mental picture" of private worlds, is locked in the prison of subjectivism.

To avert dangers posed by bad psychology and psychologism, Ricoeur approaches the metaphoric image through its verbal core. He first recalls the word of Aristotle: *lexis* makes discourse appear. Although discourse is not a body, its different ways of signifying and expressing do exhibit something akin to bodies, namely, differences of form or figure which imply a kind of spatiality. Still, how does metaphoric discourse "spatialize" or "make a figure"? Ricoeur takes a second step by joining the notion of "figure" to metaphoric "play of resemblance." To be sure, this "figuring" play becomes visible, not in the non-space of noun-metaphor, but in the exploding space of bizarre predication. For, in bizarre attribution, distance between subject and predicate is stretched to the breaking-point. Reduction of its literal contradiction through the play of resemblance diselongates: what was "far" draws "near."[15]

Here, then metaphoric attribution becomes "figure" or "image." For the "far" of bizarre predication does not collapse into the "near" of resemblance. Tensively and persistently, far and near stand together. To "see the like" is to see both at once, each through the other.

What makes possible this "seeing" of near in far and far in near is an imagination properly semantic and productive. Ricoeur here draws upon the Kantian theory and further develops it. Productive imagination is, as Kant held, a schematizing function. But, whereas Kant understood its schematism as joining empirical and intelligible aspects of the concept, Ricoeur here gives it a linguistic twist: productive imagination schematizes metaphoric attribution.

As schematism of metaphoric attribution, productive imagination provides the point of insertion for pictural images of reproductive imagination. Ricoeur again draws support from Kantian theory. According to Kant, the schema is a *method* for producing images. Might not, then, the schema of metaphoric predication also serve to produce and combine sensory images? In point of fact, certain contemporary authors understand the iconicity of metaphor in just this way: proper to it is the power to raise up and deploy images called for by its predicative sense. [MV, pp. 263-64, 268]

Thus anchored in the schematism of productive imagination, what is the status of sensory images? Ricoeur is far from condemning these works of reproductive imagining. Indeed, to them the metaphor owes its vivacity, its power to put likeness "under the eyes." Further, deprived of its sensible element, productive imagining would not be productive; its power to deploy itself in sensory images would be aborted. Choosing between verbal and non-verbal image functions is therefore worse than futile. Their fusion within the metaphoric process is strictly required.

But how explain their fusion? Ricoeur finds their missing link in a theme of Wittgensteinian origins: "seeing as."[16] Developed by Marcus Hestor in terms of poetic language, this theme unifies verbal and non-verbal image functions at work within metaphoric iconicity.

Examined closely, "seeing as" is not only intuitive; it is also a selective act. This dual constitution is admirably exhibited in reading a poem. To read a poem is doubtless to see pictural images. These simply come upon the gifted reader; their flood or flow escapes voluntary control: in the end, one sees or does not see. And yet these images are not simply free. They are bound to poetic diction. The reader is obliged to select from the flow of sensory images those aspects more or less appropriate to the poetic text. For: "the same imagery which occurs also means."

Though two-sided, "seeing as" is one event. Its selective act requires the flow of sensory images; inversely, the flow of sensory images requires its selective act. Within one and the same event, the light of meaning is joined to the plenitude of imagery. Or, in the Kantian formula proposed by Ricoeur, "seeing as" plays the role of schema uniting empty concept and blind impression.

Beyond uniting verbal and quasi-visual image functions, "seeing as" joins the "is" and "is not" of tensive metaphoric interaction. Hitherto this tension appeared incompatible with a theory of fusion between image and meaning. But the "is" of "as" includes "is not." To see X *as* Y is to see, not only that X is Y but also that, in other respects, X is not Y. Though the "is" of figurative predication crosses frontiers of meaning, it does not obliterate them. Tension is thus sustained. No longer, then, need interaction theorists emphasize the "impertinence" of logical contradiction at the expense of the new pertinence effected in figurative predication. Thanks to "yes and no" of "seeing as," both semantic impertinence and its tensive reduction are saved. [MV, p. 270]

Why Ricoeur works to assure the fusion of meaning and sensory image now emerges. At stake is the secret of *epiphor*, a transfer of meaning which makes kinship appear through conflict. Precisely, this secret resides in the iconic nature of intuitive passage. Face-to-face with metaphoric iconicity, semantic theory of metaphor encounters its limit. Irreducible to language though suffused with its sense, the sensory image makes possible the seeing of likeness.

Irreducible to language, the non-verbal image function nonetheless draws from it life and power. Ricoeur here cites the work of Gaston Bachelard, namely, his "phenomenology of imagination." For, rightly, Bachelard accords preeminence to the poetic work. Of the poem, after all, the poetic image is born. And, if the poetic image becomes "psychic origin," it is because it puts us at "the origin of our speaking being."[17] As a new being of language, it becomes an increase of consciousness. Or, more exactly, it becomes an increase of being.

But how does the poetic image, work of poetic imagination, give an increase of being? And is poetic imagining one with metaphoric imagining? These questions turn on a prior problem, that of metaphoric reference.

3. *Metaphoric imagination and reference*

What Ricoeur intends by "reference" is best approached through two sources: the logician, Frege; the linguist, Benveniste. [MV, pp. 273-75] To Frege belongs credit for the classic sense/reference distinction. By "sense," he understands the meaning of a sign, *what* it says. By "reference," he understands the denotation of a sign, that "about which" meaning is said. Each sign has a definite sense and, corresponding to it, a definite denotation. Still, a single denotation may involve more than one sign: thus, though "morning star" and "evening star" denote the same star, the sense differs in each case. Whereas Frege applies the sense/reference distinction to noun words, Benveniste applies it to the sentence. Because the sign of semiotics belongs to a closed system of signs, its sense is determined by its difference from other signs within the system. But, since "discourse" is the proper field of semantics, its primary unit is not the sign but the sentence. Unlike the sign which refers only to other signs, the sentence refers to extra-linguistic reality.

From the different emphases of Frege and Benveniste, it appears that reference applies to both words and sentences. For these poles are not mutually exclusive. Thus, in Frege, reference proceeds from the word to the sentence which, as sum of word-denotations, refers to a "state of affairs." Inversely, reference in Benveniste proceeds from the sentence to words whose denotation is decided by their use. Moving beyond Benveniste and Frege, Ricoeur arrives at a third pole of reference: one corresponding to a text, a work. In this case, "work" refers to "world."

But here poetic works present a special problem. Applied to prosaic works, the third realm of reference may seem reasonable enough. What Frege says of nouns might also apply to them: it is our desire for truth that impels us to move from sign to thing; not content with ideal meanings, we seek to verify their claim to status in the real world. With imaginative worlds, however, things go differently. To whom does Ulysses refer? To what does a poem refer?

Indeed, the poem appears to ruin reference. Ricoeur gathers evidence for this view from works of literary criticism and the "new rhetoric" of French structuralism: insofar as a poem calls into play the poetic function, it blocks movement from sign to thing. For the poem is itself quasi-thing. An arresting synthesis of rhythms, sounds, the dance of images, it speaks not of something else but of itself. In speaking of itself, the poem says what it is, a shaping or structuring of "mood." [MV, p. 285] Could anything say better its centripetal movement? French structuralism, assuming a positivist epistemology, draws the conclusion: opaque, satisfied with itself, poetic discourse "refers to no reality." Whereas "the function of prose is denotative, the function of poetry is connotative."[18]

Ricoeur does not deny an initial ruin of reference in poetic works. What he denies is the assumption that reference is simple or singular. Metaphor, "poem in miniature," clearly exhibits a doubling of reference. At a first moment, reference is counterpart of literal predication. Exposed as contradictory through metaphoric predication, literal predication destroys itself as meaning and, with itself, its referential counterpart. But this destruction is only the reverse side of positive metaphoric strategy which, on the ruins of literal meaning, makes new meaning arise. To the upsurge of new meaning there corresponds an upsurge of new reference. In terms of proportional analogy, the new reference would be to semantic pertinence what the old reference was to semantic impertinence. [MV, p. 289-90]

Through another proportional analogy, the doubling of metaphoric reference is confirmed and further explained: the model is to scientific language what the metaphor is to poetic language. As recent studies show, scientific models function as heuristic fictions; they are designed to break the grip of explanations no longer adequate and to replace them with theories more fitting and fecund. Some traits of these models deserve notice: 1. Descriptive only, their factual existence or constructibility is irrelevant. 2. By means of them, scientific imagination can see and formulate new connections. 3. Necessity of resort to them follows from the impossibility of obtaining a strict deductive relation between *explanans* and *explanandum*. 4. What is seen through them, the *explanandum*, is changed by metaphoric redescription: "Rationality consists precisely in continuous adaptation to a world continually expanding; metaphor is one of the principal means of accomplishing this." [MV, pp. 305-6]

Theory of scientific models rebounds upon theory of metaphor in helpful ways. Thus, it confirms the principal traits of the general theory: interaction of focus and frame, the cognitive import of metaphoric statement, its untranslatability and inexhaustibility. Of special interest, however, is a dual advance bearing upon metaphoric imagination and reference. First, the model corresponds, not to the chance or isolated metaphor, but to the radical and expansive metaphor embodied in poetic works. Just as the model builds systematic and complex networks of meaning, so the poetic work organizes and projects a world. To this totalizing metaphoric creation, a philosophy of imagination owes most careful attention. Second, by joining heuristic fiction and description, the scientific model recalls Aristotelian *mimesis* and *mythos*. Aristotle also understood poetic works as "imitating" human life through myth. Achieved in fiction, this *mimesis* is clearly irreducible to copying. Rather, it is denotative description and, thanks to it, we see human life *as* myth exhibits it.

Nor is the *mimesis* of *mythos* reserved to tragic poetic works. In the lyrical poem, "mood" is myth. Suspension of mood from ordinary reference, its distanciation as fiction, makes possible a descriptive deployment. Thanks to it, that "world" is uncovered which, in resonating, mood implicitly denotes. What does it mean, then, to say of mood that its movement is centripetal? Consider the "lake of ice" in Dante's *Inferno*. Though Dante turns from cosmological reference, he does not thereby dismiss the world. Does he not rather describe a way of dwelling in it whose truth is as "ice"? To oppose "inner" and "outer" here is utter folly. These are but reverse sides of a unitary phenomenon. Poetically structured, mood is the inside of outside. [MV, pp. 308-10]

Implicit in metaphoric reference is the question of metaphoric truth. Here everything depends on keeping the tensive unity of "is" and "is not." To assert the "is" without its mediating negation is to lose interaction of identity and difference. Then metaphor is no longer a discursive work of making kinship through conflict. Thus, instead of reconciling subject-object oppositions, it reverts to the murky indistinction that precedes them. Altogether other, indeed, is the poetic work. For the poet, in raising from indistinction the bi-polar unity of "inner" and "outer," never confuses the "textural feel-of-things" with prosaic things-of-feeling.

But metaphoric truth is as much ruined by inflating "is not" as by denying it. Eclipsed by negation magnified, "seeing as" disappears into timid "as if." Cautious vigilance then counsels "ontological abstinence": use metaphor, but be not seduced by its claim to disclose the truth of reality.[19] Within creative metaphoric process, however, disbelief does not prevail. Ricoeur, indeed, finds "metaphoric faith" among its conditions of possibility: can we create metaphors without believing that, in some way, they say "what is"?

As enabling metaphoric creativity, belief works against dogmatic slumber. For this "seeing as" builds new meaning on the ruins of accustomed reality and truth circumscriptions. Thus, its refusal of ontological abstinence concedes nothing to ontological naïveté. In sum, metaphoric "as" mediates extremes of ontological fideism and skepticism.

Reconciling these extremes has long been a major concern of Ricoeur. All the more thought-provoking, then, is his insistence on the mediation that makes it possible: the interlacing of verbal and pictural image functions in metaphoric "seeing as." Could it be that he here identifies the hinge of all those various mediations assigned to imagining throughout his major works? And, if so, what else might hinge upon that?

IV. CONCLUSION

Taking the "hinge" as rightly identified, I propose to work from it in revisiting briefly the major works. On the strength of it, I hope to support three conclusions: 1. Major works of Ricoeur sketch a unified and coherent philosophy of imaginal mediation which, by joining metaphoric creativity to person-constitution, sustains the fundamental project of ethics insofar as this project depends upon an "imagination of freedom."[20] 2. Considered from the side of method, these works exhibit a philosophic exercise of metaphoric strategy. 3. As creative, metaphoric strategy entails the collapse of positivist "reality" and "truth" definitions.

In drawing my first conclusion, I do not deny gaps and difficulties in accounts of imaginal mediation prior to *La Métaphore vive*. In fact, it is useful to stress them. Otherwise, the critical importance of reinterpreting earlier accounts in light of metaphoric "seeing as" fails to emerge clearly.

Need of this reinterpretation is nowhere more evident than in *Freedom and Nature*. The image is there badly exposed to psychologism. Though charged with mediating will and need, its reproductive "picturing" appears confined within the individual consciousness. How, then, assure its public status, its reference to the common world where needs are named and specified, multiplied, and manipulated? True enough, public status is implied in the culminating mediation of voluntarist subjectivism and fatalist objectivism. In evoking "consent to the Whole," poetic images combine verbal and pictural functions. But, even so, union is here only supposed; the "why" and "how" of it are not shown.

Placed in context, however, the image that mediates willing and need is safe from all threat of psychologism. For rightly understood, it presents an object under the aspect: "need-fulfilling." Thus assimilated to aspect-seeing, it exhibits a three-fold irreducibility. First, it resists reduction to mere picturing since, of itself, picturing cannot yield the sense: "need-fulfilling." This sense, like any other, depends on context. Second, the imaged object of aspect-seeing is irreducible, not only to reproductive perception, but to perception simply. Even when aspect-seeing occurs during perception, the aspect itself is not a percept. Rather, in visual aspect "dawning," as when a drawing is seen alternately as duck and rabbit, the image comes "in contact with" a percept.[21] Third, an aspect-image cannot be reduced to the intra-psychic. Brought to expression, it can be presented to anyone who is not generally "aspect-blind." But, then, who today will deny communicability of need-fulfilling aspects? A massive and thriving industry depends on it.

Precisely as tensive, metaphoric "seeing as" does more than assure presentability. It gives also the vivacity that comes of mediating extremes of opposition. In *Freedom and Nature*, imaginal mediation of will and need sorely needs this livening. For, clearly, the young Ricoeur distrusts creativity. Perhaps his reserve toward Sartrism plays a large part here. In any event, though he carefully develops the complexity and multiplicity of vital needs, the stress is on "levels." And, at all levels, need-imagining is firmly held to the "inner-worldly" frame ruled by perception. [FN, pp. 97-98]

Oddly enough, however, perception itself requires for its possibility a mediating image-schema. This key affirmation of *Fallible Man* marks a development of decisive importance. If, understood transcendentally, the image-schema is always already operative in perceiving, then imagining and perceiving do not simply exclude each other. A way is thus opened to a "seeing as" which would be "perceiving in the imaginal mode."[22] Nor can the image now be confined to reproductive and pictorial instances. What makes perception possible is a productive schema. Of special interest, indeed, is the nature of schematic productivity: the schematizing act is assimilated to noun and verb functions.

Does it follow that *Fallible Man* needs no reinterpreting through metaphoric "seeing as"? Such an inference is unfounded since, apart from this seeing, its image-schema fails to emerge fully. In fact, left as it stands, the schematizing function solves only the transcendental problem of object-constitution. How it works within experience of objects is a further and unanswered question.

As enabling a response to this question, metaphoric "seeing as" exhibits anew its hinge status. For, in *Fallible Man*, Ricoeur proposes the solidarity of two processes: (a) constitution of the "person" as "value without price," and (b) assimilation of objects whose sense refers to basic modes of human relationship, namely, relations of having, power, and esteem. [FM, pp. 172-191] To the last of these, he gives priority. Objects which promote esteem, i.e., works of culture and art, preeminently disclose the absolute worth of the human being insofar as they "search out man's possibilities." But this early work searches out neither how such possibilities arise nor how they are assimilated. Its completion thus depends on developing the sense of metaphoric "seeing as."

Dependence, however, need not be a one-way street. To achieve their sense, imaginal mediations also rely on a unifying, coherence-giving context. I think it possible to develop this contextual field by adapting the sketch of person-constitution set forth in *Fallible Man*. In *Freud and Philosophy*, Ricoeur himself indicates its amplitude and responsivity to innovation. For he there returns to the triple objectivity which mediates "person" or "humanness." But now objects of having, power, and esteem are no longer understood as the work of prospective consciousness alone. For these objects "figure" human possibilities only in fusing the regressive movement of deep-lying instinctual interest with the progressive movement of symbols and values.

When the Freud work encounters metaphoric "seeing as," however, two notable advances become possible. First, nothing now prevents the sense of "unconscious psychism" from appearing as tensively stretched between opposing poles of Freudian repetition and Jungian creativity. This development would seem welcome. How, for example, can an adequate philosophy of imaginal mediation ignore the theory of archetypes? Further, any temptation to imagine "regions" of person-constitution as separate or merely side-by-side is fully overcome. For the "as" of poetic metaphor lights anywhere. Nothing prevents it from transfiguring accustomed senses of having and power.

But, as *The Symbolism of Evil* shows, esteem-objectivity includes a rational mode not properly confined to the interhuman. In mediating person-constitution, its sense embodies also an imagination of Transcendence, the "more than human." Here Transcendence is approached only through symbolic-mythic figures of defilement, sin, and guilt. Becoming human or "person" involves entry into myths whose great images span the extremes of external and internal evil, of guilt and pardon.

And yet, though surely important, symbols and myths of evil leave much to be imagined. Of this, the works of poets and mystics leave little doubt. To examine these works anew seems to me a pressing need. For, perhaps especially in our time, it is tempting to regard all imagination of Transcendence as a relic of human infantilism. A lingering positivism may help to explain so unimaginative a view. But it must also be granted that crude and destructive images of Transcendence have led, rightly I think, to distrust if not disgust.

As needing new lines of development, this account of imaginal mediation is clearly unfinished. But, then, is there anywhere a "finished" philosophy of imagination? In any case, the foregoing sketch makes a more modest claim which, in summary, comes to this: inserted within the unifying problematic of person-constitution and reinterpreted through metaphoric "seeing as," imagining mediates the triple objectivity of having, power, and esteem. Thus, rescued from psychologism, need-imaging traverses all three objectival dimensions. Among these dimensions, however, the esteem-objectivity of poetic works is both preeminent and comprehensive. For its tensive "as" can extend and transform the sense of all relational modes.

Not only do imaginal mediations now appear interrelated and interwoven; their ethical importance at last comes to light. If ethics is understood in the large sense of Spinoza, namely, as the passage of the human being from bondage to freedom, then it can be said: here imagination, ethics, and freedom are indissolubly joined. Unlike Spinoza, Ricoeur joins freedom, not simply to necessity understood, but to possibilities uncovered. And, insofar as uncovering possibilities occurs above all through the "as" of poetic seeing, he further implies the mediation of ethics by works of poetic imagining.

Much depends on drawing out implications of this mediation. Ricoeur himself has underlined a dual predicament of contemporary ethics. There is first the dilemma acutely posed by Sartrism: are values invented or discovered? Second, there is the recognized impossibility of producing by fiat the hinge-value of ethics: respect for the "person" as value without price. To both problems, poetic "seeing as" effectively responds. For, in its "as," discovery and creativity interlace. Further, precisely as communicable, its "seeing" permits a work of education whereby, in and through poetic works, an eye for "value without price" is cultivated.[23]

Nor does ethics alone hinge on metaphoric "seeing as." The method of Ricoeur also turns on it. From its beginning until now, his work exhibits the strategy of metaphoric tensivity: a field is sketched out between polar extremes; oppositions are set out in sharpest relief; then, beneath and within oppositions, hitherto hidden exchanges and reciprocities are brought to light; in the end, what first appeared external and opposed is shown to be mutually inherent and solidary. What could more aptly describe this dynamic than the formula: "kinship through conflict"?

Not that philosophical and metaphorical modes of discourse are identical. Indeed, Ricoeur is surely right to insist on their difference. Still, Ricoeur also insists on the kinship of scientific models and poetic metaphor. Is it not fitting, then, to acknowledge a kinship between philosophic and metaphoric methods? Or, more precisely, is the time not ripe for recognizing a similarity of strategy in works proceeding from scientific, poetic, and philosophic modes of metaphoric imagining?

Admitting a properly philosophic use of metaphoric strategy furthers, in the first place, methodic interests of philosophers themselves. Negatively, this recognition counters the tendency to methodic insularity and isolationism. Indeed, a spur to creativity is contained in the exigencies of an integrative work which gives no quarter to the expediency of "scissors and paste." Positively, a philosophic use of metaphoric strategy corresponds to a sense of expanding reality. If, as Mary Hesse points out, "a world in continuous expansion" obliges practitioners of scientific method to "continuous adaptation of their language," their philosophic counterparts are no less obliged. [See MV, pp. 305-6] It thus appears that metaphoric strategy enables, not only scientific and poetic creativity, but philosophic creativity as well.

To arrive here is to be roused less from dogmatic slumber than from nightmare. Nor is it by chance that positivist definitions of "real" and "true" raise up a nightmarish world. When the "is" of "X" lacks the play of imagination, it must become:

"The vital, arrogant, fatal, dominant X."[24]

But now at last, thanks to metaphoric "seeing as," the "is" of "X" opens to disclose a creative tension of "yes and no." Awake to this disclosure, the philosopher attempts to think it. Doing so, however, entails return to the cornerstone rejected by positivism: the productive imagination that brings kinship from conflict.

NOTES

1. Thus, in a bicentennial address, the late Hannah Arendt avers that, though lying is nothing new in politics, "Image-making as global policy is indeed something new in the huge arsenal of human follies. . . ." ("Home to Roost," *The New York Review of Books*, June 26, 1975), pp. 3-6.

2. Paul Ricoeur, "Creativity in Language," David Pellauer, trans., *Philosophy Today*, Vol. XVII, Summer 1973, p. 109.

3. My argument rests on a close study of the following major works of Ricoeur: *Freedom and Nature, Fallible Man, Symbolism of Evil, Freud and Philosophy*, and *La Métaphore vive*. [Editor's note: Since the English translation of the last work is not yet available, references to it will be abbreviated as MV and will refer to page numbers in the French version.]

4. Paul Ricoeur, "Recerches phénoménologiques sur l'imaginaire: Seminaire 1973-1974," (Paris: Centre de Recherches Phénoménologiques, 1974), pp. 1-8.

5. *Freedom and Nature*, pp. 88-134. Taken strictly, "corporeal involuntary" refers to the régime of vital needs. Having shown these needs to be, not reflexes but pre-actions (pp. 88-93), Ricoeur is "led to seek the crossroads of need and willing in imagination—imagination of the missing thing and action aimed towards the thing" (p. 95). As presentative, the image is intentional; as prefiguring satisfaction, it conceals a latent valuation. Cognitive and evaluative, need-imagining assumes key importance. For, if a good part of our wisdom lies at the intersection of need and will (p. 93), does not the image that mediates need and will thereby mediate a good part of our wisdom?

6. *Ibid.*, pp. 250-318. Ricoeur distinguishes affective and emotive aspects of the image. *Feeling* refers to its presentative or intentional side (p. 58); what is presented, however, is never without "a host of organic accompaniments" which incite to action (pp. 259 ff). Thus, as not only motive but *motor*: "Desire is the body which dares and improvises, body brought to action pitch" (p. 266).

7. In his early battle with fatedness, Ricoeur accords to freedom only the power of "consent." For the "Whole" is here understood as encompassing an inexorable order of Being; this necessity of the Whole easily translates to the "order of Creation," work of a Creator-God in whose "will is our peace."

8.   More than twenty years later, Ricoeur ties metamorphosis to the strategy of metaphor which, in ruining the reference of literal language, metamorphoses both language and reality: "Creativity in Language," p. 111. Thanks to this development, the sense of "belonging to the Whole" undergoes a decisive shift: *see* below, pp. 78-80. But the shift is not sudden; it is already announced in *The Symbolism of Evil*: see below, pp. 63-64.

9.   In 1970, Ricoeur expressed serious reservations about the type of analysis presented in *Freedom and Nature* in his article, "The Problem of the Will and Philosophical Discourse," in James M. Edie, Francis H. Parker, Calvin O. Schrag, eds. *Patterns of the Life World* (Evanston: Northwestern University Press, 1970), pp. 273-89.

10.   Stanislas Bréton remarks a present need to renew and deepen Kantian theory of schematism; in particular, he urges its extension to aesthetic works: "Symbole, schéma, imagination," (*Revue Philosophique de Louvain*, tome 70, 1972, p. 86.) By implication at least, Ricoeur has already effected this extension in *Fallible Man*.

11.   This reluctance appears early in *Freedom and Nature* when, having admitted the "suggestive power" of metaphors (p. 78), Ricoeur speaks of "inadequate concepts" which "barely rise above the level of metaphors" (p. 136).

12.   *La Métaphore vive* examines first the Aristotelian origins of substitution theory (pp 13-61), then its nineteenth-century demise (pp. 63-86).

13.   Aristotle, *On the Art of Poetry*, translated by Ingram Bywater with a preface by Gilbert Murray (Oxford: Clarendon Press, 1920), pp. 71-2. [Italics added.]

14.   Thus, in the interaction theory of Richards, "vehicle" is to the resemblance of "tenor," not as one idea is to another, but as an image is to an abstract meaning. *See* MV, p. 263.

15.   Intended or not, Heideggerian overtones are here discernible. But, if this passage draws Heidegger near, it is to show how far from him Ricoeur remains. Heidegger's position is explicitly considered. [MV, pp. 356-74]

16.   MV, pp. 268-71. In Wittgenstein, to be sure, "seeing as" refers neither to metaphor nor to imagination; it refers rather to ambiguous figures.

17.   MV, p. 272. Ricoeur had cited this passage many years before: *The Symbolism of Evil*, p. 13.

18.   Underlying the denotative/connotative opposition is a positivist definition of reality; Ricoeur proposes a "generalized theory of denotation" to surmount this opposition. MV, pp. 288-301.

19.   Ricoeur here refers to the stance of Colin Turbayne: *The Myth of Metaphor* (Columbia, S.C.: University of South Carolina Press, 1970); at the opposite extreme of Turbayne's "ontological abstinence" is the "ontological naïveté of Philip Wheelwright: *Metaphor and Reality* (Bloomington: Indiana University Press, 1962). MV, pp. 313-21.

20.   Like Kant, Ricoeur understands the "person," not as an "is" but as an "is to be" which we are obliged to "make be" through the act of "respect": precisely, that act which treats the "human" or "person" always as an end and never simply as a means. *See Fallible Man*, pp. 110-12.

21.   Virgil C. Aldrich, "Pictorial Meaning, Picture Thinking, and Wittgenstein's Theory of Aspects" in *Essays in Metaphor*, edited by Warren Shibles (Whitewater, Wisconsin: The Language Press, 1972), p. 97.

22.   Aldrich proposes a helpful distinction between "observational" and "imaginative" modes of perceiving. *See* pp. 100-1.

23.   To be sure, this "education" in no way involves the reduction of art works to didactics.

24.   Wallace Stevens, "The Motive for Metaphor" in *The Palm at the End of the Mind* (New York: Random House, Vintage, 1972), p. 240.

V

Patrick L. Bourgeois

FROM HERMENEUTICS OF SYMBOLS TO THE INTERPRETATION OF TEXTS

In this essay, the author traces the evolution of Ricoeur's views of symbols and hermeneutics from the hermeneutics of symbols through the polysemy and more general symbolic function common to all language, to the hermeneutics of texts, with their depth semantics giving rise to new creative interpretations on the far side of what Ricoeur has come to call the "hermeneutical arch." In the process, both extremes of the arch, the objective side and the subjective side, must be dealt with. Three phases of his treatment will be discussed: symbols as expressions with double meaning and hermeneutics as making the passage to the hidden level of meaning; hermeneutics in the context of polysemy and rooted in the symbolic function of all language; finally, hermeneutics in the context of reading and appropriating the depth meaning of texts.

Patrick L. Bourgeois is Associate Professor of philosophy at Loyola University, New Orleans, Louisiana. He has previously published a monograph on Ricoeur's philosophy, *Extension of Ricoeur's Hermeneutics.*

From Hermeneutics of Symbols
to the Interpretation of Texts

PATRICK L. BOURGEOIS

Philosophers have especially manifested a serious interest in symbols and in the symbolic function of behavior since the modern period of philosophy. The entire tradition of hermeneutics from Schleiermacher is at least implicitly taken up with that concern. On the contemporary scene, Cassirer interprets the whole of human activity in terms of symbolic forms and function, getting his impetus from the promptings of Kant, especially about the schemata and the transcendental imagination.[1] As diverse thinkers as Karl Jaspers and Alfred North Whitehead turn to symbols at one point or another.[2][3]

Many contemporary philosophers have confronted the various enigmas of language because of the emphasis and priorities placed on language by most current philosophic schools and movements. Among the problems emerging from any focus on language, the problem of symbols, symbolic form, or symbolic structure must be confronted in order to deal adequately with the phenomenon of language and the symbolic function. Anyone attempting to be attuned to these problems in contemporary thinking and to be informed in the whole scope of these traditions, with a view to continuing the development of contemporary thinkers, has undertaken a Herculean task. Paul Ricoeur has undertaken such a project and has done as much as anyone in contemporary thinking to cross barriers from one framework to another, to promote a deepening and a broadening of reflection and philosophy. He has written so prolifically and extensively that any consideration of his thinking must necessarily at the outset restrict itself in some way, or lose coherence, unless such a treatment goes on at great length.[4] Consequently, this focus will be specific and narrow, keeping in mind that a full treatment of the evolution from one phase of his treatment to another would require a more explicit treatment of the continuity from one phase to another.

The specific focus of our consideration is the several phases of treatment of symbols and hermeneutics of symbols. The focus traces the evolution of his views of symbols and hermeneutics from the hermeneutics of symbols through the polysemy and more general symbolic function common to all language, to the hermeneutics of texts, with their depth semantics giving rise to new creative interpretations on the far side of what Ricoeur has come to call the "hermeneutical arch."[5] In this last phase, appropriation and recreation is accomplished by the hermeneutist, who is bound to and bound by the Word and Being. In the process, both extremes of the arch, the objective side and the subjective side, must be dealt with. Thus, three of the phases of his treatment of symbols and hermeneutics will be brought to light: symbols as expressions with double meaning and hermeneutics as making the passage to the hidden level of meaning; hermeneutics in the context of polysemy and rooted in the symbolic function as the root of all language; and finally, hermeneutics in the context of reading and appropriating the depth meaning of texts. This passage is not at all obvious without a serious consideration of the movement from one phase to another and a focus on the problems which gave rise to the move to the next stage.[6]

I. FIRST PHASE: SYMBOLS AND HERMENEUTICS

The first phase of Ricoeur's treatment of symbols within the context of his philosophy of the will was an attempt to grasp the fullness of experience and the language in which it is expressed. Realizing that symbols are more basic than myths, and focusing on religious symbols expressing the experience of evil, he began to investigate the structure and nature of symbolic expression. Without dwelling further on the particular interest he had in the symbols and symbolisms of evil, this article will focus on his insights into symbols and hermeneutics in these writings as a first phase of development.[7]

Ricoeur uses a brief eidetic description in imaginative variation to derive a characterization of symbols and hermeneutics in which he defines symbol and interpretation in their relation to one another, thus limiting one by the other.[8] His procedure of treatment is similar in each case, contrasting narrow and broad definitions of each, and defining symbol and interpretation as intermediary between these extremes. Symbols, therefore, are situated between the symbolic function the way Cassirer develops it, and Aristotle's doctrine of analogy.

The most general delineation of the symbol is that it is a sign. As such it is an expression which communicates a meaning. But this is too broad. Every symbol is a sign, but not every sign is a symbol. What characterizes a sign as a symbol for Ricoeur is the double meaning, or the double intentionality which the symbol conceals in its aim.[9] This is the intentional structure of the symbol, which is so important for Ricoeur, and especially relevant to his theory of interpretation. There is the literal intentionality which implies the triumph of the conventional over the natural sign. The second intentionality to which he refers is built upon this first intentionality, and is not given except in the first, the literal, patent meaning which points to the second.[10]

For Ricoeur, this duality of the symbolic function must be distinguished from the duality of the sensible sign and its signification, and from the signification and the thing or the object designated. [FP, p. 12] The symbol presupposes the signs which already have a primary, literal, manifest sense, and which, by this sense, returns to another sense. He deliberately restricts the notion of symbol to the expressions with a double sense. The semantic texture of these is correlative to the work of interpretation which explicates its second sense. [FP, p. 12]

Thus it is not difficult to arrive at Ricoeur's definition of symbols. "*I call* symbol every structure of signification in which a direct, primary, literal sense designates by excess another sense, indirect, secondary, figured, which cannot be apprehended except across the first." [CI, p. 16/ pp. 12-13]* This definition captures to some extent what Ricoeur speaks of as the common structure of symbols. He distinguishes the analogous bond between the literal and the symbolic meaning from analogy as a reasoning process through a fourth proportional term.[11] In the symbolic structure, the analogous relation which binds the second meaning to the first cannot be objectivated. By living in the first meaning I am drawn by it beyond itself. The symbolic meaning is constituted in and through the literal meaning. Symbol is the movement of the primary meaning making us share in the latent meaning, thus assimilating us to the symbolized without our being able intellectually to dominate the similarity. This is one sense in which the symbol "gives"; it "gives" because it is a primary intentionality giving the second meaning.

By its exigency of interpretation the problem of symbol inscribes itself in the broader problem of language, for this bond to interpretation is not exterior to the symbol. The symbol is an enigma in the Greek sense of the word, not blocking understanding, but provoking it.

Precisely the double sense as the intentional aim of the second sense in and by the first feeds and gives to the understanding; Ricoeur admits that he was able to show in the figured expression of the servile will constituting the symbol of confession, that it is the very surcharge of sense, by relation to the literal expression, which puts the interpretation into movement. [FP, pp. 18-19]

Ricoeur considers interpretation, therefore, to belong organically to symbolic thought and to its double sense. [FP, p. 19] This is why, as has been said above, he attempts to limit one by the other, so that in discussing the symbol and its structure, the need for interpretation comes to light. We have seen how the need for the interpretation of the double sense of the symbol's intentional structure arises from the very nature of the symbol.

Ricoeur proceeds in much the same fashion as he did in delineating the definition of symbol, first opposing his position to the too broad view of interpretation by Aristotle, then, to the too narrow view of Scriptural exegesis, placing his view somewhere in the middle. Aristotle's view, with his use of analogy and *pros hen* equivocals, is too broad. The Biblical tradition, on the other hand, has too limited a view. [FP, p. 20]

Ricoeur sometimes speaks of hermeneutics or interpretation as an exegesis. [FP, p. 26] However, we must not misunderstand him. He has in mind an enlarged concept of exegesis consisting of rules or the science of rules of exegetics. We have to see that "the text can be broader than is usually understood in a more narrow acceptance of exegesis. The text can be every ensemble of signs able to be considered as a text to be deciphered, such as a dream, a nervous symptom, a rite, a myth, a work of art, a belief." [FP, p. 26/ p. 35]

II.   SECOND PHASE POLYSEMY AND SYMBOLIC FUNCTION

The second phase of Ricoeur's treatment of symbolic language might be considered one of transition. For Ricoeur at the time of his books *The Symbolism of Evil* and *Freud and Philosophy,* still

> defined symbolism and hermeneutics in terms of each other. On the one hand, a symbolism requires an interpretation because it is based upon a specific semantic structure, the structure of double meaning expressions. Reciprocally, there is a hermeneutical problem because there is an indirect language. Therefore I identified hermeneutics with the art of deciphering indirect meanings.[12]

Before going on to the context of general hermeneutics and of the text, he confronted the challenge of semiology, with its strict scientific view of language. This confrontation eventually made him realize that structuralism and semiology had something to say to the phenomenologist of language, and to the hermeneutist. The semiologist's understanding of language as a closed system of signs must be taken as a challenge to the phenomenologists' view of language. Without belaboring the many treatments of Ricoeur confronting this challenge, we will focus on his discussion where he takes up the heart of the matter.[13]

Ricoeur reaches the crux of his consideration when he focuses on putting words together and selecting words. In order to put words together coherently, to select them from the whole system, a delimitation, a *dédoublement,* is necessary. This means that the problem of polysemy has a place even in the sciences of language. It also means that polysemy and symbolism belong to the constitution and function of every language. How does the word, put in relation to other words, according to the science of language, derive its meaning? Surely, from its relation to other signs in the system with which it is connected. "So the possibility of symbolism is rooted in a function common to all words, in a universal function of language. . . ." [CI, p. 78/ p. 76] "When I speak, I realize only one part of the signifying potential; the remainder is obliterated by the total significance of the sentence which operates as the unity of speech." [CI, p. 72/ p. 71]

But this has not yet established the priority of semantics. It shows how symbolic function and polysemy are presupposed and belong to all language. It shows that the context, the sentence, acts as the sifter of which meaning is meant. The further point Ricoeur makes is that the meaning arising from this closed system of signs is not adequate. It does not do justice to the fullness of meaning. There is meaning still unaccounted for. It yields only an abstract language and an abstracted meaning. It yields the constitution of symbolics but not a semantics. Thus, there are two ways of giving an account of symbolism: by that which constitutes it, the elements, structures; and by that which it wants to say or which it expresses.

This marks the break in the hierarchy of levels, arising from the difference in the ways of considering the sign, the transition from semiology to semantics. This break is constituted by the closed system of signs of semiology, but is not so absolute as it might at first appear. Ricoeur has come to consider semantics in semiology; and semiology in semantics—or, in other words, system and structure in speech, and meaning in structure. But to remain at the level of semiology and its meaning is unacceptable to him because he cannot accept the absoluteness of such a break. Therefore, the passage to the broader view of signs doing justice to the fuller meaning is necessary.

The same signs are seen from different levels. There are not two definitions of signs, but rather, two aspects: one expressing the relation to the sign in the system; and the other to its function in the sentence. [CI, p. 88/ pp. 87-88] Ricoeur writes:

> To oppose the sign to sign, that is the semiological function; to represent the real by signs, that is the semantic function; and the first is subordinated to the second. The first is in view of the second, or if one wishes, it is in view of the signifying or representative function that language is articulated. [CI, pp. 248-49/p. 252]

However, so far the problem of the subordination of semiology and system to semantics and speech has not been settled. The second part of the above quotation has been well stated by Ricoeur, but not yet established. How can this subordination of the semiological function to the semantic function be necessary? Can we simply presume that the essence of language is to say something about something: that expressivity should not be left out of any consideration of language?

The clarification of this point demands a deepening in the view of polysemy. In approaching this question of polysemy as the "pivot of semantics" [CI, p. 94/ p. 93] from the side of synchrony, polysemy signifies in the system, and at a given moment a word has many meanings which belong to the same state of the system. This view of polysemy misses the essential and crucial point, which is the process and history of usage.

> Now this process of the transfer of meaning—of metaphor—supposes that the word is a cumulative entity, capable of acquiring new dimensions of meaning without losing the old ones. It is this cumulative, metaphorical process which is projected over the surface of the system as polysemy. [CI, p. 93-94/p. 93]

However, this expansion of sense, this history, is limited by the return to the system. "Words have more than one sense, but they do not have an infinite sense." [CI, p. 94/p. 94] Thus, Ricoeur has brought system into semantics, through this dialectic between expansion and limitation of meaning in system. But it brings out too the subordination of of semiology to semantics, of synchrony to diachrony, at the semantic level. Both limitation and expansion are process:

> regulated polysemy is of the panchronic order, that is, both synchronic and diachronic to the degree that a history projects itself into states of systems, which henceforth are only instantaneous cross-sections in the process of sense, in the process of nomination. [CI, p. 94/p. 94]

Thus, the importance of the word as sign in the articulation of structure and of function is clear. However, it is the *context* which brings about the univocity or plurivocity of words in use or in discourse. The extent of the limitation of the semantic richness depends on the context. If the structure of a discourse allows several frames of reference, themes, topics, isotopies [CI, p. 94-95/p. 94], then more than one interpretation of the multiple meanings is justified. But the crucial focal point is the word. Ricoeur brings tradition and history to the system, and system to process, to semantic flux. The priority of semantics over structure becomes clear, as well as the interrelation between them.

But this discussion is not yet adequate or complete. Ricoeur's attempt to bridge the gap between semiology and semantics and to subordinate semiology to semantics has been reflected on, but the two ways of taking the sign have not been seen in the polarity, except insofar as the *semiological perspective* is not sufficient by itself, and therefore cannot be considered the adequate and full treatment of the sign or of language. "The semiological order does not constitute the total of language." [CI, p. 256/ p. 260] Considered alone it is only the condition of articulation. [CI, p. 250/ pp. 253-54]

The word as the point of articulation of the various levels of language calls for a distinction of the sign in semiology or syntax, and the sign in semantics. On the one hand, the sign is "meaningless" in semiology, and on the other hand, it is a word in semantics, "and words are the point of articulation of the semiological and the semantic in each event of speech." [CI, p. 93/ p. 92] We have already seen how Ricoeur puts semantics into semiology, and at what price, i.e., the closure of the sign system; and we have seen how he puts semiology or system into semantics. We have also seen that semantics or (Ricoeur's) phenomenology of language cannot accept the closure of the sign system, which is the overextension of a method or theory. Semiology can be considered to root the symbolic function and polysemy. This insight demands an adjustment in interpreting the relation between diachrony and synchrony, because of what Ricoeur calls the surcharge of sense and the semantic regulation of the context. Further reflection on the closure of the sign system reveals how the meaningful use of signs as words does not allow for a closed system, but rather demands an openness.

In attempting to evaluate the strength of the argument favoring the opening of the universe of signs, the distinction within the sign given above must be recalled. We saw that sign can be regarded from the point of view of its constitution, and from the point of view of what it says, so that there are not two definitions. All Ricoeur has said, then, is simply, yes, a sign is in a system: but that is not all it is. That does not do justice to or exhaust the full consideration of sign. We have already seen the subordination of semiology or system to function and to semantics, allowing for the opening of the sign system at a different but more essential level. At this higher level, signs have a reference function and a manifesting function. They point to and stand for things. They are expressions. As such they express, i.e., they show or reveal the world, and they manifest or posit the subject. The semiological sign system is a lower level which cannot do adequate justice to this aspect of sign. On this level, there is no saying of something about something, nor a positing of the I who appropriates language in speaking; the uniqueness of the I and the situation or occasion of the speaker and the speaking (e.g., tense, demonstratives) go beyond the limits of this level. Thus the closure of the sign system is not tenable on this level. And it is the more fundamental level, once the new unity of language in the sentence is accepted. Thus semantics gives the unity not only to the sentence, but to the sign. The dual nature of signs of the semiologist is superseded on this higher level by accepting the reference, that to which the sign points, as giving it unity.

III.   THIRD PHASE: GENERAL HERMENEUTICS AND TEXTS

In recent years Ricoeur has come to consider symbols and interpretation more generally. After his confrontation with semiology and contemporary problems of language, he links interpretation especially to discourse in texts. He has given more consideration to the objective side of reading texts:

> Today I should be less inclined to limit hermeneutics to the discovery of hidden meanings in symbolic language and would prefer to link hermeneutics to the more general problem of written language and texts. . . .Nevertheless such was the way I was introduced to the hermeneutical problem.[14]

This linking of hermeneutics to written language and texts allows for an extensive treatment of texts: a text is considered to reveal a depth meaning, if interpretation does not move too quickly to the subjective side of the hermeneutical arch in appropriating the meaning before letting the text speak and interpret for itself. This possibility is due to the *distanciation* effected in the fixing of a discourse in a text.[15] The insights springing from the *interarticulation* of semiology and structuralism with phenomenology of language have been carried over to his recent studies in the broader context of explaining and interpreting texts.[16] Still maintaining the important insights gained from the overthrowing of the absolute claims of these sciences and the interarticulation with phenomenology, he shows at least implicitly the same insights when he treats the fixing of discourse in texts. Furthermore, what has been gained from semiology and structuralism in the more narrow context of sign and words in sentences is likewise carried over into the more general context of discourse in text and text-interpretation. Just as a phenomenology of language had to be instructed by semiology, so too, hermeneutics and interpretation of texts must be instructed by a structural approach to the text. Just as phenomenology of language and semiology dealing with the sign each learn from the other, so too, the explanation approach and the interpretation approach can learn from one another.

Ricoeur has been adamant in both the narrow and the broad contexts of interarticulating structuralism and language about the basic aim of discourse as saying something about something to someone. He has adhered to the priority of the semantic over the structural. Discourse in speech and in writing has been fundamentally important, emerging as a focal point and unifying element in much of his recent work. Reading of texts, such as those of the great philosophers of history, requires a reconciliation of explanation and interpretation as two modes of reading a text, bringing together in an interarticulation the contribution of structuralism, as explanation of the text, and interpretation. This interarticulation allows the text to speak for itself before its discourse is appropriated in the final stage of appropriation into the soil of subjective lived experience. Before the discourse of a text can be appropriated in new interpretations, the depth history and depth meaning must be attained, so that, finally, Being can be heard. This is possible because of the transcending of the event of discourse by the meaning. This distanciation allows for a two-fold reading of the text. Although these two modes are opposed, they can be interarticulated in such a way as to allow for arriving at the depth meaning of discourse in texts, and thus let the text itself interpret.

Ricoeur considers a new concept of interpretation which highlights his full extension of this concept from his former or narrow view limiting interpretation to double meanings, or moving from one level of meaning to another relation to symbols. He briefly highlights two different modes of reading thus:

> Two ways of reading, we have said, are offered to us. By reading we can prolong and reinforce the suspension affecting the text's reference to the environment of a world and the audience of speaking subjects; this is the explanatory attitude. But we can also bring an end to this suspension and complete the text in actual discourse. It is this second attitude which is the genuine aim of reading. The other sort of reading would not even be possible if it were not first of all apparent that the text, as writing, waits and calls for a reading; if a reading is possible, it is indeed because the text is not closed in on itself but opens out onto something else. By any supposition reading is a linking together of a new discourse to the discourse of the text. The linking reveals, in the very constitution of the text, an original capacity of being re-enacted, which is its open character. Interpretation is the concrete result of this openness and of this linking together.[17]

Ricoeur shows the failure of the first concept of both structuralism and interpretation as ways of reading texts, as the first step in bringing about a reconciliation in these two modes of reading a text. Structuralism as such has too formal or abstract a conception of sense (or meanings). He says:

> We tried to hold ourselves to a notion of sense (or meaning) which would be strictly reducible to the arrangement of the elements within the text. As a matter of fact no one remains with a conception as formal as this of the sense (or meaning) of a narrative or myth.[18]

In fact, this type of formal approach presupposes this fuller sense or meaning. In attempting to overcome the contradiction, the myth expresses the contradiction in meaningful relationships. Ricoeur holds that it is impossible to bracket or exclude the function of the myth "as a narrative of the origins."[19] Rather, structural analysis allows us to be withdrawn from a superficial reading of the text, brackets the superficial semantics, "that of the apparent narrative, so as to make manifest a *depth-semantics,* which is the latent narrative."[20] Thus through structural analysis of the text we are brought from a naïve or superficial interpretation of a text to a depth or critical interpretation. But what does this do to his initial concept of interpretation as appropriation?

What this actually does for interpretation as appropriation is to postpone such an appropriation in order to let the text speak, to allow the text and its language to interpret first. The concept of the first level of interpretation, then, is now an objective interpretation which postpones the subjective or other end of the arch of hermeneutics. The reader must let the interpreting text have its say before too quickly appropriating it and reactualizing or enacting it. Thus structural analysis has extended the initial (subjective) concept of interpretation to admit a separation or bracketing of the reference of the supposed intentions and references of the author, and allow the reader to focus on and hear what the text itself wants to say and let it orientate our thinking according to it and its direction. "The sense of the text is the direction which it opens up for our thought."[21] Ricoeur goes on to repeat this new definition of interpretation:

> This concept of sense as direction for thought leads us to a new definition of interpretation which would be less a subjective operation than an objective process; less an act on the text, than an act of the text. This process of interpretation has something to do with the depth semantics of the text delivered which is to understand in dynamic terms; whereas the structure constitutes the statics of the text, the depth semantics is itself a process of meaning; it requires a fresh interpretation, this interpretation which I called the act of the text.[22]

This new understanding of interpretation does not eliminate the idea of it as appropriation, but only postpones it until the end of the process. "It is the other end of what we have called the hermeneutical arch: it is the last pillar of the bridge, the anchor of the arch in the soil of lived experience."[23] What the reader must do, then, is enter the process of the text, and let it first interpret and reveal the process of depth meaning, before appropriation by "re-saying" as "re-enacting." Thus the objective interpretation necessitates a postponement of the subjective interpretation.

We can see clearly the direction of Ricoeur's deepening development in extending the meaning and application of interpretation. Now he considers the text the focal context for any consideration of general hermeneutics. And this has enriched his whole scope of consideration in philosophy of language. It has also given him more adequate scope and tools for raising again the long-dormant questions of his philosophy of the will, which he has recently done. But to understand that present endeavor on his part, one must understand the different phases he has gone through in his developments on language, especially dealing with the symbolic aspect of language and interpretation. Then one can approach the question of Being with the proper disposition.

NOTES

1. Ernst Cassirer, *The Philosophy of Symbolic Forms*, trans. Ralph Manheim (New Haven & London: Yale University Press, 1955).

2. Karl Jaspers, *Truth and Symbol, from Von der Wahrheit*, trans. and introduction by Jean T. Wilde, William Kluback and William Himmel (New York: Twayne Publishers, 1959).

3. Alfred North Whitehead, *Symbolism, Its Meaning and Effect* (New York: Capricorn Books, 1959).

4. For full length treatment of Ricoeur's thought, *see*:
Don Ihde, *Hermeneutical Phenomenology* (Evanston: Northwestern University Press, 1971).
David M. Rasmussen, *Mythic-Symbolic Language and Philosophical Anthropology*, (The Hague, Martinus Nijhoff, 1971).
Michael Philibert, *Ricoeur* (Paris: Editions Seghers, 1971).
Patrick L. Bourgeois, *Extension of Ricoeur's Hermeneutic* (The Hague: Martinus Nijhoff, 1975).

5. Paul Ricoeur, "What is a Text? Explanation and Interpretation," an article at the end of *Mythic-Symbolic Language and Philosophical Anthropology*, David M. Rasmussen (The Hague: Martinus Nijhoff, 1971), *passim*.

6. For a simple and clear statement of the problems and development, *see*: Paul Ricoeur, "From Existentialism to the Philosophy of Language," *Philosophy Today*, 17, No. 2 (Summer, 1973), pp. 88-96.

7. It must be kept in mind that for our purposes we can distinguish three phases of development in his view of symbols and in his general focus on language with more than one meaning. But a full elaboration would reveal that at the time of *Le volontaire et l'involontaire* Ricoeur did not realize that symbols and not myths had to be the focus in the empirics of the will. *See* my book: *The Extension of Ricoeur's Hermeneutic* (Martinis Nijhoff, The Hague, 1975).

8. *See* FP, pp. 8-9. SE, pp. 14-18. CI, pp. 12-13.

9. *See* SE, pp. 14-15, "The Hermeneutics of Symbols and Philosophical Reflection," *International Philosophical Quarterly*, 2, (May 1962), p. 194. FP, p. 8.

10. SE, p. 15.

11. "Hermeneutics of Symbols," p. 194. SE, pp. 15-16, FP, p. 13.

12. Paul Ricoeur, "From Existentialism to the Philosophy of Language," p. 91.

13. *See* chapter VII of my book for a lengthy treatment of this phase: "Phenomenology and the Sciences of Language: Further Extensions," in *Extension of Ricoeur's Hermeneutic*; or, *see* my article "Phenomenology and the Sciences of Language," *Research in Phenomenology*, vol. I, pp. 119-136.

14. "From Existentialism to the Philosophy of Language," p. 91.

15. The term "distanciation," used by Ricoeur in several of his recent writings, needs some clarification. He uses it in the context of refusing certain basic points of Gadamer's position in *Truth and Method*. It will be helpful to see two statements of Ricoeur about distanciation from his article "The Hermeneutical Function of Distanciation," *(Philosophy Today*, Vol. 17, No. 2, pp. 132 and 134). "The very first distanciation therefore is the distanciation of the saying in the said." He goes further in speaking of the distanciation brought about in writing: "Such is the triple distanciation introduced by writing: 1. distanciation from the author; 2. from the situation of discourse; 3. from the original audience. But once again this does not mean that the problematic of the text is reduced to that of writing. First, because writing only realizes a trait that is virtual in all discourse—the distanciation of meaning and event. And furthermore, because the problematic of the text passes through other modalities of distanciation that can affect discourse outside of writing, even at the level of oral discourse. This is what I have called the realization of discourse as a work."

16.   When Ricoeur speaks of "interarticulating" semiology or the sciences of language with a phenomenology of language, he does not mean simply to indicate reciprocal influences, nor a mere juxtaposition of one with the other, nor the taking of elements from one for the other. Rather, each has a particular truth about the language phenomenon which must be brought together or integrated in a whole and unified view of language, so that the truth or essential aspect of each view is brought together into a new and unique view of language. For a complete treatment of this interarticulation *see* chapter VII of my book, *Extension of Ricoeur's Hermeneutic*; or *see* my article, "Phenomenology and the Sciences of Language," *Research in Phenomenology*, vol. I, pp. 119-136.

17.   Paul Ricoeur, "What is a Text?", p. 144.

18.   *Ibid.,* p. 146.

19.   *Ibid.,* p. 147.

20.   *Ibid.*

21.   *Ibid.,* p. 149.

22.   *Ibid.,* p. 148.

23.   *Ibid.,* p. 150.

* [Editor's Note: The author has used his own translation of certain passages of Ricoeur's work. Therefore, the first numbers indicate pagination in the French edition and the second indicate that of the English translation.]

VI

David Pellauer

THE SIGNIFICANCE OF THE TEXT IN
PAUL RICOEUR'S HERMENEUTICAL THEORY

In order to assess the recent development of Ricoeur's hermeneutical theory, the author presents a brief examination of the growth of that theory since the publication of *The Symbolism of Evil*. Due to considerations of length, he does not attempt a detailed historical analysis of Ricoeur's many recent writings; instead, he schematizes them in terms of the hypothesis of the growing importance of the text for his reflection. This approach has the advantage of emphasizing the scope of Ricoeur's theory if we accept the price of imposing a system on the elements which appear in it which may not have been intended in each instance of their occurrence. The author suggests, however, that a proper appreciation of Ricoeur's contribution in this area requires such an approach, at least so long as we do not have a complete statement of his position from him.

David Pellauer is a doctoral candidate at the Divinity School, University of Chicago, Chicago, Illinois. He has been Ricoeur's assistant for several years.

The Significance of the Text in
Paul Ricoeur's Hermeneutical Theory

DAVID PELLAUER

It is no secret that the thought of Paul Ricoeur has taken a hermeneutical turn, nor, as Don Ihde has so admirably demonstrated, is this turn unanticipated in Ricoeur's earlier writings.[1] What has been lacking is a detailed consideration of the development of his hermeneutical theory subsequent to its explicit appearance in *The Symbolism of Evil*. This lacuna may be due in part to the fact that this aspect of Ricoeur's thinking is still very much a theory in the process of being formulated and the fact that he has undertaken this process in numerous essays which suffer the limitations of that genre of philosophical writing, i.e., frequent repetition of points developed at length elsewhere and the necessity to limit one's topic to the space available. Yet despite these drawbacks, the shape of his hermeneutical theory can be discerned and is worth our consideration even though a book-length treatment of the topic has not yet appeared.

Such consideration is important because it reveals that Ricoeur's understanding of the significance of philosophical hermeneutics has broadened considerably, especially as he has advanced beyond the analysis of Western myths and symbols to the problem of hermeneutical understanding in general.

In order to assess this recent development of his hermeneutical theory, I shall present a brief examination of the growth of that theory since the publication of *The Symbolism of Evil*. More specifically, I shall focus on the significance of the text in that theory for I believe that it not only has assumed an ever more central emphasis in his thinking, but also that a better understanding of this central concept will help us to appreciate better the horizon of Ricoeur's hermeneutic and its fundamental continuity with his basic philosophical project.

Due to my own considerations of length, I shall not attempt a detailed historical analysis of Ricoeur's many recent writings; instead, I shall schematize them in terms of my hypothesis of the growing importance and centrality of the text for his reflection. This approach has the advantage of emphasizing the scope of his theory if we accept the price of perhaps imposing a system on the elements which appear in it which may not have been intended in each instance of their occurrence. I suggest, however, that a proper appreciation of Ricoeur's contribution in this area requires such an approach, at least so long as we do not have a complete statement of his position from him.

To anticipate our course, I will consider (1) how the concern for understanding the symbols of evil gives rise to concern for a general theory of interpretation; (2) the place of the text in that theory; and (3) the scope of the concept "text" in Ricoeur's writing, and its significance for understanding his hermeneutic theory.

I. The Move Toward A General Hermeneutic

The Symbolism of Evil, which may conveniently be taken as a starting point for any analysis of Ricoeur's hermeneutic, is really part two of volume two of Ricoeur's major philosophical undertaking, a philosophy of the will. Volume one, *Freedom and Nature*, presents an eidetics of willing, a description of an act of the will in terms of the three interconnected steps of decision, movement, and consent. This description takes place within an epoché which does not take into account either Transcendence or the fault, where Transcendence is anticipated to be "a presence which constantly precedes my own power of self-affirmation," [FN, p. 33] and the fault "expresses the awareness that all is not right with the world, that existence as I live it is always a flawed existence."[2]

It is the presence of this initial double epoché that necessitates the subsequent study of finitude and guilt which reintroduces the problem of the fault, and also the as yet unpublished *Poetics of the Will* which will take Transcendence into account.

The study of the fault, entitled *Finitude and Guilt*, itself consists of two volumes because of the inherent incapacity of reflection rationally to explain the fault. Part one, *Fallible Man*, demonstrates the possibility of evil through an analysis of the fragility of existence, but it cannot show the necessity of or the reason for its occurrence, for if evil were necessary or rational it would no longer be the fault in the requisite sense that human beings are responsible for its existence even though paradoxically it precedes each one of us. This is why *The Symbolism of Evil* has to undertake the indirect approach of trying "to surprise the transition in the act by 're-enacting' in ourselves the confession that the religious consciousness makes of it." [SE, p. 3] It attempts to do this through reflection upon the symbols of stain, sin, and guilt, and the myths which embody and already interpret them.

Here the hermeneutical turn is self-consciously taken, its purpose being to discover the symbolic meaning of the myth which the philosopher wagers shall lead him to "a better understanding of man and of the bond between the being of man and the being of all beings." [SE, p. 355; see also

p. 308] Such understanding in turn may give rise to a return to coherent discourse and reflection capable of making sense of our lives. It is this desire for self-understanding that provides the continuity between Ricoeur's hermeneutical theory and his philosophy of the will.

Clearly the use of hermeneutics in *The Symbolism of Evil* is a means to an end. It is applied to concrete symbols and myths in order to advance a larger philosophical project which is as yet unfinished, although to the best of our knowledge, not abandoned. In the interim, however, Ricoeur has undertaken a series of "detours" which have delayed its fulfillment while adding to its richness. It is one of these detours, the concern for philosophical hermeneutics which interests us, and I will henceforth set aside any direct concern for Ricoeur's philosophy of the will to examine this path he has taken.

A first sign of this detour is indicated in Ricoeur's next major volume following the publication of *The Symbolism of Evil*, his work on Freud, *Freud and Philosophy*, where he notes that his investigation is intended to contribute to the solution of a problem left unresolved by *The Symbolism of Evil*, namely "the relationship between a hermeneutics of symbols and a philosophy of reflection." [FP, p. xii] In turning to this problem he moves beyond the particular problem of the symbols of evil to "the epistemology of symbolism," [FP, p. 14] and from reflection upon particular symbols and myths to those areas of experience where symbols make their appearance—the cosmic, oneiric, and poetic dimensions—along with consideration of how these dimensions of human experience are brought to language. Clearly, in this work the problem is no longer one of interpreting concrete symbols, but one of understanding symbolic language in general, and as his thought on this topic develops it becomes more and more a question of grasping such language as it is inscribed in "texts."

Ricoeur's study of Freud is at least partially motivated by what he has come to call the conflict of interpretations. That is, Freud's own hermeneutic or theory of interpretation is one of suspicion, as are the hermeneutics of Marx and Nietzsche. Such a theory tends toward a form of reductive explanation which Ricoeur cannot accept, but which he also cannot refute. Such a hermeneutic has its legitimacy, so the only course open is to confront its claims and if possible show that they can be situated within a larger hermeneutic field which would incorporate them while recognizing their proper limits.[3]

Hermeneutics, Ricoeur says, "seems to be animated by this double motivation: willingness to suspect, willingness to listen; vow of rigor, vow of obedience." [FP, p. 27] So what is needed is, if not a complete theory of interpretation, at least a basic comprehension of the breadth and structure of such a theory, and understanding of its capabilities and its limits. It is this need, I believe, that underlies much of Ricoeur's recent work on topics in this area of inquiry. More and more he has come to articulate what could become a general theory, although he did not begin with such a project in mind. In fact, from one point of view, his recent essays may be seen as attempts to elucidate those areas of hermeneutics which are important to his own concern for the philosophy of language, structuralism, and post-Bultmannian theology.[4] From another, more retrospective view, their insight and capacity to resolve the difficult problems raised by hermeneutics suggest the possibility of a more complete and systematic presentation of his theory, if he should decide to undertake it.

What is significant for our inquiry into the notion of the text and its significance is that in every instance just cited, i.e., language, structuralism, and post-Bultmannian theology, Ricoeur has seen analysis of and reflection upon the notion of the text as the proper way to proceed.[5] Let us turn therefore to more direct consideration of this pivotal concept.

II. The Place of the Text in Ricoeur's Hermeneutic

The central problematic of *The Symbolism of Evil* deals with understanding symbols, where a symbol is defined by its structure of double-meaning.[6] This structure gives rise to reflection because it is mediated by language, particularly in the form of myths, where the myth itself is already a form of interpretation. Thus at this early stage we are already faced with the requirement to make sense of interpretation since, as we shall see in more detail below, language in all its forms calls for an effort of interpretation. But at the same time the way beyond the problem of interpretation within the philosophy of language is also indicated and opened, for myths are a special use of language. They are ordered wholes and as such may be considered as texts to be interpreted. The crucial question is whether forms of language such as myths, and more generally texts, introduce a new problematic for understanding.

Ricoeur's answer is affirmative in at least two senses. Texts introduce new questions in so far as they (1) are complex works of discourse which transcend the problem of understanding at the levels of both the word and the sentence, and (2) because many texts, especially myths, are culturally and methodologically distanciated from us. We must discover whether this distance constitutes an unbridgeable form of alienation or if it is a necessary aspect of the basic structure of understanding.

Let us consider each of these aspects which contribute to the centrality of the text in Ricoeur's reflections in turn. The mediating term which connects them is "appropriation."

A. *Language*

In attempting to come to grips with the structural modes of analysis and their claim to objectivity, Ricoeur has developed a philosophy of "discourse" as a way of incorporating both syntactic and semantic analysis into his philosophy of language. The notion of the text is crucial to the development of this theory.

Structural linguistics beginning with Ferdinand de Saussure demonstrates that language as *langue* can be made the object of scientific investigation if we assume certain postulates which may be summarized as follows.

(1)   Language is to be treated as a synchronic system.
(2)   This system may be treated as a finite set of discrete elements.
(3)   The significance of the elements of this system depends on the oppositions between them and not on any element taken by itself.
(4)   The system is closed. It does not refer beyond itself.

The fruitful results of such analysis are well known, but they are costly in the sense that language so considered no longer says anything since it neither refers to the world nor is it spoken by anyone to anyone. It is intelligible because it has a discernible structure, but meaningless in so far as it has nothing to say.

At first glance it might seem that there is no problem of interpretation implied here because there is nothing to be interpreted. But Ricoeur's fundamental assumption (or wager) is that discourse (as including both *langue* and *parole*) does say something. It is spoken by someone to someone about something. Hence it is necessary to show how this is possible. This task is doubly urgent if we recall that Claude Levi-Strauss has undertaken to generalize structural methods and apply them to the study of myths, Ricoeur's topic in *The Symbolism of Evil*. The possibility that structuralism might demonstrate that myths too do not really say anything must be seen, I believe, as a primary motive underlying the development of Ricoeur's theory of discourse.

The key to this undertaking is the refusal of any ultimate reduction of language to *langue*, a refusal that in a way brings him close to Anglo-American philosophy of language for the event that unites *langue* and *parole* as discourse is use. Language is meaningful when it is used by somebody to say something about something to somebody. As soon as we admit this, interpretation becomes a necessary step toward understanding at every level of discourse, from the simplest speech-act to the most complex written accounts. We can see this if we consider (1) the event of discourse and (2) its fixation in texts.

As opposed to *langue*, discourse is characterized by the following fundamental features. It is a temporal event, not an atemporal system. It requires a speaker because it is said by someone and this someone can be indicated by such grammatical devices as the first person singular personal pronoun "I." It has an audience who can also be designated. It is not a set of elements, but a combination of them, and it refers to something which is part of the context of the act of discourse. In short, discourse is an occurrence in the real world; it is not an ideal, atemporal, subjectless system of relations.[7]

If this is true, we are already confronted with a task of interpretation and that task occurs on two levels. First, at the level of the word, there is the problem of polysemy. Since languages are finite lexical systems, words must have a plurality of meanings for reasons of economy. This plurality is partly reduced by the use of the words in sentences where the structure of the sentence helps determine the words chosen and their meanings. It is also affected by the word's sensitivity to the context in which it is used, but the threat of ambiguity remains. Even if we introduce such strategies of discourse as scientific language,[8] the possibility of misunderstanding remains. The need, therefore, is for some general theory of interpretation which can help us to combat this threat and so we are driven beyond the problem of analyzing particular instances of discourse to the question of interpretation in general. Let us keep in mind, however, that the problem already arises at the first level of discourse.

Discourse interpreted is discourse understood. This maxim may be said to guide the next steps in the development of Ricoeur's theory of interpretation. The question is what is to be interpreted or understood in discourse, and the answer is its meaning. An act of discourse, we recall, is an event. It passes away. But something remains. Something, so to speak, is fixed and can be interpreted. This something is not the event of speaking, but rather the "said" of speaking, its meaning.[9] We do not need to go into great detail concerning Ricoeur's theory of meaning here for it will suffice simply to indicate its major components. What is important is to see that it is concern for the "text" that allows these components to be recognized and that they in turn determine how a text is to be interpreted.

Meaning, in brief, is not an event. It can be identified and reidentified as the same. It arises out of the conjunction in the sentence of a singular identification (the subject) and a general predication (the act of predicating something about the subject). It can be expressed as the propositional content of any illocutionary act, and, following Frege, it includes both sense and reference, where the reference is both to reality and to the self.[10]

Texts enter into consideration here because they make clear these characteristics of meaning. A text, in effect, "fixes" discourse, preserving its meaning when the event of speaking passes away. So consideration of the "textuality" of the text is first of all important because it reveals how meaning can be expressed, preserved, and conveyed over temporal and cultural distance. The text, in other words, makes clear how language can continue to be meaningful even though the transference of such meaning calls for an act of interpretation which recovers it in appropriation.

From this insight, it is only a small step to consideration of the nature of the text taken as such, a step necessitated by the realization that texts are not always, and in fact need not be, transcriptions of spoken language. Writing does not presuppose speaking since it is possible to proceed directly to writing as a form of discourse. This is the basis of any attempt to recover the meaning of ancient writings such as religious scriptures.

Let us next consider the characteristics of the text as such which reveal these characteristics. In comparison to the prominent event character of speech-acts, texts "fix" discourse. They endure and this has the important consequence that it gives rise to what may be called the autonomy of the text. That is, a text, because it endures, escapes an author's intention. It has consequences which he or she could not have foreseen or anticipated and it may be used in a way never intended by the writer, as, for example, when we publish an important historical personage's private correspondence. In a similar way, a text outlasts and thereby escapes both its original audience and its original situation. It passes over to that indefinite audience of anyone who knows how to read.

This threefold autonomy of the text with respect to its author's intention, its original audience, and its original situation, implies that its meaning, both as sense and reference, is not determined in the same way as is the meaning of spoken discourse. In conversation, certain devices or strategies such as inflection and gesture are available which cannot be directly reproduced in writing. So any theory of text interpretation must recognize what means are used in writing to replace or compensate for these changes. In the case of sense, the most important things are the underlying syntactic and narrative structures, which accounts for the importance of structuralist analyses for hermeneutics. However, the case of reference is more complex. In conversation, ostensive reference is possible because the interlocuters share a common present and a common situation, something not necessarily true when we read a text. Its author, original audience, and original situation may all have disappeared or may even be unknown.

What then is the reference of a text? What do we understand a text as referring to, as being about, when we interpret it? Here is the point perhaps of Ricoeur's most significant contribution to hermeneutical theory for he proposes, in effect, that a text refers to its own "world," where this world is to be understood in an existential sense as a possible world for self-understanding and a potential mode of existing. It is, in a word, a new way of understanding reality.

In saying this, Ricoeur undercuts the Romanticist tradition's contention that the purpose of interpretation is to understand an author better than he or she understood himself or herself. In a striking metaphor, Ricoeur responds that our purpose is not to understand the author (or the author's intention) behind the text, but the text itself whose meaning is in front of it as its world. Sometimes he has even spoken of this world of the text as the "issue" of the text, to indicate better that we are concerned with what is at stake in the text and that what is at stake is what the text proposes to our self-understanding.

It follows that one task of hermeneutical theory must be to show how interpretation appropriates this meaning and its world by bringing the written text back to discourse, "if not as spoken discourse, at least as a speech-act actualized in the act of reading."[11] Ricoeur has not yet spelled out the details of this process, but it is evident that he conceives it as a movement from understanding to explanation to understanding. In the first instance, understanding refers to our initial pre-judgment or guess as to what the text is about. Explanation which utilizes the structural approaches developed by theorists such as Lévi-Strauss and A. J. Greimas is the effort to work out the consequences of this first step and its plausibility in terms of the sense of the text as conveyed by its deep structures. Then reflection upon how these structures are connected to the text's referent or world leads finally to a second level of understanding, understanding as appropriation.

This theory of reading deserves greater attention than we can devote to it here, but we need here instead to continue our examination of the textuality of the text to see how it is the structure of the text that makes interpretation not only necessary, but also possible.[12]

We have seen that the need for interpretation is grounded in the very elements of language, its words and sentences. Now it is necessary to grasp that a text reintroduces this need for interpretation at a higher level. Hermeneutics as the theory of text interpretation is not just due to the polysemy of words or the ambiguity of individual sentences. It also stems from the plurivocity which arises from the very nature of the text as a structured work.[13] That is, Ricoeur maintains that a text cannot be simply analysed into its elements. It is more than a mere collection of sentences as can be demonstrated if we recall that the sequence of a text cannot be altered without affecting its meaning, nor may a poem be reduced to a series of propositions that "say the same thing." So the existence of a text introduces a new problematic into any general theory of interpretation.

This new level of ambiguity is due to three aspects of the text which make it a structured whole. First, it is the product of a composition. It is made, a work, and therefore governed by rules of production. Second, it is shaped by its genre, and, third, it has a style which determines its individuality. These are the elements which go beyond the semantics and syntax of the word and sentence that a theory of text interpretation or reading must take into account. Ricoeur has given some indication of what this theory might look like, especially in his work on the parables of Jesus, but in effect we here reach the current state of his reflections.

The only definite indications he has given of how these elements are themselves to be interpreted is to say that he believes genre must be understood as a productive as well as a classificatory category which distanciates the work from its author and its original situation and audience.[14][15] Style conveys the author's presence, although not in terms of his or her intention, but rather as what Wayne Booth has called the "implied author."[16] If we are to appropriate the meaning of a text, our reading must take these factors into account. Such an undertaking will mean that the way to understanding is through explanation, although at the same time, as we indicated above, explanation must be said to begin with and presuppose some understanding.[17] This understanding should be taken in the sense that Heidegger speaks about when he discusses the fore-structure of understanding and that Gadamer discusses in terms of the role and status of prejudice in interpretation.[18][19]

B.   *Distanciation*

Distanciation we said is the second major area of reflection in Ricoeur's hermeneutic which reveals the significance of the text for that theory of interpretation. It appears in two forms, cultural (or temporal) distanciation and methodological distanciation.

Cultural distanciation is important because it suggests the reason we do hermeneutics, which began after all as a response to religious and literary texts which had lost their former, immediate authority. This sense of loss gave rise to the development of exegetical and literary critical techniques whose differences reflect this double origin. What is important here, though, is the sense that older texts have lost their meaning for us and that it needs to be recovered. Ricoeur's own interests in the myths and symbols of the fault and of the Christian tradition correspond to this general problematic. To this may be added the influence on him of Gadamer's *Truth and Method*, probably the most influential work on hermeneutics in this century. This book formulates the problem of interpretation in such a fashion that its title almost appears to be a strict disjunction: truth *or* method—although this undoubtedly was not the author's intention.[20][21] Yet if participation in the meaning of the text means the refusal of all distanciation as alienating, as Gadamer does at times seem to imply, it is difficult to see how any critical (or post-critical) appropriation of a text is possible. Are not all earlier texts lost due simply to temporal distance, while more contemporary examples succumb to the requirement that method "objectify" its object, thereby introducing another form of alienating distance. The question is whether the hermeneutical situation or hermeneutical method has any resources for overcoming the very conditions which give rise to that situation and method. Ricoeur believes that distanciation itself provides one such resource.

His reflections on distanciation are directed therefore to reformulating the problem of distanciation, his goal being to show that all distanciation is not alienating.[22] It is not always something imposed on a situation of participation. In fact, it is a necessary condition for the preservation of meaning, which at the same time creates the need for interpretation. Once again, it is reflection on the text that makes this evident, although distanciation antedates the text in that it already occurs in the event of discourse or speech-act. It is the text, however, which reveals the broader horizon of this phenomenon.

Distanciation first occurs in the event of discourse itself in the distanciation of meaning and event. "The very first distanciation therefore is the distanciation of the saying in the said."[23] We indicated above that the ambiguity of discourse calls for interpretation. This first occurrence of distanciation further grounds this requirement.

A similar double structure appears at the level of the text as a written work of discourse. Distanciation is one of the constitutive elements of the text as such and it insures that the text requires interpretation.

Distanciation is constitutive of the text in terms of the basic traits of the text discussed in the preceding remarks on language. It assures the autonomy of the text with regard to its author, original situation, and audience. As such, "it is not the product of our methodology and therefore is not something added and parasitic, rather it is constitutive of the phenomenon of the text as written."[24] Like genre, distanciation thus helps to preserve the text from the perishing of the moment. But in so doing it also decontextualizes the text from its original setting. This decontextualization, in turn, becomes a condition for all subsequent interpretation for in preserving the text it also keeps it open for new interpretations. In other words, it makes possible the subsequent recontextualization of its message.

Distanciation, then, need not be seen simply as alienating. It is also a necessary, though not a sufficient, condition for any participation beyond the original situation. This productive sense of distanciation may be further illuminated by considering two other aspects of the role of distanciation in the text: its effect on the reference of the text, and through the reference, on the reader or subject.

The reference of a text, we saw, is the world of that text. This world may be the known world as in a scientific or a historical text or it may be a different, but perhaps no less real world in the case of fictional texts. Since it is fictional narratives which most interest Ricoeur, his emphasis here is on the ability of such works to abolish, so to speak, a first-order reference to the familiar world in favor of a second-order reference "which reaches the world not only at the level of manipulable objects, but at the level Husserl designated by the expression *Lebenswelt* and Heidegger by "being-in-the-world."[25] Distanciation, in other words, contributes to a text's ability to "redescribe reality." In this sense, the world of the text "constitutes a new kind of distanciation which we can call a distanciation of the real from itself."[26] It proposes a kind of being in the world which is unfolded in front of the text which my interpretation seeks to explicate. In so doing, I discover "a world that I might inhabit and wherein I might project my ownmost possibilities."[27]

This proposed world introduces the final form of distanciation: "The distanciation of the subject from himself" which is the precondition for self-understanding and action.[28] This distanciation comes about through the appropriation of the text which is the result of reading. It will suffice to note here that "in the last analysis the *text* is the mediation by which we understand ourselves."[29] Clearly this understanding is not to be conceived as some form of alienation or as alienated reason, instead it is to be conceived as tied to the distanciation proper to discourse and discourse fixed in texts as revealed by reflection on the textuality of the text.

III.   THE EXTENSION OF THE CONCEPT "TEXT" IN
RICOEUR'S HERMENEUTIC

The preceding reflections centered on how the text functions in Ricoeur's hermeneutic inquiries as a means of discovering the nature and limits of the hermeneutical task. It is now necessary to turn our attention to the text itself as the object of interpretation to broaden our analysis and appreciation of this hermeneutic.

It is necessary to consider the extension of the concept "text" in Ricoeur's thought in order not to be misled by the preceding section with its emphasis on the text as fixed, written discourse. In fact, as a cursory survey indicates, "text" also covers an extremely broad spectrum of application in Ricoeur's work. Our task in this section of our essay will be to account for this extension and to show that it does not contradict the results of our earlier analysis.

That the concept "text" has a broad extension for Ricoeur may be demonstrated by enumerating a few examples. In *Freud and Philosophy*, all of the following are called texts or are said to be worthy of consideration as texts: Freud's work; the "text" of the dream account; the primitive speech of desire; the metaphor of the book of nature; the object of psychoanalytic and phenomenological decipherment; and what analysis penetrates to.[30] In the essays collected in *The Conflict of Interpretations* we find: the object of exegesis; the object of philosophy; that which characterizes the level of hermeneutics; the object of the problem of multiple meanings; the text of consciousness; effects of meaning in Freud; and penitential literature.[31] From other sources may be added: previously living values regarded from the perspective of objectification and distanciation; culture; historical reality and its interconnections (following the nineteenth-century historians); and the paradigm of distanciation in all communication.[32] Nor is this all. As is implicit in these references, "text" becomes a paradigm for any object of hermeneutical inquiry. It delimits the field of hermeneutics proper [CI, p. 298], so that any group of signs which may be characterized as a work—i.e., as constituted by composition, a genre, a style—may be viewed as a text.[33] Taking it to its limit, the entirety of human existence becomes a text to be interpreted and we rejoin the title of Ihde's study of Ricoeur's philosophical project: hermeneutic phenomenology.[34]

Part of this breadth of the concept "text" is already implicit in the tradition of hermeneutics from within which Ricoeur undertakes his reflections. This may be seen in the references given from the book on Freud. Freud himself, in his interpretation of dreams and secondary forms of repression, uses the analogy of the text as a means of explicating the psychoanalytic interpretation of these phenomena. And Ricoeur's own interpretation of Freud's theory argues that psychoanalysis is a combination of an energetic and a hermeneutic—which implies that there is something (the text) which the analyst interprets, even though this text is a written document only when it is recorded in the analyst's notes or the subsequent case-history.

Even more influential for understanding this practice of taking "text" in a broad sense is the modern history of hermeneutics as it was shaped by Romanticist thought beginning with Schleiermacher and culminating in the work of Wilhelm Dilthey who spoke of the object of hermeneutics as any inscribed expression of life.[35] Ricoeur has retained this definition even though he, like Gadamer, severely criticizes this tradition for its psychological emphasis. Using "text" in this sense as a paradigm for the object of hermeneutical research as well as an analytical device makes sense when we recall that hermeneutics as a set of problems arising out of concrete instances of a need for interpretation points to a general theory of interpretation.

Hermeneutics may have begun when certain specific texts became problematic and in need of translation in terms of a changed situation, but it did not and does not end there. In becoming a theory of interpretation, hermeneutics moves beyond concern for a specific text to texts in general, from texts in general to the concept "text," and from the concept "text" to the analogical application of this concept to other groups of signs susceptible of being considered as texts. As Dilthey perceived, any "work" of culture, that is, any inscribed expression of existence, is a possible object for hermeneutical interpretation and appropriation.

Of course, the problem of precisely delineating the object of inquiry at these levels becomes increasingly difficult, but this does not gainsay the analogical application of the paradigm "text" to such expressions of life or existence.

There are two clear examples in Ricoeur's recent work which illustrate such an analogical application of the concept "text" which are worth briefly considering. The first considers human action as a text; the second is related to his work on metaphor.

The application of the hermeneutical concept of the text to human action is found in an article entitled "The Model of the Text: Meaningful Action Considered as a Text."[36] There Ricoeur draws upon the characteristics of the text in relation to discourse to discuss their implications for the human sciences, especially as regards the question of method. The analogy which may be drawn between a text and the object investigated by such sciences suggests that they should be interpreted more as hermeneutical disciplines and less on the basis of the more explanatory natural sciences. They must also include something like the appropriation which is the goal of hermeneutical understanding.

He chooses the concept of "meaningful action" as the primary example suggesting this conclusion because meaningful action, like discourse, must be subject to a kind of fixation and distanciation if it is to be a suitable object for scientific investigation. And, in fact, there are characteristics of action which parallel the fundamental characteristics of the text, giving rise to this possibility. Corresponding to the fixation of meaning of discourse in a text while its event character disappears is the fact that an action may be said to have the structure of both a locutionary and an illocutionary act. It is like a locutionary act in that it has "a propositional content which can be identified and reidentified as the same" and which therefore may become an object of interpretation.[37] It is like an illocutionary act in that a typology of actions may be drawn up based on the constitutive rules for each action. These two characteristics of an action give rise to its "sense content," a sense content that is inscribed insofar as it leaves its mark on the temporal and social dimensions of our existence.[38]

This process of leaving its mark accounts for the autonomy of the act with regard to its agent and original setting. Meaningful actions leave a trace; they make their mark on the course of events, eventually becoming sedimented into social institutions.

Corresponding to the third way the meaning of a text surpasses the event of discourse is the fact that "a meaningful action is an action the importance of which goes 'beyond' its relevance to its initial situation."[39] It may even be re-enacted in new social contexts, thereby establishing a new world of reference which in a sense it bears within itself.

Finally, like a text, meaningful action is addressed to an indefinite audience which includes anyone who knows how to read an action where reading is to be understood as a "kind of practical interpretation through present praxis."[40]

If this correlation between meaningful action and the paradigm of the text is valid, important methodological consequences follow which are themselves correlative with the place of explanation and understanding in text interpretation. Attempts to explain an action in terms of its motivational basis, for example, are similar to construing the meaning of a text. They begin with understanding even if it is just a guess. And as explanation requires understanding, so too understanding is dependent upon explanation. The world discovered through this process is a "*Welt* . . . which is no longer an *Umwelt*, the projection of a world which is more than a situation."[41] It follows that the human sciences insofar as they are hermeneutical sciences must include a moment of appropriation as a climax of this process of reading.[42]

The second example drawn from the broad sense of "text" and the theory of interpretation may be seen in Ricoeur's treatment of metaphor.[43] Although we cannot consider this magisterial work in detail here, it will suffice to indicate that he thinks there is a fundamental similarity between text interpretation and the problem of understanding a metaphor. To a certain extent we may even consider them as similar processes applied to different levels of discourse, the one at the level of a work, the other at the level of a sentence. More specifically, we may say that "the process of understanding a metaphor is the key for that of understanding larger texts, say literary works" when we consider the question of the immanent sense of the object in question.[44] On the other hand, when it is a question of the reference of an act of discourse insofar as this reference is directed toward a world and self-understanding, it is understanding the work as a whole which provides the key to understanding metaphor.[45]

A metaphor is a semantic innovation which cannot be explicated through simple substitution or translation if it is a live metaphor. It must be construed in such a way that the metaphorical twist is both an event of discourse and of meaning. More specifically, it is the emergence into being of a new meaning.[46] We construe texts in a similar way, not only because a text, is written down and needs to be brought to speech again, but because it is a work, a closed structure of meaning which is more than a linear succession of sentences.

Here once again interpretation depends on an initial guess and a process of validation which establishes our interpretation as at least probable.

Then when the question becomes one of reference, "text understanding gives the key to metaphor understanding."[47] This is because reference stands before the text instead of behind it and interpretation aims at "the appropriation of world hypotheses opened by the non-ostensive references of the text."[48] Similarly, metaphors, even though they do not fully embody the dialectic of self and world disclosure due to their short length, must be understood by means of it. What is at stake is the effort to capture the emergence of meaning in both cases. It is this emergence which guarantees their mutual relatedness. Both the metaphor and the text are trying to say something important, something we want and ought to understand.

To sum up, the "text" occupies a central place in Ricoeur's hermeneutic and must be recognized as doing double duty in it. It serves both as an analytical device and as a key theoretical term in the theory which results from his reflections on the problems of interpretation and understanding.

As an analytical device, it serves three purposes in that (1) it helps him to move beyond a concern for particular symbols to concern for extended works of discourse which may themselves be symbolic of something beyond the world of ordinary, everyday, taken-for-granted reality; (2) it allows him to integrate results garnered from linguistics, structuralism, and the philosophy of language into a unifying framework; and (3) it assists him in evaluating and modifying the received Romanticist model of hermeneutics in light of the results obtained in the first two steps.

As a theoretical term the text serves to identify the object of hermeneutics and to delineate its task. Hermeneutics is concerned with the interpretation of any expression of existence which can be preserved in a structure analogous to the structure of the text. In interpreting these structures it must take account of and utilize their elements which are revealed by the analysis of the text as inscribed discourse. The end result of this process of interpretation is appropriation which leads to self-understanding. This self-awareness functions on both a theoretical and a practical level. As a redescription of reality, it helps us to recognize both who we are and what we might do. In this way Ricoeur's hermeneutic rejoins his original project of a philosophy of the will.

NOTES

1. Don Ihde, *Hermeneutic Phenomenology: The Philosophy of Paul Ricoeur* (Evanston: Northwestern University Press, 1971).

2. E. Kohak, "Translator's Introduction" to Paul Ricoeur, *Freedom and Nature: The Voluntary and the Involuntary* (Evanston: Northwestern University Press, 1966), p. xvii.

3. "The hermeneutic field, whose outer contours we have traced, is internally at variance with itself . . . . According to one pole, hermeneutics is understood as the manifestation and restoration of a meaning addressed to me in the manner of a message, a proclamation, or as it is sometimes said, a kerygma; according to the other pole, it is understood as a demystification, as a reduction of illusion." [FP, p. 277] "Our entire hermeneutic problem . . . proceeds from this twofold possibility of an 'innocent' analogical relationship or a 'cunning' distortion." [FP, p. 17]

4. See "From Existentialism to the Philosophy of Language," *Philosophy Today*, 17 (Summer 1973): 88-96; "New Developments in Phenomenology in France: The Phenomenology of Language," *Social Research*, 34 (1967): and "Preface to Bultmann," in CI, pp. 381-401.

5. See, for example, "From Existentialism to the Philosophy of Language," pp. 90-91, 93, 95.

6. More specifically, a symbol is a sign which conceals in its aim a double intentionality. This double intentionality points to a double meaning where one meaning is literal and the other is symbolic, the symbolic meaning being constituted in and through the literal meaning. Symbols in this sense are not allegories or the "symbols" of symbolic logic. They are more primitive than the myths which embody them. See SE, pp. 14-18; "The Symbol . . . Food for Thought," *Philosophy Today*, 5 (1960): 196-207. For Ricoeur's most recent reflection on symbols, see "Parole et Symbole," *Revue des Sciences Religieuses*, 49: 1-2 (1975): 142-161. A slightly revised version of this essay appears in English in Paul Ricoeur, *Interpretation Theory: Discourse and the Surplus of Meaning* (Forth Worth, Texas: Texas Christian University Press, 1976), essay three: "Metaphor and Symbol."

7. See "Structure, Word, Event," in CI, pp. 86ff; "Creativity in Language," *Philosophy Today*, 17 (Summer 1973): 98-99; "Metaphor and the Main Problem of Hermeneutics," *New Literary History*, 6 (1974): 97-98; "The Model of the Text: Meaningful Action Considered as a Text," *Social Research*, 38 (1971): 534-537, 546; "The Hermeneutical Function of Distanciation," *Philosophy Today*, 17 (Summer 1973): 133, 139-141. Another translation of "Metaphor and the Main Problem of Hermeneutics" with notes and commentary by Jeff Close may be found in the *Graduate Faculty Philosophy Journal* of the New School for Social Research, 3:1 (Fall-Winter 1973-74): 42-58.

8. See "Creativity in Language," pp. 102-103.

9. "The Model of the Text," p. 532.

10. "Metaphor and the Main Problem of Hermeneutics," pp. 97-98.

11. "Biblical Hermeneutics," *Semeia*, no. 4 (1975), p. 67.

12. See ibid., pp. 29-148 for Ricoeur's interpretation of the parables of Jesus; see also "Listening to the Parables of Jesus," *Criterion*, 13: 3 (Spring 1974): 18-22, reprinted in *Christianity and Crisis*, 34: 231 (January 6, 1975): 304-308. On the relationship between explanation and understanding, see *Interpretation Theory*, essay four: "Explanation and Understanding." This essay is the final version of Ricoeur's essay "Interpretation Theory" (presented to a colloquium of the faculty of the University of Chicago Divinity School, May 1971), which has circulated in manuscript form and which is widely quoted in the literature on Ricoeur.

13. "The Hermeneutical Function of Distanciation," pp. 134-139; "Biblical Hermeneutics," pp. 66-71.

14. "The Hermeneutical Function of Distanciation," pp. 135-136; "Biblical Hermeneutics," p. 70.

15. *Ibid.*, p. 68; see our discussion of distanciation below.

16. Wayne Booth, *The Rhetoric of Fiction* (Chicago: University of Chicago Press, 1961).

17. "The Hermeneutical Function of Distanciation," p. 139.

18. Martin Heidegger, *Being and Time*, trans. by John Macquarrie and Edward Robinson (New York: Harper & Brothers, 1962), pp. 182-195.

19. Hans-Georg Gadamer, *Truth and Method* (New York: Seabury, 1975), pp. 235-274.

See also Hans-Georg Gadamer, *Philosophical Hermeneutics*, trans. and ed. by David E. Linge (Berkeley: University of California Press, 1976).

20. "The Hermeneutical Function of Distanciation," p. 129.

21. Hans-Georg Gadamer, *Philosophical Hermeneutics*, p. 26.

22. Besides "The Hermeneutical Function of Distanciation," *see* "History and Hermeneutics," *The Journal of Philosophy* 73, no. 19 (November 4, 1976): 683-695; esp. pp. 690-694.

23. "The Hermeneutical Function of Distanciation," p. 132; see also p. 134.

24. *Ibid.*, p. 133.

25. *Ibid.*, p. 140.

26. *Ibid.*, p. 141.

27. *Ibid.*, p. 140.

28. *Ibid.*, p. 141.

29. *Ibid.*, italics mine.

30. *See* FP, pp. xi; 5, 401; 5; 25; 392, cp. and CI, pp. 263, 401.

31. CI, pp. 3, 14, 16; 22; 66, 70, 80, 95; 64; 215, 442; 263; 425.

32. "Ethics and Culture: Habermas and Gadamer in Dialogue," *Philosophy Today*, 17 (Summer 1973): 164-165; "Two Essays: The Critique of Religion and The Language of Faith," *Union Seminary Quarterly Review*, 28: 3 (Spring 1973): 207; "The Task of Hermeneutics," *Philosophy Today*, 17 (Summer 1973): 116; "The Hermeneutical Function of Distanciation," p. 130.

33. FP, pp. 8, 26; "Two Essays," pp. 219-220.

34. "If we succeed in understanding that the entirety of human existence is a text to be read, we will be at the threshold of the general hermeneutic, by means of which I have tried to define the task of the next philosophy." "Two Essays," p. 223.

35. *See* CI, p. 382; Wilhelm Dilthey, *Pattern and Meaning in History*, ed. by H. P. Rickman (New York: Harper Torchbooks, 1962), pp. 75, 77, 107, 116-117, 121, 161, 164.

36. *Social Research*, 38: 3 (1971): 529-562. Also in *New Literary History* Vol. V, (Autumn 1974), pp. 92-117.

37. *Ibid.*, p. 538.

38. *Ibid.*, p. 540.

39. *Ibid.*, p. 543.

40. *Ibid.*, p. 544.

41. *Ibid.*, p. 560.

42. "The paradigmatic character of text-interpretation must be applied down to this ultimate implication. This means that the conditions of an authentic appropriation, as they were displayed in relation to texts, are themselves paradigmatic. Therefore we are not allowed to exclude the explanatory procedures which mediate it." *Ibid.*, pp. 561-562.

43. *See* "Metaphor and the Main Problem of Hermeneutics," "Creativity in Language," "Biblical Hermeneutics," especially Chapter II, The Metaphorical Process, pp. 75-107, and above all *La Métaphore vive* (Paris: Le Seuil, 1975).

44. "Metaphor and the Main Problem of Hermeneutics," p. 100.

45. *Ibid.*, p. 101.

46. *Ibid.*, pp. 96, 99, 103; "Creativity in Language," p. 107.

47. "Metaphor and the Main Problem of Hermeneutics," p. 105.

48. *Ibid.*, p. 106.

VII

Beatriz Melano Couch

RELIGIOUS SYMBOLS AND PHILOSOPHICAL REFLECTION

The aim of this essay is to outline Ricoeur's theory of the symbol in an attempt to demonstrate what there is of philosophical importance in the interpretation of symbols, and more specifically, religious symbols. The inquiry is further circumscribed to the symbolism of evil as expressed in the Judeo-Christian tradition. Ricoeur's hermeneutical theory and method will be assumed, since they are treated elsewhere in this volume. The author focuses on three questions: Why does Ricoeur take the long detour through the interpretation of signs and symbols to arrive at an acceptable notion of existence? How is it that the necessity and contingency of evil are simultaneously manifested and hidden in symbolism? What new roads for further reflection are opened by Ricoeur's treatment of symbols?

Beatriz Melano Couch is Professor of theology and modern literature at Union Theological Seminary in Buenos Aires, Argentina. She holds degrees from the University of Buenos Aires, Princeton Theological Seminary, and the University of Strasbourg.

Religious Symbols and Philosophical Reflection

BEATRIZ MELANO COUCH

The aim of this essay is to outline Ricoeur's theory of the symbol in an attempt to demonstrate what there is of philosophical importance in the interpretation of symbols, and more specifically religious symbols. Our inquiry is further circumscribed to the symbolism of evil as expressed in the Judeo-Christian tradition.

I will not discuss the *theory of the text*, even though our author has given a great deal of attention to it lately, and relates it to philosophical and theological hermeneutics.[1] Nor will I expand his *hermeneutical theory and method*; elsewhere in this collection both themes are discussed. It is assumed that this essay will be understood within this double context: Ricoeur's hermeneutical method and theory of the text.

As a way of introduction to the theme I will try to answer why Ricoeur takes the long detour through the interpretation of signs and symbols to arrive at an acceptable notion of existence, or in other words, why the starting point of his philosophical reflection is language. Here we will find a basic difference between Ricoeur and both Heidegger and Merleau-Ponty. Then we will follow a gradual progression in the limitation of the field of inquiry, from language to symbol and from symbol to its manifestation of evil. It is in symbolism that Ricoeur finds the necessity and contingency of evil manifested and at the same time hidden; therefore, the need of interpretation. Up to this point we let ourselves be instructed by Ricoeur's reflection on the understanding of our being-in-the-world. In a third and final stage of our itinerary we can ask which new roads are opened before us for further investigation and reflection. The first two parts will be analytical and descriptive, the last, synthetical and critical.

I

Ricoeur contends that the apodictic character of the Cartesian affirmation has been confused with its adequateness. The undeniable "I am" is confused with the "I am just as I see myself"; and apodictic judgment is mixed with a judgment of perception (to be such) or, using Kant's terminology, an apodictic judgment with a problematic (contingent) one.

Already in one of Ricoeur's first publications, *Freedom and Nature*, the notion of *broken* thinking (*Cogito brisé*) appears; lately under the influence of Freud he calls it *wounded* thinking (*Cogito blessé*). He inscribes himself in the *school of suspicion* of his predecessors Marx, Nietzsche, and Freud, and starts from the premise that the false or illusionary consciousness needs to be unmasked. Our first task on the road to truth is to unveil the non-truth of our own "faulty" thinking. The subject who poses itself as the foundation of all meaning is de-centered. The preponderate nature of reason and truthfulness of the immediate conscience are challenged. It is for this reason that Ricoeur situates reflexive philosophy before a double semiological challenge: psychoanalytical and structuralist. The task of the philosopher is that of a hermeneut, that is, he must decipher the signs of culture as manifested in language.

The fundamental purpose of the philosopher's investigation becomes a creative encounter between hermeneutics and phenomenology in an ontological search. "My purpose is to explore the paths opened to contemporary philosophy to what could be called the graft of the *hermeneutic problem* onto the *phenomenological method*."[2] In order to realize this task Ricoeur begins with language, or to be more precise, from the fullness of language as it is to be found in the symbol in order to arrive through reflection as a mode of being, at a new understanding of existence. In other words, he follows the path from semantics towards ontology. This indirect path through the symbol and through interpretation is the key to Ricoeur's philosophical hermeneutics.

Language becomes not only a means to understand being but a mode of being, and symbols and myths become the anchorage of the pre-reflexive in the reflexive. Ricoeur leans on the final works of Husserl, where he finds a more exact consciousness of the nature of the operation by which language refers back to the experience which precedes it. Husserl calls this socle which is before language *Lebenswelt* (the world of life). But this *Lebenswelt* is not something immediate, pure and simple. It is directed by an operation which is exercised at once in language and upon language and consists in referring us back—in a process of returning—in a "back-questioning attitude" (*Rückfrage*) through which language grasps its own basis in that which is not in itself language.

Since symbolism is language at its maximum point of condensation and thickness, it expresses indirectly dimensions of human existence which cannot be reduced to conceptual abstractions, it takes hold of reality in a way which is not possible through philosophical or scientific thought. More so since it unifies the reflexive with the pre-reflexive; symbols have a capacity to describe limit-situations of human existence that exceed the capacity of philosophical thought. That is to say, there are no other means of access to the understanding of certain experiences such as evil, for example, except through the interpretation of symbolic language, which points towards the human existential situation. The revealing power of the symbol is closely related to the hermeneutical task and both the symbolism and its interpretation are closely related to the understanding of one's self and the world. "All the symbols of guilt—deviation, wandering, captivity,—all the myths—chaos, blinding, mixture, fall,—speak of the situation of the being of man in the being of the world. The task, then, is, starting from the symbols to elaborate existential concepts—that is to say, not only structures of reflexion but structures of existence, insofar as existence is the being of man." "The symbol gives reason to think that the *Cogito* is within being, and not vice-versa." [SE, p. 356]

In summary, the way to decipher "what I am" is provided by the interpretation of symbols and signs, whether they be expressed in a myth, a dream, or a poem.

Now, we face the problem that there is not a single theory and method of interpretation but a "conflict" between different ways of interpreting the manifestations of our being in the texts of culture—in art, institutions, documents, dreams, symptoms, rites, symbols, beliefs, etc. Ricoeur assumes that each interpretation discloses a certain aspect of the same truth and that it is in the dialectical relationship between different interpretations that we may arrive at a fuller and more profound knowledge of the subject under treatment. This is not an eclecticism or a juxtaposition of different hermeneutics, but a confrontation between them. His method expresses his vision of truth. Truth is for Ricoeur an *itinerary in common* with others, it is a future and a road to follow: it is "to put himself under the law of another, and to conduct his investigation as an exercise of communication." [HT, p. 44]

Just to present one example of the confrontation of hermeneutics, Ricoeur analyzes the symbolism of fatherhood,[3] interpreting its meaning by using three different areas and methods of investigation: the psychoanalytical field (a regressive movement towards the *arché*); the phenomenological field, and more explicitly a phenomenology of the Spirit of the Hegelian type (a progressive movement towards the *telos*) and a phenomenology of religion (interpretation of divine names and designations of God in the Judeo-Christian tradition). What is the outcome of this triple interpretation?

Ricoeur discovers in Freud the death of God on the level of fantasy and repression which leads to the dispossession of oneself in order to find the authentic Ego. In Hegel the death of God is the death of the separated transcendence: this is not a religious death, but an atheistic death which places God in the beyond instead of the spirit among us. In his biblical exegesis he offers us an interpretation which is far removed from the punitive theologies of the death of Christ which confirm Freud's position. Death is considered a gift in place of assassination or punishment. He has not reduced the meanings of the religious sphere to psychoanalysis, as many others have tried to do; whatever the libidinal burden that these meanings might possess, what he has done is to pass from phantasm to symbol.[4] The phantasm is deceitful (illusory, idolatrous) but the symbol carries implicitly the *arché* and the *telos*, because "by its power to reveal it constitutes a simple argumentation of *self-awareness*, a simple extension of reflexive circumscription, (. . .) a philosophy instructed by the symbols has for its task a qualitative transformation of reflexive consciousness." [SE, p. 356]

II

We find throughout Ricoeur's work a triple dialectical analysis which will serve as a framework to grasp the importance of the interpretation of symbols for the philosophical task. The dialectic assumes these forms:

1. The deciphering of primary symbols in relation to myths; at this point the *power of the symbol* is revealed.

2. The interpretation of myths in relation to each other; here appears the problem of the *demythologization* already started by biblical myths.

3. The exegesis of rationalizations of myths in relation to primary symbols helps us to discover different layers of meaning which point to the limitations of speculative thought concerning the tragic aspect of human existence.

Let us consider each form in turn:

1. Ricoeur elaborates three cycles of problems around the phenomenon of the symbol: the *semantic problem*—the symbol as a word which accomplishes something in relation to being (the unitive action of being and saying, "ontological openness of the symbol"); the *semiotic problem*—the symbol in relation to polysemy (several meanings within sychronism) and transference of sense (changes of meanings within diachronism); and lastly the *syntactical problem*—within the broadest discourse where it is located, that is, myths.

From the semantic point of view the symbol gives one meaning by means of another, "in it a primary, literal, worldly, often physical meaning refers back to a figurative, spiritual, often existential, ontological meaning which is in no way given outside this indirect designation." [CI, p. 28] In other words the literal expression points to an existential meaning. But its value is not only cognitive, but operative, that is to say, it not only represents but also operates a relation with that which it designates. Ricoeur calls this characteristic the "ontological openness of the symbol".[5] It is here that the analytical philosophy of language of Austin's school comes to help the thesis of Ricoeur as I see it. For Austin the "performatives" are expressions which by their being said carry out an action; they are the very operation of that which is said. In this sense also the symbol "works the ontological relation which it designates obliquely."[6] I believe that the following example clarifies the relatedness of both notions, "performatives" and symbol. If I say, "I baptize you in the name of the Father, of the Son and of the Holy Spirit," the sentence "I baptize you. . ." will be for Austin a performative since by saying the sentence itself I execute the action. If I add another act and another element, "the water" which I use for baptism, we find: the action of baptizing, in itself symbolic, the sentence "I baptize. . ." and the water which are symbols too. All these symbols: act-word-element, point to the ontological relation which they designate.

Furthermore, it is unitive action which is the genius of the symbol; it relates unequal terms in different ways and works a union with that which it signifies. Ricoeur quotes a beautiful expression of Belin-Milleron with regard to this operative-unitive function of the symbol, which this author calls "ana-work" (*ana-travail*). "It is an ana-work which relates temporally the time of origin and the promised time, spatially man and things, socially the individual and the community, cosmically man and the totality".[7] The symbol unites the being-said (*être-dit*) with the saying of being.

The most archaic form of man's dealing with the experience of evil suffered and performed is found in the image of the *Stain*. Evil is explained and expressed through a scheme of exteriority to the human being. The stain is a quasi-material "event," which "infects" humanity by concrete contact. The "stained being" needs, therefore, purification rites to be washed, cleaned, purified. Contact with the stain acquired a religious and moral meaning. There was wonder and fear related to the existential phenomenon of evil and suffering and the symbol of stain explained both evil and suffering, uniting the cosmic to the biological world and these to behavior, private and communal. Suffering was loaded with an ethical meaning which sprang from the fact of the stain and which afterwards was rationalized.

Later the external image of stain is transformed in the internal concept of *sin*. The Hebrew prophets developed this theme, especially Isaiah, Amos and Jeremiah. The scheme of exteriority becomes a scheme of interiority. Evil is no longer a "material thing" which attacks man from the outside but an internal reality which humanity experiences before the sacred. The idol is supplanted by a name (Yahweh), the sacred acquires a face and a voice that speaks to man. Sin is understood in the context of the Alliance between God and a people; evil is the expression of a broken relationship, a failure to keep the commandments. If stain was a "thing," sin is an absence of God, a nothingness which is expressed in the symbols of wandering, loneliness, abyss, nakedness, solitude, exile, desert and death. But the archaic symbol does not disappear. The scheme of exteriority reappears at an ethical level instead of a "magical" one. Sin, even though understood as a breaking of the covenant between man and God—a personal relation, subjective, spiritual—continues to have the weight of the primitive trait of the "stain," the objective, physical impurity which contaminates from the outside. *Guilt* appears as the interiorization of the notion of sin with its subjective connotation but the objective dimension of the stain is not lost. From the symbol of the stain one passes to the concept of sin and from the latter to guilt without the accumulative "load" of the archaic meaning ever disappearing in this evolution. In the prophets and in the psalms, for instance, we find that the confession of sins is parallel to the necessity of purification from the stain, and it appears in expressions such as this: blot out, wash me, purify me; it does not say "forgive me," which would correspond to a violated covenant.[8]

These three levels of the human experience of evil, stain-sin-guilt, are interwoven in the narrative form of the myths. Ricoeur points out a three-fold function of the myth and two basic dimensions of evil present in the Adamic myth. The functions are: 1. Represent by means of symbolic language concrete universal human experience; 2. Introduce a historical tension in this experience (there is a beginning and an end); 3. Explore the cleavage between innocence and guilt.

In the Adamic narrative the scheme of interiority is present in the instance of the "fall" (evil by choice, by human decision). This trait, philosophically speaking, would correspond to the contingency of evil. But the scheme of exteriority is also present through the introduction of a mythical figure, the serpent, which represents an evil "there," a pre-given reality which humans find "outside" themselves and which they do not initiate. In philosophical language, this would correspond to the necessity of evil.

The Adamic narrative presents the tragic aspect of evil. Even if freedom of choice is a human trait and the evil committed or suffered becomes man's responsibility, the experience of evil is not exhausted in its ethically contingent dimension. There is an unfathomable presence of evil "already there" when and where we are born, whose origin we don't know but under whose power we live, and the inexhaustible depth of this experience has been revealed through the centuries not by abstract speculation but by symbolic language, the characters and plot of the myths.

An anthropology of ambiguity is also expressed in the Adamic narrative: the human being is good by creation (original destiny) and evil by election (radical evil), he does not initiate evil but continues it, in this sense the figure of the serpent is a limit between the scheme of exteriority and interiority.

2. In a second movement of this triple dialectic we find that the interpretation of myths is done in relation to each other. The Adamic

narrative represents what we could call a breaking point with the oriental and Babylonian cosmologies. This breaking point is that of the beginning of *demythologization*. Ricoeur points out that if we interpret Genesis 1 and 2 we find a desacralization of nature: the earth is to be worked and dominated by man, the heavenly bodies—sun, moon, stars—are no longer mythological figures but empirical realities; there is an expressed will to make worldly all the mythological figures of oriental cosmologies.[9] In the whole narration there is only one mythological figure which the writer introduces to account for the pre-given reality of evil, the serpent.

In Greek tragedy man is caught between the wrath and fatal will of the gods and his own *hubris*, and such is the case of Prometheus and also of Oedipus. In the Adamic myth man is no longer a prey of the ill will of the evil gods; God has been demythologized to the extent that he is presented as a creative force which enters into a face-to-face communication with his creatures. Yet man also appears, I would say, as Prometheus and Oedipus, as a creature who is guilty-innocent. [*See* SE, pp. 225ff]

Ricoeur states that in the case of Prometheus his freedom is "a freedom of *defiance* and not of *participation* . . . [it] has its roots in the chaotic depths of being" [SE, pp. 224-225] and his gift is a stolen gift, and I would add, a product not of generosity towards man but of defiance and wrath against Zeus. Therefore, the hero becomes a guilty benefactor and guilty victim.

In the case of Oedipus the tragedy of incest and parricide described by a psychoanalytical type of interpretation becomes secondary to the *tragedy of truth*, of self-knowledge. Besides his double guilt (of which he is in a way innocent) our author discovers a truly adult guilt, the guilt of Oedipus' own justice. It is not a question of an irreversible destiny determined by uncontrollable instincts, but rather a destiny motivated by human pride and anger. It is a *hubris* for truth which is the instrument of his own condemnation. The guilt of it is expressed in his anger against Tiresias. It is not sexual guilt but rather anger due to lack of knowledge. The process of this development is represented by the seer Tiresias: Oedipus is only the king; he is not the center of truth. Oedipus represents the force of human vanity which is revealed in relation to the figure who possesses the truth, Tiresias. For this reason the tragedy is, for Ricoeur, the tragedy of Oedipus *King*, not Oedipus the parricide or the incestuous. "The connection between Oedipus, anger and the power of truth is the core of the real Oedipus tragedy, and it expresses the problem of light, whose symbol is Apollo, and not that of sex." [CI, p. 116]

Self-punishment belongs to two interrelated dramas: the tragedy of truth belongs to the drama of self-knowledge and it springs from the relationship between Oedipus (the seer who is blind) and Tiresias (the blind man who is seer). When Oedipus loses his sight he knows the truth; the external destiny becomes an internal destiny: the accursed man is converted into a blind seer like Tiresias. On the other hand, the final meaning of the tragedy appears veiled in this work until the moment when Oedipus not only knows the origin of his birth but also the meaning of his anger and his self-inflicted punishment.

If I may go one step further in this dialectical interpretation of myths, we will find some traits of human nature in relation to both freedom and evil in the Adamic narrative and which relates Adam (primordial man) to Prometheus and Oedipus.

Adam wants also to possess the truth, to be the center of truth not because he is a proud king like Oedipus but because this will give him the power to be like God. The "fall" from his original destiny is, as I see it, the tragedy of *power* and *pride*. Adam has already been given dominion and power over all creation (Genesis 1 and 2), yet he craves for more power: "your eyes will be opened, and you will be like God, knowing good and evil" (Genesis 3:5). Here the zeal for truth is fed by a zeal for power and pride.

In both figures *hubris* is the factor that unchains their drama. When Oedipus curses the unknown person (the other) who is the cause of the plague, he excludes himself. Adam blames the serpent, the woman, and God (he also tries to exclude himself, even by blaming God). Adam and Oedipus acquired self-knowledge, but it is a self-knowledge born not of the exercise of freedom but the product of *hubris* and zeal for power; this very acquisition meant guilt, "nakedness," and exile.

"Nakedness" in the biblical account and "blindness in Greek tragedy are powerful symbols which point in a very concrete way to man's ontological nature and existential condition. In both cases the exile from Thebes and from the Garden expresses another dimension of the human condition, or as a psalmist sings so beautifully, they were *lost* in the *desert* because of their "solitude with no roads ahead" (Ps. 107:4).*

3. A third form this dialectical interpretation assumes is between the rationalization of myths and primary symbols. We are warned by Ricoeur of the danger of falsifying the meaning of symbols and myths by reducing them to allegory or to rationalizations (the trap of gnosis). To avoid these perils one must be willing to be taught by the enigma of symbolic language and bring out the meaning through interpretation in a systematized order. To carry on this task Ricoeur sets out to demythologize evil in its rationalized forms in order to arrive at the true meaning of the primary symbols. He states that the doctrine of *original sin* as is found in Augustine, even though anti-gnostic in its intention, falls into a quasi-gnostic conceptualization.

For Augustine evil is not a substance, a matter, but a power, a nature-will. But if the ill will or deviated will accounts for the contingency of evil, it does not account for the dark experience of a pre-given reality of evil. If Adam is prior to every man, the serpent is prior to Adam, who does not originate evil but continues it. How can this "dark experience" be made intelligible philosophically? Augustine introduces a scheme of heritage to explain the nature of evil. Within the scheme of heritage, sin is contingent and original. Therefore we run the risk of falling into a reification of evil in a nature or quasi-nature. Augustine has unified the juridical concept of imputable guilt to a biological concept of heredity. Ethics and biology are mixed in one single discourse which produces a pseudo-knowledge of the nature of evil but also of the nature of man and the nature of freedom. This attempt falls into a rationalization of the myth. The surplus of meaning of primary symbols is lost. [*See* CI, pp. 269-86]

Only by the interpretation of constellations of myths in a dialectical relation to each other and these in relation to the layers of meaning sedimented in the primary symbols can we break the false knowledge of late rationalizations and arrive at the non-ethical aspect of evil which no philosophy can fully account for. This face of evil is a dimension of our human experience which is complementary but not reducible to ethics. The experience of radical evil goes beyond the realm of ethical decision. Ricoeur describes it by means of paradoxes, such as servile-will, bound-freedom, and involuntary in a voluntary.

The problem posed to the philosopher is precisely how to include the necessity and contingency of evil in a coherent system. "For *either* the thought of necessity leaves contingency aside, *or* it so includes it that it entirely eliminates the 'leap' of evil which posits itself and the 'tragic' of evil which always precedes itself." [CI, p. 311] Ricoeur illustrates this failure in the first case with the non-dialectic philosophies of Plotinus and Spinoza, and in the second with the dialectical approach of Hegel. He asks as a working hypothesis "must we not seek the answer to our quest for intelligibility in a *meaningful history* rather than in a *logic of being*? Does not the movement from the Fall to the Redemption, a movement so full of meaning, exclude a "logic," whether it be non-dialectical or dialectical? Is it then possible to conceive of a meaningful history, wherein the contingency of evil and the initiative of conversion would be retained and encompassed? Is it possible to conceive of a *becoming of being* in which the tragic of evil—of this evil always already there—would be both recognized and surmounted?" [CI, pp. 313-14] This question will lead us to some final reflections on the roads opened up for us by Ricoeur's investigation.

III

Even though Ricoeur does not answer this pertinent question, he opens a road ahead which is yet to be explored and which we could very well call the interpretation of the *symbolics of hope*. His *heremeneutics of suspicion* have been nurtured by the philosophical hope to arrive at an acceptable notion of existence. Rightly so, he has been called the philosopher of hope. Yet we find only scattered essays that treat the symbols of hope in a very schematic manner.

There is a whole constellation of symbols and narratives where the human experience of deliverance, freedom, and liberation are expressed. This kind of symbolism expands the ethical and non-ethical aspects of evil; it expresses the counterpart of evil. Sin and redemption, captivity and deliverance, exile and return, wandering and promised land, guilt and justification, old creature and new creature, first Adam and second Adam, have to be interpreted not as separate systems of symbols, but in a dialectical relationship. The symbolics of evil and the symbolics of hope each do not describe a different "half" of the human being but its totality. If the experience of radical evil is manifested through symbols which point to the human state of alienation, oppression, captivity, loneliness, etc., the symbols of hope are produced out of this very experience as the possibility of reconciliation, liberation, community "thanks to," "in spite of" evil. The Pauline statement "where sin abounded, grace did *much more* ($\pi o \lambda \lambda \tilde{\omega}$ $\mu \tilde{\alpha} \lambda \lambda o \nu$) abound" (Romans 5:20) is a key for Ricoeur to begin to explore the symbolism of hope. It is in the midst of the evil suffered and inflicted that the Hebrew prophets, the Sapiential literature and the writers of the New Testament not only foresaw but lived under the hope of the promises of justice and *shalom*. The symbolism of a beginning is illuminated with a new light by the symbolism of the end. The reserve of meaning, or surplus of meaning of these symbols is to be understood within the structure of thought and therefore of the language in which they are expressed.

One more thing, man's relation to himself and to the world was interwoven by his relation to the Sacred, no longer an idol, as I have already pointed out, but a face and a voice that acted within history, individual and communal. These events in which both man and God intervened gave meaning to both human life and God's action, and are present in the structure of society and therefore of language and culture. The symbols and language of hope express a human relation to the Sacred very different from the *deus ex machina* of the Greeks; they represent a presence among the people which does not sweep away the "injustice of evil" or the "gratuity of reconciliation."

This dialectical exegesis and interpretation of the symbolism of evil in relation to the symbolism of hope poses a true challenge not only to the theologian but to the philosopher as well. "No symbol *qua* opening and uncovering a truth of man is foreign to philosophical reflection." [CI, p. 305]

Before finishing this point I believe it is important that I add some further reflections on the power of the *symbol*. The meaning of the expression "the symbol gives food for thought," is according to Ricoeur, the axis on which his whole work, *The Symbolism of Evil*, turns. If it "gives food for thought," if it speaks to us "as an index of the situation of man at the heart of the being in which he moves, exists and wills . . ." [SE, p. 356], the symbol has in itself a "capacity for action" similar to the verb in the sense that it not only accumulates meanings like the polysemic nouns, but also, and rather, generates, produces new meanings. This capacity for generating meaning I call "the verb" of the symbol, and the personal, existential appropriation of this capacity I call "lived experience." This terminology does not belong to Ricoeur, although it has been suggested to me by the dimensions of the symbol which he points out. The Greek origin of this word connotes implicitly a dynamism, as I see it, very close to verbal dynamism as opposed to the static character of a noun, or, for example, an adjective. The σύμβολον was a commercial contract, therefore, a relation between two persons, a treaty. The verb συμ-βάλλω means "to bring together," "to unite," "to meet with," "to join," "to reach an agreement with." Both the substantive and the verb mentioned connote implicitly a dynamic, personal relation; that is why I call "lived experience" the appropriation of the symbol, in the sense of an entering into a relation with the symbol, establishing a "vital relation" with its meaning.

Now, if we analyze any symbol of the Old Testament in relation to its use in the New, we find, as I see it, this capacity for generating meaning, this verb and this lived experience of the symbol. Let us explain: when we read Deuteronomy 30 we find the symbol of death facing the symbol of life; ". . . I have set before you life and death, blessing and curse; therefore choose life" (vs. 19). Life represents good, blessing; death on the contrary evil, cursing. These two symbols are closely related to ". . . *obey* his voice in all that I *command* you this day" (vs. 2), "*love* the Lord your God that you may live" (vs. 6), "keep all his *commandments*" (vs. 8), "keep his *commandments* and his statutes which are *written* in this book of the *law*" (vs. 10). Death is disobedience, the lack of love for God on the part of the individual and of the people before the law and the Covenant.

When Paul speaks of passing from death to life, especially in Romans 6, these symbols acquire a new meaning: "we who died to sin" (vs. 2) and "we shall also live with him" (vs. 8) because "we *were buried* therefore with him" (vs. 4), ". . . our old self was *crucified* with him" (vs. 6), "baptized into his death" (vs. 3). The emphasis is not on the fulfilling of the law, on obedience to the commandments, but rather on dying and living with Christ. These two symbolic forms point to another reality, point out another action (verb) and another "lived experience" of the symbol. This does not mean that the old meaning disappeared, was annulled or that there is a transposition of meaning from the law to Christ, because although now we live "not under law but under grace," Christ did not come to abolish the law but to fulfill it. Obedience retains its place, "obedience which leads to righteousness" (vs. 16), "the wages of sin is death . . . but the free gift of God is eternal life" (vs. 23), ". . . in order that the just requirement of the law might be fulfilled in us" (8:4). In this new symbol of death and life there is no transference, nor mutation, nor addition of meaning. There is, rather, the generation of a new meaning as a consequence of the death and resurrection of Christ. That is, it is the death and the resurrection of Christ that generated a new sense in the very symbolics of human life and death, without losing the previous sense. The symbol has thus a dynamism similar to that of the verb, it produces new meanings just as the verb points to the realization of an action. It is interesting to note that the symbol of death is, semantically speaking, related to verbs and in the indicative mode: buried, crucified, baptized. There is a whole amplification of the symbol of death as "verb" related to personal "lived experiences," which are also verbs. Do not this verbal capacity and this existential experience of the symbol point to an ontological dimension of the being-in-the-world and a historical dimension of the becoming of that being? Do we not find in the symbols of death and life different layers of meanings related to both the symbolism of evil and the symbolism of hope expressed not as two separate dimensions but as one single reality of human existence?

Furthermore, could we not say that the "verb" and the "lived experience" of the symbol point to a kind of anthropogenesis of becoming and of the human present? If this is so, the understanding of the structure of the symbol, of the transference and mutation of sense, of the generation of new meaning, does it not give us a certain basis for understanding history? I would venture to suggest that without this foundation of historical understanding, without this "memory" which man has of himself and which he expresses through a whole symbolics, every attempt at the existential appropriation of sense succumbs like a tree whose roots have been cut. If my interpretation of the place occupied by symbolics in relation to historical understanding is correct, we may affirm that the purpose of the philosophical hermeneutics proposed by Ricoeur is confirmed through the very process of his work.

It is interesting to point out that Ricoeur, when he turned to the study of the finitude of man and the problem of evil, did not find the resources of philosophy sufficient, just as historical resources would not have been sufficient—that is, history in the way it has been written, conceived as the description of conquests, the taking of power, wars, expansion of influence, etc. Ricoeur turns to symbolics to decipher the ways in which the human being explains to himself his origin and his end, his finitude and his guilt, his eternity and his hope. Could we not say then that the study not only of symbols but also of all literature (tragedy-narration-poetry) may give us a more correct vision of history? At least, a vision perhaps less inclined to perspectivist subjectivism, to racial and nationalistic prejudices. If this is the case, another specific task of hermeneutics would be to discern within the global events pointed out by history the course of the human being as such, and this would give us perhaps certain dimensions of historical and human totality which escape historicist analysis.

If the interpretation of the religious symbols of Semitic and Hellenistic cultures are an important place to start in our search for the truth of our being-in-the-world because they account for dimensions of our human experience that go beyond speculative thought, I believe that we need to go one step further. We need to enter into a serious and scientific dialogue with the language of oriental philosophy in order to have a deeper understanding of the wholeness of human experience. Ricoeur has not done this explicitly, but if I read him correctly he has suggested an amplification of our field of inquiry when he speaks of a "beyond ontology."[10] For a Westerner there is no such thing as a "beyond ontology," beyond the primary and fundamental reality of being. Yet "is it not the idea itself of being called into question by a fundamental experience, at the same time primitive and so simple, which nothing in the philosophical discourse of Greece and of the West is really adequate for?"[11]

I believe that when Ricoeur speaks of a "beyond ontology" he is not speaking of "a beyond" being as such but "a beyond" our own rational Western interpretation of being. We have inherited and incorporated in our own manner of thinking some basic prejudices of the Enlightenment. Our access to truth has been limited by our own *fixed horizons* of what is the truth and how to reach it.[12]

Finally, one further road of investigation which is open before us is the relation between word and praxis, between saying and doing, or to be more explicit between *work, word* and *power*. If it is true that man's fallibility and transcendence are expressed through language in general and symbols in particular and that we may reach a fuller and deeper understanding of ourselves through the continuous interpretation of the signs of culture, it is also true that language has been at the service of the structures of power—political, economic, cultural, religious, racial, sexual—a power exercised by some humans over others. Therefore, we must include in Ricoeur's "vast philology" (his interdisciplinary approach to the study of language) at least one more discipline, sociology, to understand more clearly the relations between work and power and between these two and language. New dimensions will no doubt be added to our understanding of evil and freedom, of man's existential captivity and redeeming hope.

To the task of unmasking a false consciousness we must add the challenge of unmasking a language that has been the product of structures of oppression and that shapes our lifestyles and limits our creative imagination. At this point once more we will find in the symbolic language of the Hebrew prophets and New Testament writers an immense reserve of sense. In the Adamic narrative the alienation between man and woman, between man and work, man and nature are the product of human zeal for power; as I stated earlier, this narrative is, in my own understanding, the tragedy of man's search for power. Work was a blessing and becomes a curse precisely because the nature and destiny of work were conceived as a gift to share (dominating and using the whole of creation for the benefit of all: humans, animals, plants, etc.), and becomes a means for egoistic and individual survival.

I bring this essay to an end with words pronounced recently by Ricoeur and which point in the direction I have just stated:

> All the discussions concerning language today are abstract because two great dimensions of human existence are missing—the work of men and power, that is, the domination which some men exercise over others. To the extent that one places language in this context the problem of liberation appears . . . certainly liberation from exploited work but also liberation of the word which has been deviated, falsified by the fact that it is at the service of certain relations of power. Consequently a philosophy of language is a liar if it forgets that the language on which we work is already a language which has been deviated by the fact of being 'taken' in this relation between domination and work. There is also a whole aspect which needs to be introduced into the field of hermeneutics: the criticism of ideologies. . . . Very often hermeneutics is simply a kind of recuperation of sense from old discourses forgetting, first that the present situation is one of domination, second that the future relation is one of liberation. . . . It is my purpose now to take up again a philosophy of action in which the philosophy of language receives language anew as that which is given.[13]

This new study will amplify, without doubt, both the conception of the philosophy of language and the horizons of our future hermeneutical task.

NOTES

1. Paul Ricoeur, "Philosophical hermeneutics and theological hermeneutics," *Sciences Religieuses/Studies in Religion*, Summer 1975, Canada, pp. 14-32.

2. CI, p. 3. For Ricoeur there are two ways of bringing about this encounter between phenomenology and hermeneutics: what he calls the *short way*, the ontology of understanding following Heidegger, and the *long way*, which undertakes an indirect approach to the question of existence through the analysis of language. The short way enters directly into the ontological problem without going deeper into the methodological demands of exegesis, history or psychoanalysis. Right from the beginning, the question is raised, what is being whose being consists in understanding? The short way is kept apart from the circle of interpretation, the hermeneutical problem is only accessory, it is only a part of the analysis of *Dasein* which exists in understanding.

The long way which Ricoeur proposes, starts from the same level on which understanding takes place, that is to say from the level of language, and arrives at an ontology. But the process is a step-by-step one, passing through successive stages by means of a series of investigations at the semantic level and also at the level of what is called reflexive philosophy applied to semantics.

The semantic approach has two advantages which Ricoeur points out. It keeps hermeneutics in touch with other methodological disciplines and thus does not run the risk of separating method and truth; and on the other hand it makes sure that hermeneutics is grafted on phenomenology at the level of meaning.

The task of philosophical hermeneutics (at the semantic level) is three-fold, to investigate the symbolic forms and analyze their structures, to compare hermeneutical methods and criticize their systems of interpretation and in the third place to act as a true umpire between the totalitarian pretensions of each one of the various interpretations.

Semantics gives way to reflection, as an intermediate step in the movement from linguistic analysis towards ontology. The grafting on of hermeneutics to phenomenology is made at the level of the problem of the *Cogito*, just as semantics was analysed at the level of meaning.

In summary, Ricoeur wants to arrive at a general hermeneutics which embraces the whole question of *human discourse*, treated at the moment separately by logic, symbolics, exegetical science, anthropology, psychoanalysis, the phenomenology of religion, and so on.

Another short way is that of Merleau-Ponty, who follows Husserl faithfully with respect to method but his phenomenology is existential and it is a phenomenology of speech. In his perceptualist emphasis there is an advance from the perceptualist sense to the linguistic sense. Language is in a central position but excludes all connection with modern linguistics. This is the weak point of his phenomenology. The return to the speaking subject, to the *parole*, is too rapid. He sets opposite one another two positions: one objective, language as a residue of past meanings and another subjective, speech. Ricoeur develops the philosophical aspect of this phenomenology of speech, but in distinction from Merleau-Ponty, he does it through a serious dialogue with the semiological disciplines and with modern linguistics. In the last works of Merleau-Ponty there is a turn towards ontology, an indirect ontology involved in phenomenology. Ricoeur challenges us to continue the task already begun by him, to relate this phenomenology of expression to linguistics, a linguistics attentive to the creative aspects of language.

3. *See* "Fatherhood: From Phantasm to Symbol", in CI, pp. 468-97. The German term *Phantasie* is translated in French as *fantasme* and in English as *phantasm*.

4. What does it mean to pass from phantasm to symbol? Ricoeur is dealing with the psychoanalytic use of the term phantasm and it needs to be understood in that context. So to pass from phantasm to symbol means to go beyond the Freudian interpretation of symbolic language to other dimensions of this language which psychoanalysis does not deal with, precisely because they are outside its own field, purpose and techniques. We may also recall that the symbol has for Ricoeur three dimensions: cosmic, oneiric and poetic. While Freud often limits the notion of the symbol to the oneiric dimension, our author explores the other dimensions too. " . . . Whereas ritual and myth fix symbols in their hieratic stability and dreams close them in upon the labyrinth of desires where the dreamer loses the thread of his forbidden and mutilated discourse . . . The power of the poet is to show forth symbols at the moment when 'poetry places language in a state of emergence,' to quote Bachelard. . . . In order to give consistency and unity to these scattered manifestations of symbol, I define it by a semantic structure that these manifestations have in common, the structure of multiple meaning." FP, p. 16. *See also* pp. 494-551.

5. "Language Religieux, Mythe et Symbole," *Le Langage II:* Sociétés de Philosophie de Langue Francaise, Actes du XIIIe. Congrès, Genève (Neuchatel: La Baconnière, 1966), p. 130.

6. *Ibid.*, p. 131.

7. *Ibid.*

8. The prophet Isaiah exclaims: "Woe is me! For I am lost; for I am a man of unclean lips, and I dwell in the midst of a people of unclean lips, for my eyes have seen the King, The lord of

hosts!" (Isaiah 6:5). "Behold, this hath touched your lips; your guilt is taken away, and your sin forgiven" (Isaiah 6:7). "Have mercy upon me, O God, according to thy steadfast love; according to thy abundant mercy *blot out* my transgressions. *Wash me* thoroughly and *cleanse me* from my sin" (Psalm 51;1,2).

9.   Cf. "Démythologisation et Herméneutique", *Centre Européen Universitaire*, Nancy, Année 1966-67, p. 1-32.

10.   Cf. "Ontologie", *Encyclopaedia Universalis*, France, Vol. XII, 1972, pp. 94-101.

11.   *Ibid.*, p. 101.

12.   In the thirteenth Congress of the Sociétés de Philosophie de Langue Française, which took place in Geneva in 1966, Ricoeur presented a paper entitled "Religious Language, Myth and Symbol," followed by a discussion. Precisely in that discussion Henri Corbin—who had presented a paper entitled "Philosophie Prophétique et Métaphysique de l'Etre en Islam Shi'ite"—quotes some examples of difficulties and differences between occidental and oriental vocabulary. In my view they are highly important because I believe that they point in the same direction as Ricoeur when he questions himself concerning the adequateness of our western philosophical vocabulary and a simple and primitive experience of being.

Corbin expresses, for instance, that the term "oriental" corresponds to an Arab word which is also used in Persian, it is the word *Ishrâq*: it means the rising of the sun. For oriental philosophers this word contains something more than a geographical designation, it expresses a spiritual meaning: the rising of the soul to its orient is a *presence* in the soul. This oriental knowledge is not a *Volksgeist* (folklore) but rather the other way around, it is this *oriental* knowledge which has made the Iranians oriental persons. Corbin explains himself: this knowledge is not representative, one can therefore not argue with it, it is a presence and a presence imposes itself, it is not argued. *Ishrâq* "is a presence which imposes itself on the soul, which invades it all of a sudden and which at the same time liberates it, it is the absolute of all other beforeness, of all other deduction. . . . What calls the oriental's attention more than anything else when he participates in a Western Philosophical Congress is precisely the absence of such presences. Truly one has sometimes the impression that the Western universe is a devastated, unpopulated universe." "Language Religieux, Mythe et Symbole," p. 138.

13.   From taped personal conversation with P. Ricoeur.

*   I am fully aware that the use of "man" to designate the human race is a classic and undesirable case of male chauvinism and clear proof of the deficiency of our language. Yet I have decided to use it here because I have not yet found a substitute in English which satisfies me.

*   My translation.

VIII

Michel Philibert

THE PHILOSOPHIC METHOD
OF PAUL RICOEUR

Philosophical thinking has been for some twenty-five centuries in the Western world issuing from three sources: our difficulties in living; contradictions in our sayings; the work of previous philosophers.

Each new philosopher endeavours to interpret the difficulties and contradictions of his time in the light of what he finds still illuminating or provocative in the work of one or several among his predecessors; he attempts at the same time to reinterpret their works in the light of those events, comments and changes, produced between his predecessors' times and his own, that he finds meaningful.

The trait that makes Paul Ricoeur unique in our time, and no less unique in the history of philosophy, lies in the way he combines an eager and humble attention to practically all previous philosophers with a feeling for our present situation and a modest but strong determination to speak his own mind on any problem he deals with.

Michel Philibert is Professor of philosophy at l'Université des Sciences sociales de Grenoble, France, and the director of the Centre Pluridisciplinaire de gérontologie. He has written *Paul Ricoeur ou la liberté selon l'espérance* and *L'Echelle des âges*.

The Philosophic Method of Paul Ricoeur

Michel Philibert

Philosophical thinking has been for some twenty-five centuries in the Western world issuing from three sources: our difficulties in living; contradictions in our sayings; the work of previous philosophers.

Each new philosopher endeavours to interpret the difficulties and contradictions of his time in the light of what he finds still illuminating or provocative in the work of one or several among his predecessors; he attempts at the same time to reinterpret their works in the light of those events, comments and changes, produced between his predecessors' times and his own, that he finds meaningful.

The balance between interpretation of present situations in the light of the philosophical tradition and re-interpretation of the philosophical tradition in the light of present situations is a delicate one. Depending on emphasis given to one or the other side, we usually classify philosophers into two classes: (a) creative thinkers, usually so involved in their own thinking that their interest for previous philosophers seems dried up and the interpretation they give of their works turns into creative and brilliant mis-interpretation; (b) historians of philosophy, usually so engaged in interpreting past philosophers that they do not have much energy left to cope with contemporary problems and elaborate original answers.

The trait that makes Paul Ricoeur unique in our time, and no less unique in the history of philosophy lies in the way he combines an eager and humble attention to practically all previous philosophers with a feeling for our present situation and a modest but strong determination to speak his own mind on any problem he deals with. It lies, more specifically, in the way his attention to past philosophers and his involvement in designing new and original approaches to contemporary problems instead of inhibiting each other, keep on reenforcing each other. A French proverb says, "He who embraces too much has a poor hold." The larger the ground you attempt to cover, the feebler your control! The paradox of Ricoeur's thinking is that whatever theme, concept or problem he studies in any of his predecessors, he uses it to both ends: better to understand (and help us understand) the philosopher under consideration; and to take (and give us) a better hold either on some other philosopher, or on some traditional or new issue, or on both.

Any thinker dealing with a problem or situation will use or refine concepts, methods and schemes to analyze, solve or control it. His attention will oscillate between the elements and difficulties of the situation, and the tools and approaches he has to select or adapt to cope with it. Inevitably some of his moves and attitudes in analyzing the situation, including his most efficient and successful moves, will be spontaneous, either by force of habit, or by way of innovative talent and trial; such will not be themselves fully analyzed: the attention of the creative thinker passes through them to carry on the situation and absorb whatever evolution it undergoes from the moves he made.

Now the careful reader of his works may give his attention in turn to the situation, as approached by the author, and to the author's moves and skills. The reader is not so much involved in the situation as was the author, and he also keeps a distance (however strong his admiration and identification) from him. He may thus acquire clearer views and a better understanding (than the original thinker) of the reason why such a move was successful (or failed), and also of a pattern or style which appears progressively in the way the thinker passes from one move to the next and uses his skills—and the more so when the thinker is observed repeatedly in several situations.

The careful reader may then borrow the tools, acquire the skills, remake the moves of the thinker, so as to try his own hold and develop his mastery in the same situations; he will next be in a position to use, transfer and adapt the same kind of approach (or more consciously different ones), either to his own problems (which the former thinker did not face), or even to some of the difficulties that the original thinker attempted to solve but could not, despite his talent, fully grasp and control: partly because he could not perceive the situation as we can later, after it has developed a chain of unexpected consequences and revealed in retrospect "aspects" that were not visible in the anticipation; and partly because he did not himself analyze, systematize and fully develop all possible uses and effects of his own techniques.

This may explain *technically* how Ricoeur, a most careful reader, is in the same process humble and faithful in his interpretation of past philosophers and creative in applying their techniques better to understand either their past or his own present situations.

One might add that Ricoeur—trained by a constant practice to pay an undivided attention to the ground covered by past philosophers and to their moves on this ground, to interpret the ground through their moves, and their moves by the ground (eventually by what he also learned about that ground from other explorers or through his own explorations)—is probably more aware than many of his colleagues not of all his own moves (nobody possibly can), but of the usefulness in reflecting on them, in analyzing them and experimenting with them.

Let us quote for illustration the beginning of the last essay ("Metaphor and Philosophic Discourse") in his last book *La Métaphore vive*. This chapter

> aims at exploring the philosophical frontiers of an inquiry the poise of which has been moving into the domain of hermeneutics, from rhetoric to semantics, from problems of meaning to problems of reference. This last move has implied as postulates some philosophical assumptions. No discourse can ever contend to be free of assumptions, for the simple reason that the thinking work which organizes into a series of themes an area of what is to be thought utilizes operative concepts that cannot be themselves and in the same time looked on as themes. But if it is true that no discourse can be completely free of assumptions, no thinker however can dispense from doing his very best to explicate his own assumptions. [MV, p. 323]

The technical explication we suggest may help understand *how* Ricoeur, uniting attention to others and creative thinking, became a champion in *creative attention*. The *why* is another problem. Our suggestion would be to look at the relationship, inside the thinker (i.e., inside the thinking as expressed in his works), between the professional philosopher and the Christian believer, or rather, to use his own phrase, the "listener of Christian preaching."

The Christian is instructed not to fear anything, anybody, "convinced that there is nothing in death or life, in the realm of spirits or superhuman powers . . . , nothing in all creation that can separate him from the love of God in Christ" (Romans 8, 38-39); "to be patient and stouthearted" (James 5,8); "to live as free men" (I Peter 2, 16, also Galatians 5, 13). He must be "always ready with his defense whenever he is called to account for the hope that is in him, but make that defense with modesty and respect" (I Peter 3, 14). He has "no power to act against the truth, but only for it" (II Corinthians 13, 8). He is instructed to "give due honor to everyone" (I Peter 2, 17); to "love even his enemies" (Matthew 5, 44, also Romans 12, 20-21); to "call down blessings on his persecutors" (Romans 12, 14); to "pursue the things that make with peace and build up the common life" (Romans 14, 19); "so far as it lies with him, to live at peace with all men" (Romans 12, 18); to "accept one another as Christ accepted us" (Romans 15, 7). He is called "not to be conceited or think too highly of himself, but to think his way to a sober estimate based on the measure of faith that God has dealt to each" (Romans 12, 3). He must "humbly reckon others better than himself" (Philippians 2,3), for "if a man imagines himself to be somebody when he is nothing, he is deluding himself" (Galatians 6,3).

The most casual reading through Ricoeur reveals him as genuinely practising such instructions. Whenever he quotes a philosopher (or any author, at that—theologian, psychoanalyst, linguist, or poet), he expresses admiration and acknowledges what he learns from him. Whenever he disagrees with an author, he says so; but he never belittles or mocks him;

and he never disagrees before having gone all the way he possibly could with the author, trying to understand how and why he missed the point, or took another way; in so doing he still learns from him something about the point, or about the author's technique and how it could be amended, or about his convictions and conditions; and he still expresses gratefulness to him for his challenge. Patiently, attentively, respectfully, Ricoeur will draw from the author's principles new consequences, from his method new applications, either to cope with new problems he sets up for himself, or to reopen the very problems the author was dealing with, so as to amend his solution; and Ricoeur again will in any case give due credit to the authors, even for those things he finds in them that they could not see themselves.

In *Freedom and Nature* the inspiration comes from Gabriel Marcel, whose insights are tested through a confrontation with specific psychological problems, and elaborated through descriptive analyses; the technique of description used is borrowed and adapted from Husserl, and in the process dissociated from Husserl's own doctrine.

In *Fallible Man* Ricoeur detects agreements and concordances between various authors. "Eros, the philosophising soul, is therefore the hybrid par excellence, the hybrid of Richness of Poverty. Descartes, and especially Kant say the same thing in their judicious treatises on the imagination. . . ." [FM, p. 17] "The Platonic myth foreshadows the Kierkegaardian meditation . . . ." [FM, p. 19]

The same book offers several instances of the Ricoeurian remarks we alluded to. Ricoeur looks for "la faillibilité" (mankind's frailty to failure as fault) in "disproportion." But where to look for disproportion? Here there comes in handy the Cartesian paradox of man: finite-infinite. "Let us say at once that the connection that Descartes makes between this paradox and a faculty psychology is entirely misleading." [FM, p. 4] We cannot link finite to understanding, infinite to will. But Descartes should be amended, not sentenced. He must be "repris"—the french verb "reprendre" conveying both meanings of reprehend and remake. Descartes himself opens the way to a larger and deeper understanding of man as a paradox when he sees man as "un milieu entre Dieu et le néant," if we interpret "milieu" not as a place between two regions, but as mediating, and man as an active go-between. "This is why we shall not explain Descartes by Descartes, but by Kant, Hegel and Husserl: the intermediacy of man can only be discovered via the detour of the transcendental synthesis of the imagination, or by the dialectic between certainty and truth, or the dialectic of intention and intuition, of significance and presence. . . ." [FM, p. 6]

By an "admirable analysis" Aristotle opens the way for a decisive progress; but he did not engage in this way. Ricoeur explores it and explains why Aristotle, on his own way, heading to a specific aim, did not detour to explore the possibilities of his discovery. [FM, p. 52] A footnote, same page, explains how two different analyses, one dealing with action in an ethical perspective, the other with the verb, made by Aristotle in two different books, two different purposes, within different theoretical frames, did not communicate in Aristotle's thinking, but will, if connected, cross-fertilize each other. Thus Ricoeur himself acts as a go-between, matching philosopher to philosopher, discipline to discipline, concept to concept.

Again *Fallible Man* uses freely Kant's material to relate what he wrote on "respect" to what he wrote on the person. "I am fully aware here of changing the gist of the Kantian analysis of respect. . . . However, in betraying Kantian orthodoxy, I think I bring out the Kantian philosophy of the person which is outlined in the *Foundation* and stifled in the *Critique of Practical Reason* . . . ." [FM, p. 111, footnote]

In the *Conflict of Interpretations* Ricoeur will similarly take a Kantian way. "But the Kantianism that I wish to develop now is, paradoxically, more to be constructed than repeated; it would be something like a post-Hegelian Kantianism. . . ." [CI, p. 412] We have today to "better think" Kant and Hegel, in thinking one against the other, one by another, and also in thinking differently from them both.

Past philosophies are thus storehouses not of thought, but of thinking. Ricoeur's confidence is that none of them, no part in them, is dried up, frozen, dead. Reading good books, said Descartes, is like talking with the good people who wrote them. This sounds silly at first, because conversation with a living person will allow him to elaborate on his opening statements, to answer questions, to refute unanticipated objections, or to qualify, amend and change his views when objections are well taken— whereas the book is written once and for all, closed, deaf to the reader's contribution. Yet any experienced reader will agree with Descartes and refute the objection as preposterous. I embark on a book with my own experience, what I have lived through so far, and heard, read, produced; from that springs my understanding, my questions and objections to the book, and the author's replies. Upon re-reading it, my contribution and my interpretation will have changed. Admittedly there is in the process always a risk of misinterpretation, i.e. of imposing our own views and problems on the book, and destroying its own balance. But this is only the other side of the opportunity for the book to trigger our own thinking in ways which it alone opens, and to disclose both its actual and potential wealth, or rather some of it, depending on both the reader's own experience and acute attention.

The Christian preaching of the forthcoming Kingdom, the attention, obedience and hope that this preaching demands and fosters, does not only sustain and orientate the life of the listener; it also provides a *horizon* and sets up a *task* for the "responsible thinker," i.e., according to Paul Ricoeur, the philosopher. The *horizon* is that of a concert of all philosophers (of all human thinking), in which each of them will improvise his own part on his own instrument, while contributing to an endless and harmonious celebration; the anticipation of which should prevent any of us to play solo and to remain deaf to the music of others; it should also prevent any self-appointed director or manager from prematurely inflicting his own symphony and tempo on all partners as constituting the ultimate in music.

The *task* is that of correcting and developing one's own thinking—using no other tool, making no other move, than such as can be made and used by any fellow-creature endowed with common sense (be he a believer or a non-believer)—but using freely any such tool and move—so that our thinking will approach and meet what is said in the preaching; but the listening philosopher must not include in his own discourse any saying on the authority of the preaching, he must make no other claim on his audience or look for any other support to back his contentions than (as any other philosopher) the inner consistency of what he says and the light it may throw on the interpretation and management of our common experience.

Such a work in thinking finds its ground in the listening, and yet it must be led with the ways and means of an autonomous and responsible thinking. It is an endless reform of the thinking, but within the bounds of plain reason. The conversion of the philosopher is his conversion *as* philosopher and a conversion to philosophy, without any trespassing of its inherent rules. "If there is only one *Logos*, the *logos* of Christ requires of me as a philosopher nothing else than a more complete and more perfect activation of reason; not more than reason, but *whole* reason." [CI, p. 403]

IX

PSYCHOANALYSIS AS HERMENEUTICS

Any attempt to understand Freud requires us to come to grips with his "mixed discourse." Sometimes Freud speaks the language of force, mechanics, electricity, or hydraulics. Sometimes he uses the language of motives, intentions, purposes, and meanings. Frequently he mixes them. If we take psychoanalysis as a natural science, modeled after physics or chemistry, we must admit, with Nagel and others, that it fails to meet even the minimum epistemological requirements. Many "ordinary language" philosophers want to excuse Freud for talking like a scientist and emphasize his intentional explanations. Representative views of this position, such as those of Toulmin, Flew, and Peters, are presented and criticized. Finally, Ricoeur's claim that psychoanalysis is a hermeneutic discipline is presented, in detail, by showing how psychoanalysis fits the "model of the text."

Charles E. Reagan is Associate Professor of philosophy at Kansas State University, Manhattan, Kansas. He has previously published *Ethics for Scientific Researchers, Readings for an Introduction to Philosophy* (with J. Hamilton and B. Tilghman) and *The Philosophy of Paul Ricoeur: An Anthology of his Work* (with D. Stewart).

Psychoanalysis as Hermeneutics

CHARLES E. REAGAN

INTRODUCTION

Any attempt to understand Freud and psychoanalysis requires us to come to grips with his "mixed discourse." Sometimes Freud speaks the language of a natural science, mechanics, hydraulics or neurology. Sometimes he uses the language of intentions, motives and purposes. Most importantly, most of Freud's descriptions and explanations are a mixture of both. Philosophers have traditionally tried to understand Freud as proposing psychoanalysis as a natural science or as a special extension of our everyday intentional explanations. If one adopts the first view one is forced to admit that psychoanalysis will not meet even the first conditions of a natural science and even its most fundamental concepts and explanations do not conform to the canons of accepted scientific methodology. On the other hand, if one accepts the second view, then one must do a sort of linguistic gymnastics to account for unconscious motives, always running the risk that psychoanalysis can be made to conform to this model only at the cost of losing its soul.

Paul Ricoeur advances the thesis that psychoanalysis is a "hermeneutical science" rather than an observational one. In addition, psychoanalysis as hermeneutics is very close to the view of many contemporary analytic philosophers that psychoanalytic explanations and interpretations are a species of ordinary intentional explanation. However, Ricoeur, without contradicting these philosophers, notes their limitations and attempts to account for the mixed discourse of psychoanalysis without reducing it to one or the other of its components. My aim in this paper will be to examine Ricoeur's thesis to see if it meets at least the two tests of being consistent with the Freudian *corpus* and enlightening. To do this, I will give examples of "mixed discourse" and highlight its difficulties. Then I will consider the critique of psychoanalysis of those who take seriously its claim to be an empirical science and to give causal explanations of certain kinds of behavior and certain psychological phenomena. Next I will review the accounts of those who choose the other side of the "mixed discourse" and want to see psychoanalytic explanations as intentional. Then I will focus on Ricoeur's claim that psychoanalysis is a hermeneutic science. Lastly, we will see if there are any advantages to this account over the two alternatives considered above.

I. FREUD'S MIXED DISCOURSE

The "Project" of 1895 begins with a proposal to make psychology a natural science by appending it to a general mechanics and postulating "neurones" as the material particles required by such a science.[1] But even in Freud's most ambitious attempt to tie psychology to the other natural sciences, we find strictly non-scientific hypotheses as "In this way this path of discharge acquires a secondary function of the highest importance, that of *communication* and the initial helplessness of human beings is the *primal source* of all *moral* motives."[2] In the sixth and seventh chapters of *The Interpretation of Dreams* we see Freud continue the language of forces, only now he has abandoned the neurological substratum; now the forces are purely *psychical*.[3] He says, for example, "Nor do I think we shall have any difficulty in recognizing the psychical force which manifests itself in the facts of dream displacement."[4] This work, according to Ricoeur, presents us with the clearest example of mixed discourse. "Thus dreams," he says, "inasmuch as they are the expression of wishes, lie at the intersection of meaning and force." [FP, p. 91] The key concepts in *The Interpretation of Dreams* require an account which can only be expressed at once in the language of force and the language of meaning or interpretation. For example, *Verstellung* or distortion is a "violence done to the meaning." [FP, p. 92] If distortion is the effect, "censorship" is its cause.

> But what does censorship mean? The word is well chosen: on the one hand, censorship manifests itself at the level of a text on which it imposes blanks, word substitutions, softened expressions, allusions, tricks of arrangement—with suspect or subversive items being displaced and hidden in harmless, out-of-the-way spots; on the other hand, censorship is the expression of a power, more precisely a political power, which works against the opposition by striking at its right of expression. In the idea of censorship the two systems of language are very closely interwoven: censorship alters a text only when it represses a force, and it represses a forbidden force only by disturbing the expression of that force. [FP, pp. 92-93]

Condensation, repression, censorship, displacement, wish-fulfillment all require a mixed discourse of force and meaning. These are mechanisms which respond to and control psychic energy. At the same time they make up what Freud called "dream-work" which is the inverse of interpretation. Censorship is intentional *and* mechanical.

If this seems paradoxical it is because it is. "*The Interpretation of Dreams* was unsuccessful in harmonizing the theory inherited from the 'Project' with the conceptual structure elaborated by the actual work of interpretation." [FP, p. 115]

Freud's "mixed discourse" reaches its sharpest and most paradoxical point in "Papers on Metapsychology." For example, in "The Instincts and their Vicissitudes" Freud says; "If we now apply ourselves to considering mental life from a *biological* point of view, an 'instinct' appears to us as a concept on the frontier between the mental and the somatic, as the psychical representative of the stimuli originating from within the organism and reaching the mind, as a measure of the demand made upon the mind for work in consequence of its connection with the body."[5] Instincts have a noumenal existence, in that they can never be directly known. They are known through the ideas that represent them. In "The Unconscious" Freud says: "I am in fact of the opinion that the antithesis of conscious and unconscious is not applicable to instincts. An instinct can never become an object of consciousness—only the idea that represents the instinct can. Even in the unconscious, moreover, an instinct cannot be represented otherwise than by an idea."[6]

The language of force, the economics or energetics of instincts and the language of meaning and interpretation come together at precisely this point: "the 'vicissitude of instincts' *comes to language* as the vicissitude of their psychical expressions . . . the distance between the two psychoanalytic universes of discourse, which appeared insurmountable on the level of *The Interpretation of Dreams*, seems to have vanished in the 'Papers on Metapsychology.' " [FP, p. 142]

Perhaps the "distance" between these two languages has vanished, but the problem of mixed discourse has not. In fact it is aggravated by the notion of "noumenal" instincts represented by "phenomenal" ideas. The pressing question, it seems to me, is what are we to make of Freud's language (or languages)?

Two approaches seem apparent. Concentrate on the energetics or economics, construe psychoanalysis as a natural or empirical science, apply the canons of methodology, and, as a result, either confirm or disconfirm psychoanalytic hypotheses, reformulate them, or abandon the whole project as a pseudo-science. The second approach is to concentrate on the psychoanalytic descriptions and explanations which seem most "intentional," construe psychoanalysis as an extension of our ordinary concepts of "motive," "intention," "purpose," "wish" and "desire"; and then show how by so doing Freud is actually extending our ability to give "intentional" explanations to some human behaviors where they appeared to be out of place.

Ricoeur's understanding of Freud rejects psychoanalysis as an empirical science, and is very close to the second approach. However, it does avoid some of the apparent difficulties of this approach (e.g., what does it mean—and to what extent is it possible—to "extend" a concept?), is consistent with the Freudian text (e.g. Ricoeur does not want to dismiss the economics as just an unfortunate mistake of Freud's), and allows us to see psychoanalysis as a properly interpretative science. As a consequence, we will want to apply different canons to it than those of the empirical sciences. I shall now consider each approach to psychoanalysis in turn.

II. PSYCHOANALYSIS AS EMPIRICAL SCIENCE

Because Freud's "mixed discourse" admits of different interpretations, I think it important to show that seeing psychoanalysis as a science is not a misconception nor a misunderstanding. This will cut off at once any rejoinder to the critics of psychoanalysis as a science that they are mistaken in Freud's aims or words. From the "Project" of 1895 to the posthumously published *Outline of Psychoanalysis* and "Some Elementary Lessons" it is clear that Freud conceived of his enterprise as "scientific" in the strongest and most literal sense of the word. The "Project" begins, "The intention is to furnish a psychology that shall be a natural science: that is, to represent psychical processes as quantitatively determinate states of specifiable material particles. . . ."[7]

In Freud's paper "The Instincts and their Vicissitudes" (1915) he begins by considering some of the epistemological requirements of a science:

> We have often heard it maintained that science should be built up on clear and sharply defined basic concepts. In actual fact no science, not even the most exact, begins with such definitions. The true beginning of scientific activity consists rather in describing phenomena and then in proceeding to group, classify, and correlate them. Even at the stage of description it is not possible to avoid applying certain abstract ideas to the material in hand, ideas derived from somewhere or other but certainly not from the new observations above.
>
> . . . The advance of knowledge, however, does not tolerate any rigidity even in definitions. Physics furnishes an excellent illustration of the way in which even 'basic concepts' that have been established in the form of definitions are constantly being altered in their content.[8]

Throughout Freud's work is a careful concern for scientific validity, confirmation, hypothesis formation, conceptual clarity, and the need and desirability to make psychoanalysis conform to the methodological canons of empirical science. Freud's followers, by and large, consider psychoanalysis a science and themselves scientists (as well as therapists). Some defend this view naïvely (e.g., B. Wolman),[9] others with great sophistication and knowledge (e.g., L. Kubie).[10]

On the other hand, there has been a great resistance to accepting psychoanalysis as an empirical science, for a number of reasons, most important among which is, ". . . the energy notions of Freudian theory are so vague and metaphorical that it seems impossible to deduce from them any determinate conclusions; such notions may well be suggestive, but they cannot be empirically verified; further, any coordination with facts of behavior is clouded over with an invincible ambiguity, to such an extent that it is impossible to state on what conditions the theory could be refuted." [FP, p. 346]

At this point, we can be instructed by examining in detail a representative kind of criticism of psychoanalysis as an empirical science. I have chosen Ernest Nagel's "Methodological Issues in Psychoanalytic Theory"[11] because it is clear and captures the fundamental objections of philosophers of science to Freudian psychoanalysis.

Nagel asks two general questions: 1. What is the logical structure and empirical content of psychoanalytic theory? 2. What is the general nature of the evidence used to support it?[12] To answer the first question, Nagel points out that with any theory we would empirically validate, "it must be possible to deduce determinate consequences from the assumptions of theory, so that one can decide on the basis of logical considerations and prior to the examination of any empirical data, whether or not an alleged consequence of the theory is indeed implied by the latter."[13] In other words, it must be possible to determine just what the theory claims and just which hypotheses are implied by it. Secondly, "at least *some* theoretical notions must *be tied down* to *fairly definite* and *unambiguously specified* observable materials by way of rules of procedure variously called 'correspondence rules,' 'coordinating definitions,' and 'operational definitions.' "[14]

Nagel reviews some portions of Freudian theory and concludes that "the theory is stated in language so vague and metaphorical that almost anything appears to be compatible with it."[15] With respect to the "correspondence rules" which tie theoretical terms to observation, Nagel challenges the psychoanalyst to produce such rules for the theoretical terms "id," "ego," and "super ego." Thus, Nagel claims that psychoanalysis cannot meet—even partially—the fundamental requirement of a science that we know what the theory claims and how, in principle, it could be empirically instantiated.

To Nagel's second general question, how are hypotheses to be validated, he suggests—and rejects—coherence, acceptance by the patient, and improvement in condition. His general objection is that psychoanalytic interpretations (and hypotheses) are founded on material gained in the psychoanalytic interview. These interviews are generally not open to public scrutiny. But, Nagel claims, "objectivity in science is achieved through the criticism of publicly accessible material by a community of independent inquirers."[16] Coherence—the ability to give an interpretation that accounts for all of the material (dreams, symptoms, behavior, etc.)—will not do since there may be several equally coherent but mutually inconsistent interpretations possible. In fact, if one takes as a case in point the interpretations offered by psychiatrists in recent famous U.S. court cases such wide disagreement seems to be the rule. Coherence is a necessary condition, but not a sufficient condition of the validity of an interpretation. I shall return to this difficult question in Part IV.

Neither the patient's acceptance of an interpretation nor his subsequent improvement can be taken as criteria of the *truth* of the interpretation.

Another very important objection Nagel raises is that it is not clear whether the alleged regularities in some psychoanalytic hypotheses "hold between manifest neurotic symptoms and the *allegations* patients of a certain type make concerning their childhood experiences, or between neurotic symptoms and actual childhood experiences whose occurrence has been ascertained independently of the subjects' memories of them?"[17]

In sum, then, Nagel shows that psychoanalysis as developed by Freud does not meet, in an even minimal way, the fundamental methodological canons required of any enterprise which is to be an empirical or observational science.

Interestingly, Ricoeur is in complete agreement with Nagel: "As long as one tries to place psychoanalysis among the observational sciences, the preceding [Nagel's] attack against psychoanalysis seems to me unanswerable." [FP, p. 347][18]

In order to meet the demands of a logic of the sciences, some psychoanalysts have proposed a reformulation of Freudian doctrine, with the goal of making it both theoretically unequivocal and empirically verifiable.[19] Rather than review these reformulations in detail, let us consider the general objections to any reformulation. Most importantly, a "reformulation is only a reformulation, that is, a second operation with respect to the experience on the basis of which the Freudian concepts have arisen. Reformulation can only deal with results that are dead, detached from the analytical experience, with definitions isolated from one another, cut off from their origin in interpretation, and extracted from academic presentations where they had already fallen to the rank of mere magical phrases." [FP, p. 358] A second obstacle to those who would remake psychoanalysis in order to fit it to the criteria of an observational science, is that what is important to the psychoanalyst is what his patients believe, not what the facts really are. It is not an objective fact but the *meaning* of a fact in the psycho-history of the patient. Thus Nagel's criticism on this point is irrefutable. "Strictly speaking there are no 'facts' in psychoanalysis for the analyst does not observe, he interprets." [FP, p. 365]

According to Ricoeur, reformulations must fail because the closer they approach the legitimate demands of an observational science of behavior, the more they distort all that is original and valuable in psychoanalysis. In short, they misunderstand the very nature of psychoanalysis and at most pervert it in an attempt to conform to inappropriate canons. Observational psychology and psychoanalysis diverge at the very beginning: ". . . psychology is an observational science dealing with the facts of behavior; psychoanalysis is an exegetical science dealing with the relationships of meaning between substitute objects and the primordial (and lost) instinctual objects." [FP, p. 359] Reformulation misunderstands that analysis is concerned with language, particularly with a "dissociated" or substitute language and its relation with common language. Symptoms, dreams, jokes, illusions, in short, the patient's whole story, call for interpretations, exegesis, understanding.

Ricoeur insists that it is only if we see psychoanalysis as an interpretative science rather than an empirical one can we understand Freud's mixed discourse. While Freud claims that the instincts, and all of the energy exchanges summarized under the term "economics" are the ultimate origin of behavior, they can be known only through their manifestations in consciousness, principally through distortions and substitutions of meaning. As a consequence, "as soon as the economics is separated from its rhetorical manifestations, the metapsychology no longer systematizes what occurs in the analytic dialogue; it engenders a fanciful demonology, if not an absurd hydraulics." [FP, p. 371]

It is a mistake to take psychoanalysis as an empirical science; it is much closer to historical understanding than to causal explanation. Thus,

> the validity of the interpretation made in psychoanalysis is subject to the same kind of questions as the validity of a historical or exegetical interpretation. The same questions must be put to Freud that are put to Dilthey, Weber, and Bultmann, not those posed to a physicist or a biologist. . . . Thus analytic theory is not to be compared with the theory of genes or gasses, but with a theory of historical motivation. What differentiates it from other types of historical motivation is the fact that it limits its investigations to the semantics of desire. [FP, pp. 374-75]

III. PSYCHOANALYSIS AS INTENTIONAL EXPLANATION

We have just seen that if the problem of Freud's "mixed discourse" is solved by understanding Freud to be introducing an empirical science, then we must commit it to the wayside of pseudo-sciences. Freud was never able to work out a science of forces, energy, energy transfers, as he envisioned in the "Project of 1895." Furthermore, a science which would demonstrate a causal connection between certain *events* in a person's life and some set of subsequent *events* cannot be made sufficiently rigorous to meet even the minimum norms of an empirical science. Ricoeur and Nagel stand together: psychoanalysis is not an empirical science.

The other alternative to the puzzle of "mixed discourse" is to take seriously Freud's explanations in terms of people's intentions and motives, wishes and desires, and disregard as *une façon de parler* or as a worn metaphor of a *passé* scientism Freud's energetics. That this understanding of Freud needs no justification is clear. Especially in Freud's middle and later works he speaks of looking for the purpose and meaning and motives of neurotic symptoms.[20]

As a reaction to the empiricist criticism of psychoanalysis as a science, or, perhaps as a result of it, an alternative view has arisen among Anglo-American philosophers. Briefly this view is characterized by one of its leading proponents, Antony Flew: "If you are prepared so to extend such notions as *motive, intention, purpose, wish*, and *desire* that it becomes proper to speak of motives and so forth which are not known to, and the behavior resulting from which is not under the immediate control of, the person who harbours them, then you can interpret (and even guide) far more of human behavior in terms of concepts of this sort than any sophisticated adult had previously realized."[21]

This is a very liberal and generous view. However, it is not at all clear how we "extend" the logical limits of concepts, especially such fundamental concepts as "motive," "intention," "purpose" and especially "meaning." To speak of extending these concepts implies that we already have a clear understanding of them and their "logical geography" and that while they do not normally or literally apply in the way Freud wants to use them, that they can be made to do so with suitable clarification.

Let us look at some of the difficulties involved: do we presently possess the requisite clarity concerning the concepts of "motive," "intention," "wish?" A look at the current literature on these concepts indicates there is a wide divergence of analysis. But, even where we do agree (if we do) we have diffculties with the notion of extending the concept "purpose," for example, to cases where people do not know that they are acting for a purpose that we claim is theirs. What are we to make of their denial that they have the alleged intention? We do impute purposes or intentions of people on the grounds of some goal-directed pattern in their behavior. In literary and historical explanation this may be enough because in many cases there is no possibility of first-person denial. But what are we to say of those cases where we claim a person is acting with a particular intention and he denies it honestly and sincerely? These cases raise the famous cluster of problems in philosophical psychology which travel under the group name, "the problem of self-deception."

A more important reason for questioning the possibility of extending these concepts is that they are not and cannot be isolated from moral concepts, concerns, and evaluations. For example, we think that moral responsibility requires that a person is acting intentionally, be aware of what he is doing, and have some control over it. But if we extend these concepts to just those areas of human behavior where the agent is unaware of what he is doing and/or has no control over it, as Flew suggests we do, will we also extend the concept of moral responsibility? In other words, recommending that we extend certain concepts is, like so many other things, much easier to propose than to carry out.

It seems worth mentioning again that to propose extending some concepts implies that until they are "officially extended"—however that is supposed to happen—they are used metaphorically. And, indeed, this is consistent with Flew's view. That is, what Freud is signaling are some very important—and overlooked—similarities between some of our behavior which makes no apparent sense and other explicitly intentional and sensible behavior. If we see the former as somehow "intentional," "purposeful," etc., we can understand it. But after all, we cannot focus only on the similarities to the exclusion of the differences—which in this case are enormous.

In short, if we accept Flew's view—which has much to recommend it, as I will shortly argue—Freud's "mixed discourse" is a new problem: Freud is not mixing two literal languages, one of the natural sciences and the other of intentional description of human action, he is mixing two metaphorical languages. After all psychical energy is a metaphorical energy and unconscious intentions are metaphorical intentions. But this leaves Freud with no literal language.

One may object that while Flew does not work out the extension of these intentional concepts to cover unconscious and uncontrollable action, Stephen Toulmin does. He begins by distinguishing three types of explanation, E_1 the "stated reason" ("I did that because I felt he deserved it"), E_2 the "reported reason" ("He did that because he thought he deserved it"), E_3 the "causal explanation" ("He did that because he was given an injection of cocain"). After noting some of the relationships that hold among these types of explanations, E_4, a psychoanalytic explanation will bear a close family resemblance to these three, thus, E_{14} "I found myself wishing that I was alone with her"; E_{24} "He behaves like that because his father used to beat him violently as a child." He concludes:

> The typical psychoanalytic explanation E_4 (as presented by an analyst at the end of a series of consultations) has something in common with each of the other three types of explanation. Firstly, the patient must come to recognize it as a natural (indeed, as *the* natural) expression of his neurotic state of mind: it must, that is, provide him with a plausible 'stated motive.' Secondly, third parties who are familiar with the case-history must accept it as a description of his conduct: it must, that is, provide a plausible 'reported motive.' Thirdly, such 'facts of early life' as it invokes must be a kind which could have led to this kind of conduct: the explanation must include a plausible 'causal history' of the neurosis.[22]

Illustrating some logical and semantic similarities is always interesting. But this doesn't get us very far in this case. At most what Toulmin has done is to point out the very similarities which justify Freud's use of these intentional concepts, create difficulties in understanding how intentions can be unconscious, and provoke Flew to recommend that the use of the concepts be extended.

A notable exception to Flew's proposal is R. S. Peters. He states,

> Many have claimed that Freud, by reclaiming these phenomena[dreams, hallucinations, obsessions, anxieties, and perversions] for psychology, was in fact extending the model of purposive, rule-following behavior to cover the unconscious. He showed, it is argued, that we have reasons for acts which were previously only explained in terms of causes. I shall argue later that this thesis is mistaken. Freud showed, perhaps, that the concept of "wish" has a wider application than was previously thought. But his account of the working of the primary processes creaks with causality.[23]

Peters' account of the place of psychoanalytic explanation has been very influential and is interesting in its own right. Both of these reasons are sufficient to warrant a fairly detached look at his view. First of all, Peters divides the world into two kinds of events; happenings, for which causal explanations are adequate and human actions, for which only explanations in terms of a rule-following, purposive pattern are adequate. These kinds of occurrences are exclusive:

> . . . if we are in fact confronted with a case of a genuine action (i.e., an act of doing something as opposed to suffering something), then causal explanations are *ipso facto* inappropriate as sufficient explanations. Indeed they may rule out rule-following purposive explanations. To ask what made Jones do something is at least to suggest that he had no good reason for doing it. Similarly, to ascribe a point to his action is *ipso facto* to deny that it can be sufficiently explained in terms of causes, though, of course, there will be many causes in the sense of necessary conditions.[24]

> * * *

> To make explicit the implications of my thesis for psychological theories: If the question is 'Why did Jones walk across the road?' a *sufficient* explanation can only be given in terms of the rule-following purposive model—if this is a case of an action rather than of something happening to him. Answers in terms of causal concepts like 'receptor impulses' and 'colorless movements' are either not explanations because they state not sufficient but only necessary conditions, or they are ways of denying that what has to be explained is a human action.[25]

If, indeed, we can neatly distinguish actions from happenings and then give only the appropriate explanation to each, Freud poses an obstacle. For Freud precisely mixes actions with happenings and gives intentional explanations where we at first thought only causal explanations were appropriate, for example everyday accidents, slips of the tongue, mistakes, etc.; and he gives a causal account in cases where we thought an intentional account was adequate, for example, energetic explanations of what are apparently human actions.

However, Peters' distinction between actions and happenings and their appropriate explanations is tautological: we distinguish actions from happenings on the grounds of what kind of explanation would be adequate, and we know which kind explanation is appropriate by knowing whether or not we have an action or a case of something happening to someone. His distinction must be stipulative since it is not supported by our ordinary talk of actions. In fact, I don't understand what we would say of the language of excuses and extenuating circumstances if we did accept Peters' account. The crux of an excuse is to admit *doing* something and then argue that you shouldn't be held morally responsible for it, or that your responsibility was lessened. But if something *happens* to me then the question of responsibility has no place. I don't excuse—or need to excuse— myself for things of which I am the victim.[26]

With respect to Freud's explanations, Peters allows that Freud extends the notion of a "wish," but that Freud offers causal or quasi-causal explanations of what must be—on Peters' terms—things that happen to us, not actions. In referring to Freud's *Psychopathology of Everyday Life*, Peters says Freud did not intend to explain everything we do, but only "certain performances which are apparently unintentional."[27] In order for something to be a candidate for Freud's psychoanalytic explanation it must be a faulty action, such as knocking a valuable vase off a table, it must be the result of a momentary lapse, that is, we are not chronically clumsy, and we must attribute the deed to inattention, mistake, or accident.[28] (Notice the difficulty in just such cases of describing the accident without using actions words. We want to say "I did it, but it was an accident." Obviously, Peters' rule-following purposive pattern explanation won't fit; but if we give a causal account, then the accident happened as much to the agent as to the vase. But we ordinarily don't talk like that—because Peters' dichotomy is a philosopher's distinction.)

Peters claims that "These rough and ready criteria make it clear that Freud thought his explanations relevant only to phenomena which can hardly be called actions in that they seem either to have no point or conscious objective or to fall short of standards of correctness."[28] But here Peters has simply missed Freud's main point. He wants to claim that they are actions and that, therefore, they must be explained in terms of the agent's intentions. He says that most if not all parapraxes have a sense. By this he means that they serve a purpose, are done intentionally. "In most of our researches," says Freud, "we can replace 'sense' by 'intention' or 'purpose.' "[29] Parapraxes are not to be seen only as bungled actions, mistakes, slips, errors, but as purposeful actions. "They are not chance events . . . ; they have a sense; they arise from the concurrent action—or perhaps rather, the mutually opposing action—of two different intentions."[30] Peters appears to me to overlook the kind of explanation Freud wants to give. In his account of Freud he focuses on his mechanistic, energetic, causal explanations and overlooks Freud's hermeneutic explanations. Thus Peters considers parapraxes as things that happen to us and are therefore appropriate candidates for a causal explanation.

On both counts, Peters is mistaken. He says, for example, "For it would be so inappropriate to ask for the point of a dream or a vision as it would be to ask for the point of a slip of the tongue or pen."[31] But I understand Freud's point here to be precisely that we must ask for the point, the purpose, of a slip of the tongue and that parapraxes in general are to be understood as intentional actions. As a consequence, Peters is mistaken when he says with reference to parapraxes and dreams, "They are all phenomena for which some kind of causal explanation seems appropriate."[32]

Fortunately, all is not lost. Peters struggles with the difficulties which were bound to plague his dualism. In particular, he is successful in criticizing Freud's "primary processes" which "creak with causality." But what Peters also claims is that "When Freud wants to describe goings-on of which it is appropriate to say that a man is acting, that he has a reason for what he does, and so on, he talks about the Ego; when on the other hand, he wants to say that a person suffers something, or is made to do something, he speaks of the Id."[33] This is an obvious distortion of Freud designed to fit Peters' mold of two kinds of occurrences and two kinds of explanation. This is an attempt to solve the problem of mixed discourse by stipulating an ontological dualism and then wrenching Freud's explanations into it. But even Peters understands at last that this won't work:

> Perhaps Freud's lasting contribution to psychology lay not simply in the startling discoveries which he made, but also in showing, by implication, that neither the rule-following purposive model nor the mechanical model of explanation are really adequate for conceptualizing his revolutionary insights.[34]

IV. Psychoanalysis as a Hermeneutic Science

So far we have examined two understandings of Freud's "mixed discourse." Each proceeds by taking one type of discourse as central and disregarding the other as unessential or mistaken or metaphorical. Thus, those who would see psychoanalysis as an empirical science focus on the many texts where Freud explicitly claims to be proposing such a science and talks in the *force* language of a natural science. On the other hand, certain philosophers, aware of the grave flaws in the first approach, concentrate on Freud's later works where explanations in terms of motives and intentions predominate. Freud is now excused for having used the metaphors of a "phantasy physics." My point has been that while both of these approaches are justified by the corpus of Freud's work—or at least by certain parts of it—neither does justice to the genius of Freud's work. The first approach applies methodological criteria to psychoanalytic explanation which are not appropriate because, finally, the claim that psychoanalysis is—or ought to be—an empirical science cannot be defended. The second approach is more promising; but it, too, suffers from certain defects. In the main, it overlooks or ignores the mixed discourse Freud thought necessary to describe the analytic phenomenon, and secondly because it depends on a dichotomy of explanation which cannot be ultimately defended on conceptual, linguistic, or logical grounds.

In this section I will sketch Ricoeur's position. It is clear that he views psychoanalysis as a hermeneutic or interpretative discipline. But what does this entail? In my account, I shall argue that Ricoeur's "The Model of the Text: Meaningful Action Considered as a Text"[35] can serve as a basis for understanding psychoanalysis as an interpretative enterprise.

It is important to note at the outset that Ricoeur, in his characteristically generous way, does not see psychoanalysis as hermeneutics as very different from psychoanalysis as intentional explanation:

> I agree with this [Toulmin's] analysis: the statements of psychoanalysis are located neither within the discourse of the natural sciences nor within the motive discourse of phenomenology. Since it deals with a psychical reality, psychoanalysis speaks not of causes but of motives; but because the topographic field does not coincide with any conscious process of awareness, its explanations resemble causal explanations, without, however, being identically the same, for then psychoanalysis would reify all its notions and mystify interpretation itself. [FP, p. 360][36]

I shall try to point out in due course the important differences between intentional explanation and hermeneutic explanation.

Ricoeur's two main claims are: psychoanalysis is an interpretative science whose field is the semantics of desire. [FP, p. 375] This is the non-reductionist thesis which requires us to turn away from the easy paths of solving the paradox of mixed discourse by ignoring one of its constituents. This claim, it seems to me, must be taken more as a wager, whose outcome can only be determined by the results of interpretation of particular psychoanalytic cases. Thus, I propose to set aside this claim while I work out the details of the second claim. It is that the object of psychoanalysis is essentially linguistic: ". . . the psychoanalytic experience unfolds in the field of speech and that, within this field, what comes to light is another language, dissociated from common language, and which presents itself to be deciphered through its meaningful effects—symptoms, dreams, various formations, etc." [FP, p. 367]

We may begin with the most obvious case, that of dreams. Freud says, ". . . whatever the dreamer tells us must count as his dream, without regard to what he may have forgotten or have altered in recalling it."[37] Freud's thesis is that the dream story has a hidden meaning and that the analyst can come to understand his patient better if he can interpret the patient's dreams. "The dream account is an unintelligible text for which the analyst substitutes a more intelligible text. To understand is to make this substitution. The title *Traumdeutung* . . . alludes to this analogy between analysis and exegesis." [FP, p. 25] Understanding a dream requires us to interpret its symbols.

Secondly, the analytic interview or series of interviews are linguistic. What is important to the analyst is what the patient tells him. This is evidenced by the fact that analysts do not seek corroborating evidence from third parties. The analyst's goal is to interpret the baffling text that constitutes the history of that individual patient. In fact the analyst's interpretation depends on this long narrative and as a consequence, anecdotal interpretations of bits of the story frequently seem far-fetched and insupportable in isolation. The plausibility of any partial interpretation depends on its role in the overall interpretation of the whole story.[38]

The psychoanalyst is an interpreter of "texts." To see the insight in Ricoeur's claim, we must examine his account of texts and text interpretation.[39]

But to get to the notion of a text, Ricoeur must detour through the distinction between *discourse* and *language*.[40] He points out four distinctive characteristics of discourse:

> [1.] Discourse is always realized temporally and in a present, whereas the language system is virtual and outside of time. [2.] Whereas language lacks a subject—in the sense that the question 'Who is speaking' does not apply at its level—discourse refers to its speaker by means of a complex set of indicators such as the personal pronouns. . . . [3.] Whereas the signs in language refer only to other signs within the same system, and whereas language therefore lacks a world just as it lacks temporality and subjectivity, discourse is always about something. . . . [4.] Whereas language is only the condition for communication, for which it provides the codes, it is in discourse that all messages are exchanged.[41]

Ricoeur's main point here is now to show how written discourse, texts, are different from spoken discourse. Then we can show how the psychoanalytic "text" bears the characteristics of other texts, and, consequently, how the notion of text interpretation can be taken as a model of psychoanalytic explanation.

The written text has a permanence that spoken discourse lacks. It "fixes" what is *said*. Writing does not capture the event of speaking, but the "saying," or, in another idiom, the propositional content. Secondly, spoken discourse is self-referential: it designates its speaker. On the other hand, "with written discourse the author's intention and the meaning of the text cease to coincide. . . . What the text says now matters more than what the author meant to say, and every exegesis unfolds its procedures within the circumference of a meaning that has broken its moorings to the psychology of its author."[42] This characteristic of a written text will play a central role in understanding the psychoanalytic narrative. A third difference between spoken and written discourse is that the former is tied to a situation common to the interlocutors; it depends on the particular context of the particular persons who are speaking with one another. Ricoeur says that in spoken discourse our reference is ostensive, that is, the situation provides the referents of the demonstratives, tenses, and adverbs. With a written text we are freed "from the limits of ostensive reference."[43] Thus, with literary texts we go beyond particular situations to a "possible world." "Thus we speak about the 'world' of Greece, not to designate any more what were the situations for those who lived them, but to designate the nonsituational references which outline the effacement of the first and which henceforth are offered as possible modes of being. . . ."[44] In short, literature can present us with a world as a possible world rather than only as a description of our actual world. This is the essential difference between literature and history. Lastly, only spoken discourse is addressed to a particular person. A written text is available to anyone who knows how to read.[45]

Our task now is twofold: first we must see to what extent the subject matter of psychoanalysis can be construed as a text. Secondly, we must argue for the advantages of understanding psychoanalysis as the hermeneutic science of these texts.

Writing fixes the "said" of spoken discourse. By the same token, when we interpret a dream, it is not the dream as experience but the dream account that is the object of our interpretation. Freud says dreams "are a performance and an utterance on the part of the dreamer. . . ."[46] But it is the utterance, not the performance, which we interpret. "Whatever the dreamer tells us must count as his dream. . . ."[47] If we look beyond dreams to the larger context of the psychoanalytic case history, it is the whole narrative which needs interpretation. It appears to both the analyst and especially to the patient as an unintelligible text for which the analyst will eventually substitute an intelligible one. What is wanted is an interpretation of the symbols, origins, function and significance of the patient's dreams, phantasies, symptoms, etc. If we see the patient's story as a text, then we see the legitimacy of extending psychoanalytic interpretation to historical figures (e.g., Leonardo da Vinci, Woodrow Wilson), literary characters (Oedipus, Hamlet), religious and social customs (*Totem and Taboo* and *Moses and Monotheism*). Like the individual patient's narrative, these texts share the other characteristics of written discourse.

The most important characteristic of a text is that the author's intentions no longer coincide with the meaning of the text. The close connection between "I mean . . ." and "I intend . . ." from the point of view of the speaker or agent is now broken: the text has a meaning of its own and its meaning is not dependent on the intention (meaning) of the author. Thus, we can separate the psychoanalytic text from the intentions, motives, conscious wishes, desires, and fears of its author. The patient need not (and frequently does not) know the meaning of his dream symbols, his neurotic symptoms, or the underlying intention in his parapraxes. His disavowal of certain imputed intentions is not taken as decisive and in fact may be taken as in itself symptomatic (e.g., resistance to interpretation). If we understand psychoanalysis in this way, we can make better sense of Flew's suggested extension of our concepts of "intention," "motive," "desire," etc. For now we see them in their use in text interpretation (i.e., reconstruction of the motives and intentions of a textual character) without having to consider the first-person psychological reports of the author (patient) as decisive. In this way we can avoid the paradox of intention explanations imputed on the basis of patterns of action being defeated by a first-person disavowal.

A third characteristic of a written text is that it can escape the immediate situation of its production in a way that spoken discourse cannot. If we take the patient's narrative as a text, we can escape understanding it only in terms of his personal psychological situation. This means his narrative is open, first, to interpretations by others than the original analyst. We can generalize both the narrative and the interpretations beyond the particular analysis which was its original source and home. In fact, this is the basis for psychoanalytic generalization and theorizing. We can—and want to— move beyond understanding this person's neurosis to understanding neurosis in general. If we leave behind the therapeutic aim of psychoanalysis and see it as a cultural hermeneutics, we extend it to provide *an* interpretation of history, literature, morality, art, and culture in general.

As a text, the analytic narrative is available, like a work of literature, to many interpreters, and neither the patient nor his analyst are privileged. It is open, like a text, to interpretation by "all who can read."

All of the gains which come, however, from considering psychoanalysis as the interpretation of a text (the analytic narrative) will be lost unless we can show how such an interpretation can remain therapeutic. After all, for the patient, the text being interpreted is not just another story, just one text among many. If we separate the meaning of the text from the psychology of the author (patient) in what sense are we analyzing *him*? How do we ever reconnect the meaning of the text with the intentions, motives, desires, etc., of this individual person? In short, the answer is that "this text is his story." It is a privileged story. It bears to him the connection between an author and his autobiography (as opposed to that between an author and *a* biography).

Ricoeur emphasizes that the road to self-knowledge is not the direct one of self-consciousness. Descartes and Husserl have been displaced by the "masters of suspicion," Nietzsche, Marx, and Freud. Self-consciousness is a *deceptive* consciousness, and "what all three attempted, in different ways, was to make their 'conscious' methods of deciphering coincide with the 'unconscious' *work* of ciphering which they attributed to the will to power, to social being, to the unconscious psychism." [FP, p. 34] The philosophical reflection that has self-knowledge as its goal must make a detour through understanding "the ideas, action, works, institutions, and monuments that objectify it ['I think']." [FP, p. 44] Thus I come to understand myself through the understanding of history, literature, languages, arts, and my culture in general. In the same way, a person's understanding of himself will not come from some kind of introspection, even guided by an analyst, but by the interpretation of his story. In sum, the author rejoins his text at the point that he understands it is *his* story, *his* history, *his* life that the text is about.

Our second task is now to show that there are epistemological advantages to understanding psychoanalysis as an interpretation of texts, a deciphering of hidden meaning. I shall be brief since I have already indicated these advantages in an earlier part of my discussion. First, we will no longer be tempted to see psychoanalysis as an empirical science and apply it to the methodological canons of those sciences. Nagel and others have shown, definitively I think, that psychoanalysis must fail such a test. This does not mean that psychoanalysis must meet no criteria of adequacy, but that those criteria will be the ones we apply to historical interpretation or literary criticism or Biblical exegesis, and not the ones we apply to physics, biology or chemistry.

Secondly, we can understand the extension of certain psychological concepts to "the unconscious" if we see that interpreting a text is independent of the intentions of the author. It is in this sense that we can speak of someone intending to do something even though he is unaware of his intentions.[48] We can speak of someone's dream meaning something without inferring that he means that; a dream can symbolize without the dreamer symbolizing.

The last, and most important, advantage is that this understanding of Freud is consonant with his work. In discussing psychoanalysis as an empirical science, I was careful to show how this view is in fact justified by

Freud's writings. It is not an unjust interpretation of Freud. But it is not the only one justified by Freud's work. So is the view of psychoanalysis as giving intentional, rather than causal, explanations. In fact, in many important ways, this view is very close to Ricoeur's claim that psychoanalysis is a hermeneutic science. But the "intentional" view works only by ignoring Freud's mechanistic, causal, deterministic, *force* explanations, treating them as unfortunate metaphors or as *"une façon de parler."*

But Freud's "mixed discourse" is not a mistake. Ricoeur believes that it is required by the very nature of the phenomenon, the semantics of desire.[49] "How do desires achieve speech? How do desires make speech fail, and why do they themselves fail to speak?" [FP, p. 6] Psychoanalysis as a hermeneutics does not require us to choose between an energetic interpretation (explanation in terms of force) or an intentional interpretation (explanations by intention, motive, etc., of an agent) at the outset, as did the first two views we have considered. Rather, we have a "conflict of interpretations," and if we must ultimately choose, it will be not *a priori* but as the result of a careful evaluation of conflicting interpretations.

NOTES

1. Sigmund Freud, "The Project for a Scientific Psychology," in *The Standard Edition of the Complete Psychological Works of Sigmund Freud*, James Strachey, ed. (London: Hogarth Press, 1966), Vol I, pp. 283-398. Hereinafter abbreviated S. E.

2. S.E. I, p. 318.

3. Sigmund Freud, *The Interpretation of Dreams*, 1900, S.E. Vol IV and V.

4. S.E. IV, p. 308.

5. S.E. XIV, pp. 121-22.

6. S.E. XIV, p. 177.

7. S.E. I, p. 295. *See* note p. 290 as well as remark in Editor's Introduction, "But in fact the *Project*, or rather its invisible ghost, haunts the whole series of Freud's theoretical writing to the very end."

8. S.E. XIV, p. 117. *See also* "On Narcissism: An Introduction," S.E. XIV, p. 77.

9. *See* Benjamin Wolman, *The Unconscious Mind* (Englewood Cliffs, New Jersey: Prentice Hall, 1968), pp. 6, 83, *passim*.

10. Lawrence Kubie, "Problems and Techniques of Psychoanalytic Validation and Progress" in E. Pumpian-Mundlin, ed., *Psychoanalysis as Science* (Palo Alto: Stanford University Press, 1952) and "Psychoanalysis and Scientific Method," in Sidney Hook, ed., *Psychoanalysis, Scientific Method, and Philosophy* (New York: New York University Press, 1959).

11. Ernest Nagel, "Methodological Issues in Psychoanalytic Theory," in Sidney Hook, *Psychoanalysis, Scientific Method, and Philosophy*, pp. 38-56.

12. *Ibid.*, p. 39.

13. *Ibid.*, pp. 39-40.

14.   *Ibid.*, p. 40.

15.   *Ibid.*, p. 41.

16.   *Ibid.*, p. 49.

17.   *Ibid.*, p. 52.

18.   Ricoeur was severely criticized by one French reviewer for his patient and sympathetic account of Nagel's objections to psychoanalysis: "Even so, was it necessary to examine point by point the so called epistemological discussions among neo-positivist logicians and psychologists which have flourished on the other side of the Atlantic, and to tarry over their absurdities, in order to pat himself on the back for bringing to the light of day the following truth: psychoanalysis is not an observational science like astronomy!" Michel Tort, "De l'interprétation ou la machine hermémeutique," *Les Temps Modernes*, Nos. 237-38 Feb-March, 1966, p. 1470.

19.   *See* footnote FP, p. 341.

20.   *See* Sigmund Freud, *A General Introduction to Psychoanalysis* (1916-17). S.E. Vol. XV, pp. 15-239; Vol XVI, pp. 243-464. *See* especially Lectures II, III, and IV.

21.   Antony Flew, "Motives and the Unconscious," in Herbert Feigl and Michael Scriven, eds., *Minnesota Studies in the Philosophy of Science*. Vol I, *The Foundations of Science and the Concepts of Psychology and Psychoanalysis*. (Minneapolis: University of Minnesota Press, 1956), p. 155.

22.   Stephen Toulmin, "The Logical Status of Psychoanalysis," *Analysis*, Vol. IX, No. 2, (1948). Reprinted in Margaret Macdonald, ed., *Philosophy and Analysis* (New York: Philosophical Library, 1954), p. 137.

23.   R. S. Peters, *The Concept of Motivation* (London: Routledge and Kegan Paul, 1958) p. 11.

24.   *Ibid.*, p. 12.

25.   *Ibid.*, p. 15.

26.   For a detailed and sustained attack on Peters, *see* Michael Sherwood, *The Logic of Explanation in Psychoanalysis* (New York: Academic Press, 1969), pp. 127-46.

27.   Peters, p. 54.

28.   *Ibid.*

29.   Sigmund Freud, *Introductory Lectures on Psychoanalysis*, Lecture III. S.E. XV, p. 40.

30.   S.E. XV, p. 44.

31.   Peters, p. 56.

32.   *Ibid.*

33.   *Ibid.*, p. 69.

34.   *Ibid.*, p. 94.

35.   Paul Ricoeur, "The Model of the Text: Meaningful Action Considered as a Text," *New Literary History*, Vol. V, Autumn, 1973, pp. 91-117.

36.   In another passage Ricoeur says, "Nothing is closer to my position than this article by Antony Flew," FP, p. 362. This is in reference to Flew's "Motives and the Unconscious."

37.   S.E. XV, p. 85.

38.   *See* Michael Sherwood, *The Logic of Explanation in Psychoanalysis*, especially Chapter Six.

39.   I am relying on Ricoeur's later and superior article "The Model of the Text" rather than his "What is a Text?" in David M. Rasmussen, *Mythic-Symbolic Language and Philosophical Anthropology* (The Hague: Nijhoff, 1971) pp. 125-55. The articles are in many ways similar, except that in the latter Ricoeur limits a text to a written instrument: "Let us call a text every utterance or set of utterances fixed by writing. According to this definition, the fixation by writing is constitutive of the text itself." (p. 135.) In the second article, Ricoeur takes a text to be a paradigm for the object of the social sciences. Even in *Freud and*

Philosophy, Ricoeur does not want to limit a text to a written document, "as the notion of 'text' is wider that that of 'scripture.' . . . This notion of text—thus freed from the notion of scripture or writing—is of considerable interest. Freud often makes use of it. . . ." (p. 25.) Clearly, for Ricoeur's purposes in casting psychoanalysis as a hermeneutic science, he cannot restrict "text" to written texts.

40. Ricoeur is following Saussure's and Hjelmslev's distinctions between *langue/parole* and schema/usage.

41. Ricoeur, "The Model of the Text," p. 92.

42. *Ibid.*, p. 95.

43. *Ibid.*, p. 96.

44. *Ibid.*

45. *See ibid.*, p. 97.

46. Sigmund Freud, *A General Introduction to Psychoanalysis*, trans. Joan Rivière (New York: Washington Square Press, 1952), p. 105. The *Standard Edition* gives a slightly different translation: "They are products and utterances of the dreamer's. . . ." S.E. XV, p. 100.

47. S.E. XV, p. 85.

48. *See* Peters, p. 9. "But whereas his reason—whether real or not—entails that a man is conscious of his objective, the reason why he did it does not. *The* reason why he did it might well be sex or aversion to work; *yet the individual might be quite unaware of pursuing or avoiding the relevant goals.*" (My italics.)

49. *See* FP, p. 65. "Freud's writings present themselves as a mixed or even ambiguous discourse, which at times states conflicts of force subject to an energetics, at times relations of meaning subject to a hermeneutics. I hope to show that there are good grounds for this apparent ambiguity and that this mixed discourse is the *raison d'être* of psychoanalysis." *See also* Peters' remark, "Perhaps Freud's lasting contribution to psychology lay not simply in the startling discoveries which he made, but also in showing, by implication, that neither the rule-following purposive model nor the mechanical model of explanation are really adequate for conceptualizing his revolutionary insights" (Peters, p. 94).

X

Francois H. Lapointe

RICOEUR AND HIS CRITICS:
A BIBLIOGRAPHICAL ESSAY

This is a bibliography of secondary sources. Books about Ricoeur are listed along with reviews of those books. In another section the author lists doctoral dissertations. Articles are arranged by language. In another section, the author lists reviews of each of Ricoeur's major works. A final section is on bibliographies.

Francois H. Lapointe is Professor of education, Dept. of Philosophy and Education, Tuskegee Institute, Tuskegee, Alabama. He has previously published bibliographies on Ricoeur, Marcel, and Sartre.

Paul Ricoeur and His Critics:
A Bibliographic Essay

FRANCOIS H. LAPOINTE

Paul Ricoeur's work has been widely read and reviewed and has exerted a significant influence on contemporary thought. Therefore a bibliography of the wide range of critical response to his writings is most appropriate.

The present bibliography is intended to be as complete as is technically feasible. Our purpose is to provide an accurate, fairly complete and useful arrangement of materials. Although no bibliography can claim to be exhaustive, every attempt at completeness and accuracy has been made. All of the standard reference works known to us were consulted, and many periodicals and books were searched individually. Items through January 1977 are included.

The bibliography is arranged in what seems to be the most usable form. Whenever the number of items has justified it, we have arranged them by language. In the first section, we list books; in the second, dissertations; in the third section, we have classified by language articles in periodicals as well as chapters in books. Section four contains reviews and critical notices of individual works, following generally a chronological order.

We would appreciate readers calling our attention to items that have been inadvertently omitted as well as to inaccuracies.

I   BOOKS

Asciuto, Liborio. *Volontà e corpo proprio nella fenomenologia di Paul Ricoeur*. Francavilla al Mare: Edizioni Paoline, 1973, 64 pp.

Bergeron, Rosaire. *La vocation de la liberté dans la philosophie de Paul Ricoeur*. Montréal: Les Edit. Bellarmin; Fribourg: Edit. Universitaires, 1974. 302 pp. Travaux de psychologie, pédagogie et orthopédagogie, 9.

Bourgeois, Patrick L. *Extension of Ricoeur's hermeneutic*. The Hague: Martinus Nijhoff, 1975. x, 154 pp. (bib. pp. 148-152).

Guerrera Brezzi, Francesca. *Filosofia e interpretazione. Saggio sull'ermeneutica restauratrice di Paul Ricoeur*. Bologna: Il Mulino, 1969, 263 pp.
    REVIEW
        Cullen, C. *Stromata*, Vol. 27, 1971, pp. 303-305.

Ihde, Don. *Hermeneutic phenomenology. The philosophy of Paul Ricoeur*. Foreword by Paul Ricoeur, Evanston, Ill.: Northwestern University Press, 1971, 192 pp.
    REVIEW
        Bossert, P. J. *Philosophy and Phenomenological Research*, vol. 33, June 1973, pp. 388-389.

Marsh, J. L. *Modern Schoolman*, vol. 49, 1971-72, pp. 377-79.

Sweeney, R. D. *International Philosophical Quarterly*, vol. 12, March 1972, pp. 140-142.

Philibert, Michel. *Paul Ricoeur ou la liberté selon l'espérance*. Présentation, choix de textes (Philosophes de tous les temps, 72). Paris: Seghers, 1971, 192 pp.

Rasmussen, David. *Mythic-Symbolic Language and Philosophical Anthropology*. The Hague: Martinus Nijhoff, 1971, 158 pp. At the end of this book there is text in English by Ricoeur, "What is a Text? Explanation and Interpretation," pp. 135-50.

II   DISSERTATIONS

Albano, Peter Joseph. "Freedom, truth and hope: The relation of philosophy and religion in the thought of Paul Ricoeur." Claremont Graduate School 1976, *Diss. Abstracts*, vol. 37, no. 5, Nov. 1976, p. 2954-A.

Alexander, Ronald. "Paul Ricoeur's philosophy of religious language interpreted as an alternative to Antony Flew's empiricistic rejection of religious language." Lutheran School of Theology at Chicago, 1972.

Bailey, Dennis Lee. "The modern novel in the presence of myth." Purdue U. diss. *Diss. Abstracts*, vol. 35, no. 11, May 1975, pp. 7293-7293-A [Ricoeur, Lévi-Strauss].

Bourgeois, Patrick L. "Paul Ricoeur's hermeneutical phenomenology." Duquesne 1970, *Diss. Abstracts*, vol. 31, no. 10, 1971, p. 5457-A.

Cipollone, Anthony P. "Ethical elements in the philosophy of Paul Ricoeur," *Diss. Abstracts International*, vol. 35, no. 5, Nov. 1974, pp. 3049-3050-A. [De Paul University diss.]

Cox, James William. "An analysis of Paul Ricoeur's philosophy of the will and voluntary action." *Diss. Abstracts International*, vol. 34, no. 6, Dec. 1973, p. 3463-A. [Vanderbilt University diss.]

Dornisch, Loretta. "A theological interpretation of the meaning of symbol in the theory of Paul Ricoeur and possible implications for contemporary education." Marquette University 1973. *Diss. Abstracts.* vol. 35, no. 2, Aug. 1974, p. 1211-A.

Gerhart, Mary. "The question of 'belief' in recent criticism. A reexamination from the perspective of Paul Ricoeur's hermeneutical theory." University of Chicago, 1973.

Ihde, Don. "Paul Ricoeur's phenomenological methodology and philosophical anthropology." Boston University 1964. *Diss. Abstracts*, vol. 25, no. 5, 1964, p. 3031-A.

Lowe, Walter James. "Mystery and the unconscious: A study in the thought of Paul Ricoeur," *Diss. Abstracts International*, vol. 34, no. 1, July, 1973, p. 408-A.

Pauls, Arleen Laura. "Existential political theory." University of Pittsburgh. *Diss. Abstracts*, vol. 34, no. 5, Nov. 1973, p. 2725-A.

Rasmussen, David Michael. "A correlation between religious language and an understanding of man. A constructive interpretation of the thought of Paul Ricoeur." University of Chicago, 1969.

Reagan, Charles E. "Freedom and determinism. A critical study of certain aspects of the problem in the light of the philosophy of Paul Ricoeur." University of Kansas, 1967. *Diss. Abstract*, vol. 28, no. 9, 1968, p. 3716-A.

Skousgaard, Stephen A. "Self and freedom: An interpretation of the essence, existence and symbols of human freedom based on the philosophy of Paul Ricoeur." Tulane University, 1975, *Diss. Abstracts*, vol. 36, no. 8, Feb. 1976, p. 5356-A.

Smith, Esther Diane. "Aspects of human agency in the phenomenology of Paul Ricoeur." *Diss. Abstracts International*, vol. 35, no. 12, June, 1975, p. 7967-A. [Claremont Graduate School diss.]

Stewart, John David. "Paul Ricoeur's phenomenology of evil," Rice University, 1965, *Diss. Abstracts*, vol. 26, no. 5, 1965, p. 2910-A.

Vansina, Dirk. "De Filozofie van Paul Ricoeur." Louvain University, 1962.

Wells, Harold George. "The theme of freedom in the anthropology of Paul Ricoeur." *Diss. Abstracts International*, vol. 34, no. 2, Aug. 1973, p. 859-A. [McGill University diss.]

Wesolowsky, Stanley O. "Intersubjectivity and communication in recent philosophy and theology: A study undertaken in the light of the works of Paul Ricoeur." Princeton University 1972. *Diss. Abstracts*, vol. 33, no. 7, 1973, p. 3768-A.

Woods, Jerome Patrick. An application of Paul Ricoeur's hermeneutic phenomenology to the symbols of contemplative union in Richard Rolle's *The Fire of Love*. De Paul University 1977. *Diss. Abstracts*, July 1977, vol. 38, no. 1, p. 327-A.

III *ARTICLES*

A) *English*

Alexander, Ronald G. "Paul Ricoeur: Which direction is he taking?" *Dialog* 14 (No. 1, Winter, 1975): 56-61.

Arcaya, Jose. "Two languages of man." *Journal of Phenomenological Psychology*, vol. 4, no. 1, Fall 1973, pp. 315-340.

Beshai, James A. "Is psychology a hermeneutic science?" *Journal of Phenomenological Psychology*, vol. 5, no. 2, Spring 1975, pp. 425-440.

Bourgeois, Patrick. "Hermeneutics of symbols and philosophical reflection: Paul Ricoeur." *Philosophy Today*, vol. 15, 1971, pp. 231-241.

———. "Paul Ricoeur's hermeneutic phenomenology." *Philosophy Today*, vol. 16, 1972, pp. 20-27.

———. "Phenomenology and the sciences of language." *Research in Phenomenology*. Pittsburgh: Duquesne University Press, vol. I, 1971, pp. 119-136.

Doran, R.-M. "Paul Ricoeur. Toward the restoration of meaning." *Anglican Theological Review* (Evanston, Ill.), vol. 55, no. 4, 1973, pp. 443-458.

Dornisch, Loretta. "Symbolic systems and the interpretation of Scripture: An introduction to the work of Paul Ricoeur." In *Semeia* 4: *Paul Ricoeur on Biblical Hermeneutics*. Missoula, MT.: Scholars Press, the Society of Biblical Literature, 1975.

Dwiggins, C. W. "The phenomenon of ambiguity." *Man and World*, vol. 4, 1971, pp. 270-283.

Edie, James M. "Identity and metaphor: A phenomenological theory of polysemy." *Journal of the British Society for Phenomenology*, vol. 6, no. 1, Jan. 1975, pp. 32-41.

Gerhart, Mary. "Paul Ricoeur's hermeneutical theory as resource for theological reflection." *Thomist*, vol. XXXIX, no. 3, July 1975, pp. 496-527.

Gerhart, M. "Paul Ricoeur's notion of diagnostics: its function in literary interpretation." *Journal of Religion*, vol. 56, April 1976, 137-156.

Hackett, S. C. "Philosophical objectivity and existential involvement in the methodology of Paul Ricoeur." *International Philosophical Quarterly*, vol. 9, March 1969, pp. 11-39.

Hartmann, Klaus. "Phenomenology, ontology and metaphysics." *Review of Metaphysics*, vol. 22, no. 1, Sept. 1968, pp. 85-112.

Ihde, Don. *Sense and significance*. (Duquesne Studies Phil. series, no. 31, dist. by Humanities Press, N. Y. for Duquesne University Press) 1973, Ricoeur: 108-112, 130-133, 138-142 and *passim*.

———. "From phenomenology to hermeneutic." *Journal of Existentialism*, vol. 8, no. 30, Winter 1967-1968, pp. 111-132.

———. "Rationality and myth." *The Journal of Thought*, vol. 2, no. 1, January 1967, pp. 10-18.

———. "The secular city and the existentialists." *The Andover Newton Quarterly*, vol. 7, no. 4, March 1967, pp. 188-189.

———. "Some parallels between analysis and phenomenology." *Philosophy and Phenomenological Research*, vol. 27; no. 4, June 1967, pp. 577-586.

Kockelmans, Joseph J. "On myth and its relationship to hermeneutics." *Cultural Hermeneutics*, vol. 1, April 1973, pp. 47-86.

Lavers, Annette. "Man, meaning and subject. A current reappraisal." *Journal of the British Society for Phenomenology*, vol. 1, Dec. 1970, pp. 44-49.

Magliola, Robert. "Parisian structuralism confronts phenomenology: The ongoing debate." *Language and Style*, vol. VI, no. 4, Fall 1973, pp. 237-248.

McCown, Jose. "Phenomenology and symbolics of guilt." *Southern Journal of Philosophy*, vol. 14, Fall 1976, 293-302.

Mitchell, William H. "Poetry: language as violence—An analysis of the symbolic process in poetry." *Humanitas*, vol. 8, May 1972, pp. 193-208.

Mohanty, J. N. *The concept of intentionality*. St. Louis: Warren H. Green, 1972.

Morgan, John Henry. "Religious myth and symbol: convergence of philosophy and anthropology." *Philosophy Today*, vol. 18, Spring 1974, pp. 68-84.

Muto, Susan. "Reading the symbolic text. Some reflections on interpretation." *Humanitas*, vol. 8, May 1972, pp. 169-191.

Pettit, Philip. "French philosophy." *Cambridge Review*, vol. 94, no. 2214, June 8, 1973, pp. 178-180.

Rasmussen, David M. "Myth, structure and interpretation." In *The Origin of cosmos and man*, edited by M. Dhavenony. Rome: Gregorian University Press, 1969.

———. "Ricoeur: the anthropological necessity of a special language." *Continuum*, vol. 7, no. 1, Winter-Spring 1969, pp. 120-130.

———. "From problematics to hermeneutics: Lonergan and Ricoeur." *Language, truth and meaning*. Papers from The International Lonergan Congress, 1970, edited by Philip McShane. Notre Dame University Press, 1972, pp. 236-272.

Reagan, Charles E. "Ricoeur's diagnostic relation." *International Philosophical Quarterly*, vol. 8, Dec. 1968, pp. 586-592.

Sinyard, B. "Myth and reflexion. Some comments on Ricoeur's phenomenological analysis." *Canadian Journal of Theology*, vol. 16, no. 1-2, 1970, pp. 33-40.

Spiegelberg, Herbert. *The phenomenological movement. A historical introduction.* The Hague: Martinus Nijhoff, vol. 2, 1960, pp. 563-578.

Stewart, David. "Transcendence and the categorical imperative." *Rice University Studies*, vol. 61, no. 3, Summer 1975, pp. 87-96.

———. "The Christian and politics. Reflections on power in the thought of Paul Ricoeur." *Journal of Religion*, vol. 52, 1972, pp. 56-83.

———. "In quest of hope: Paul Ricoeur and Jurgen Moltmann." *Restoration Quarterly*, vol. 13, no. 1, First Quarter 1970, pp. 31-52.

———. "Paul Ricoeur's phenomenology of evil." *International Philosophical Quarterly*, vol. 9, no. 4, Dec. 1969, pp. 572-589.

_____. "Paul Ricoeur and the phenomenological movement." *Philosophy Today*, vol. 12, Winter 1968, pp. 227-235.

Synnestvedt, Justin. "Objectivity and subjectivity in Paul Ricoeur." *Kinesis*, vol. 4, no. 2, 1972, pp. 63-78.

Thie, Marilyn C. "The 'broken' world of myth: an analysis." *New Scholasticism*, vol. 45, Winter 1971, pp. 38-55.

Wells, H. "Theology and Christian philosophy. Their relation in the thought of Paul Ricoeur." *Studies in Religion* (Toronto), vol. 5, no. 1, 1975, 45-56.

B)   *French*

Althusser, L. "Essais et propos sur l'objectivité de l'histoire." (Lettre à Paul Ricoeur). *Revue Enseignement Philosophique*, vol. 5, no. 4, 1955, pp. 3-15.

Barlow, Michel. *Le Socialisme d'Emmanuel Mounier*. Toulouse: Privat, 1971.

Blanchard, Yvon. "Valeurs économiques et liberté." *Dialogue*, vol. XII, no. 1, Mars 1973, pp. 32-49. [Lavelle-Ricoeur].

Blanchet, Charles. "L'enterprise philosophique de Paul Ricoeur." *Cahiers de L'I.S.E.A.* (série M,) [Paris], no. 23, 1966, pp. 179-190.

Brazzalo, Georges. "Réflexions sur la parole." *Revue Thomiste*, vols. LXXIXe année t. LXXI, nos. 2-3, Avril-Sept. 1971, pp. 405-412.

Bres, Y. "P. Ricoeur. Le règne des herméneutiques ou 'un long détour'." *Revue Philosophique de la France et de l'Etranger*, vol. 94, 1969, pp. 425-429.

Charles, Daniel. "Dire, entendre, parler. L'herméneutique et le langage selon Paul Ricoeur." *Algemeen Nederlands Tijdschrift voor Wijsbegeerte en Psychologie*, vol. 68, 1976, 74-98.

Charron, Ghyslain. "Du langage: la linguistique de Martinet et la phénoménologie de Merleau-Ponty." *Revue de l'Université d'Ottawa*, vol. 40, April-June 1970, pp. 260-283.

_____. "Implications de la distinction de Benveniste entre linguistique de la langue et linguistique du discours." *Revue de L'Université d'Ottawa*, vol. 41, April-June 1971, pp. 192-206.

Czarnecki, J. "L'interprétation selon P. Ricoeur." *Christianisme Social*, 1967, pp. 439-447.

Dumas, André. "Savoir objectif, croyance projective, foi interpellée," in Madison, *Sens et existence*, 1975, pp. 160-169.

Duméry, Henry. "Un philosophe de la volonté: Paul Ricoeur." in *Regards sur la philosophie contemporaine*. Paris: Casterman, 1956, pp. 147-151.

Fages, J.-B. "Claude Lévi-Strauss et Paul Ricoeur," in *Comprendre Lévi-Strauss*. Toulouse: Privat, 1972, pp. 120-123.

Fialkowski, Aline. "Paul Ricoeur et l'herméneutique des mythes." *Esprit*, vol. 35, 1967, nos. 7-8, pp. 73-89.

Finance, Joseph de. *L'Affrontement de l'autre. Essai sur l'altérité*. Rome: Universita Gregoriana Editrice, 1973.

Fontan, Pierre. "Histoire et philosophie: Présence du platonisme." *Revue Thomiste*, vol. 75, Janvier-Mars 1975, pp. 108-118.

Forest, Aime. "Le sacré fondamental." *Teoresi*, vol. 27, July-Dec. 1972, pp. 147-174.

Gisel, P. "Paul Ricoeur." *Etudes Théologiques et Religieuses* (Montpellier), vol. 49, no. 1, 1974, pp. 31-50.

Henriot, Jacques. *La condition volontaire. Elements pour une phénoménologie de la praxis.* Louvain-Paris: Nauwelaerts, 1970, 308 p.

Hervé, Alain. "Un philosophe descend dans l'arène. Pourquoi Paul Ricoeur a accepté de devenir doyen de la Faculté de Nanterre." *Réalités*, no. 284, Sept. 1969, pp. 31-33.

Jacob, André. "Paul Ricoeur: une philosophie pratique d'inspiration phénoménologique." *Critique*, nos, 171-172, 1961, pp. 749-764.

Javet, Pierre. "Imagination et réalité dans la philosophie de Paul Ricoeur." *Revue de Théologie et de Philosophie*, vol. 5, 1966-1967. pp. 481-497.

Klein, Robert. "Un colloque sur la démythisation de la morale." *Critique*, 16e année, tome 21, nos. 219-220, Aug.-Sept. 1965, pp. 787-789.

Lacroix, Jean. "Un philosophe du sens: P. Ricoeur," in *Panorama de la philosophie française contemporaine.* Paris: Presses Universitaires de France, 1966, 2nd rev. ed. 1968.

Lemieux, Jacques. "L'idée de fidelité chez Emmanuel Mounier." *Laval Théologique et Philosophique*, vol. 28, Oct. 1972, pp. 219-236.

Littérature et idéologies. Colloque de Cluny 11. April 2, 3, 4, 1970. [Special number of *La Nouvelle Critique*] Paris: La Nouvelle Critique, 1971.

Lowit, Alexandre. "D'où vient l'ambiguité de la phénoménologie?" *Bulletin de la Societé Francaise de Philosophie*, vol. 65, April-June 1972, pp. 3-68.

Madison, Gary Brent. *Sens et existence.* En hommage à Paul Ricoeur. Receuil preparé sous la direction de Gary Brent Madison. (L'ordre philosophique). Paris: Editions du Seuil, 1975.

_____. "Avant Propos," in *Sens et existence*, pp. 7-8.

_____. "Hommage à Paul Ricoeur." *rue Jacob*, vol. 16, no. 185, Avril 1975, p. 27.

_____. "Ricoeur et la non-philosophie." *Laval Théologique et Philosophique*, vol. 29, Oct. 1973, pp. 227-241.

Maqdici, Antoine. "L'ontologie kérymatique de Paul Ricoeur, approche arabe," in Madison, *Sens et existence*, pp. 170-206.

Pohier, Jacques. "An nom du Père . . ." *Esprit*, Mars 1966, pp. 480-500; Avril, 1966, pp. 947-970.

Riggio, Pietro. "Paul Ricoeur et l'herméneutique des mythes." *Dialogue*, vol. 35, nos. 7-8, 1967, pp. 73-89.

Robert, J. D. "Le sort de la philosophie à l'heure des sciences de l'homme." *Revue des Sciences Philosophiques et Théologiques*, vol. 41, Oct. 1967, pp. 573-616.

Sales, Michel. "Un colloque sur le mythe de la peine." *Archives de Philosophie*, vol. 32, Oct.-Dec. 1969, pp. 664-675.

Sarano, Jacques. "La réciprocité du pâtir et de l'agir selon P. Ricoeur." *Les Etudes Philosophiques*, vol. 10, 1955, pp. 726-729.

Schillebeeck, E. "Le philosophe Paul Ricoeur docteur en théologie." *Christianisme Social*, vol. 76, nos. 11-12, 1968, pp. 639-645.

Secrétan, Philibert. "Paradoxe et conciliation dans la philosophie de Paul Ricoeur." *Studia Philosophica*, 1961, pp. 187-198.

_____. "L'interprétation selon M. Paul Ricoeur." *Studia Philosophica*, vol. 25, 1965, pp. 182-198.

S. R. "La Semaine des intellectuals catholiques: Religion critiquée, détruite, ou purifiée." *Le Monde*, no. 8138, March 13, 1971, p. 14.

Tort, Michel. "De l'interprétation ou la machine herméneutique." *Les Temps Modernes*, vol. 21, No. 237, Feb. 1966, pp. 1461-93, no. 238, March 1966, pp. 1629-52.

Tilliette, Xavier. "Réflexion et symbole. L'entreprise philosophique de Paul Ricoeur." *Archives de Philosophie*, vol. 24, 1961, pp. 574-588.

Trotignon, P. *Les Philosophes français d'aujourd'hui*. Paris: Presses Universitaires de France, 1967.

Vansina, Dirk. "Esquisse, orientation et signification de l'enterprise philosophique de Paul Ricoeur." *Revue de Métaphysique et de Morale*, vol. 59, March-July 1964, pp. 179-208; and *ibid.*, vol. 59, July-Oct. 1964, pp. 305-320.

_____. "La problématique épochale chez Paul Ricoeur et l'existentialisme." *Revue Philosophique de Louvain*, vol. 70, Nov. 1972, pp. 587-619.

C) *German*

Bollnow, Otto Friedrich. "Paul Ricoeur und die Probleme der Hermeneutik." (I & II) *Zeitschrift für Philosophische Forschung*, vol. 30, 1976, pp. 167-189, and *Ibid.*, vol. 30, 1976, pp. 389-412.

Dumasy, Annegret. "Paul Ricoeur," in *Restloses Erkennen. Die Diskussion uber den strukturalismus des Claude Lévi-Strauss in Frankreich*. Berlin: Duncker & Humblot, 1972, pp. 155-168.

Französische Kultur. Dokumente 1961. Koln: Verlag der Dokumente, 1961.

Holenstein, E. "Passive Genesis: Eine Begriffsanalytische Studie." *Tijdschrift voor Filosofie*, vol. 33, March 1971, pp. 112-153.

Kemp, Peter. "Phänomenologie und Hermeneutik in der Philosophie Paul Ricoeurs." *Zeitschrift für Theologie und Kirche*, vol. 67, 1970, pp. 335-347.

Leick, Romain. "Die Wahrheit der Existenz, Versuch uber Paul Ricoeur." *Stimmen der Zeit*, Jahrg. 98, Nr. 10, Oct. 1973, pp. 695-709.

Mainberger, Gonsalv. "Die Freiheit und das Böse. Diachronische und synchronische Lektüre der Werke von Paul Ricoeur." *Freiburger Zeitschrift für Philosophie und Theologie*, vol. 19, 1972, pp. 410-430.

Schiwy, Günther. *Neue Aspekte des Strukturalismus*. Munich: Kosel-Verlag, 1971.

Van Peursen, C.A. "Philosophen der Kontingenz." (Thévenaz, Ricoeur, Levinas). *Philosophische Rundschau*, vol. 12, 1964-1965, pp. 1-12.

Waldenfels, Bernard. "Philosophie und Nicht-Philosophie (Frankreich)" *Philosophische Rundschau* 12, 1964, pp. 13-58; pp. 48-58 deal specifically with Ricoeur.

Wyss, Dieter. *Strukturen der Moral. Untersuchungen zur Anthropologie und Genealogie Moralischer Verhaltensweisen*. Gottingen: Vandenhoeck & Ruprecht, 1968.

D) *Italian*

Andreoni, Carlo. "Paul Ricoeur. I: La demistificazione del Dio etico. II: Il superamento del Dio etico." *Ethica*, vol. 11, 1972, pp. 127-149, 173-198.

Crispini, Franco. "Paul Ricoeur e la semantica dell'uomo." *Logos*, no. 1, 1972, pp. 41-72.

Cristaldi, Mariano. "La testimonianze delle maschere. Nota sulla critica ermeneutica di Paul Ricoeur," in *Informazione e testimonianza*, (Archivio di Filosofia), no. 2, 1972, pp. 67-85. Padova: Cedam, 1972.

Dentico, Angela Loredana. "Simbolo e interpretazione in Paul Ricoeur," in *Saggi e ricerche di filosofia*. A cura di Ada Lamacchia. Lecce: Edizioni Milella, 1973, pp. 85-111.

Forni, Guglielmo. *Fenomenologia*. Brentano, Husserl, Scheler, Hartmann, Fink, Landgrebe, Merleau-Ponty, Ricoeur. Milano: Marzorati Editore, 1973, 230 p.

Guzzo, Augusto. "Gli 'entretiens' di Cambridge su l'azione." *Filosofia*, vol. 24, April 1973, pp. 177-200.

Lanisco, Antonella. "Linguaggio sinbolico e filosofia dell 'indagine di Paul Ricoeur." *Giornale di Metafisica*, vol. 23, 1968, pp. 208-218.

Mondin, Battista. *Il problema del linguaggio teologico dalle origini ad oggi.* Brescia: Editrice Queriniana, 1971.

_____. "La filosofia del simbolismo religioso di Paul Ricoeur." *Aquinas*, vol. 14, 1971, pp. 34-48.

Obertello, Luca. "Filosofia e interpretazione." *Filosofia*, vol. 22, Jan. 1971, pp. 97-110.

Paci, Enzo. "Psicanalisi e fenomenologia." *Aut Aut*, no. 92, March 1966, pp. 7-20.

Propati, Giuseppe. "La visione etica di Paul Ricoeur." *Sapienza*, v. 28, July-Sept. 1975, pp. 393-397.

Renzi, Emilio. "Criticismo, fenomenologia e problema della relazione intenzionale secondo P. Ricoeur." *Archivio di Filosofia*, no. 1, 1960, pp. 89-97.

_____. "Ricoeur d l'*Einfuhlung* husserliana." *Il Verri*, no. 4, 1960, pp. 131-138.

_____. "Ricoeur, una fenomenologia della finitezza e del male." *Pensiero*, vol. 5, 1960, pp. 360-371.

Riggio, Pietro. "Storia e verita in Paul Ricoeur." *Dialogo*, vol. 4, 1967, pp. 179-190.

Rigobello, Armando. "Paul Ricoeur e il problema dell 'interpretazione," in *La filosofia dal '45 ad oggi*. A cura di Valerio Verra (Saggi, 65). Torino: ERI, Edizioni RAI Radio-televisione Italiana, 1976, pp. 211-233.

E) *Spanish*

Conclini-Nestor Garcia. "El tiempo en Ricoeur: Acontecimiento y estructura." *Cauardenos de Filosofia*, vol. 10, Jan-June, 1970, pp. 49-61.

Maceiras Fafian, Manuel. "Paul Ricoeur: una ontología militante." *Pensamiento*, vol. 32, 1976, 131-156.

Maceiras, Manuel. "La antropologia hermenéutica de Paul Ricoeur," in *Antropologías del siglo XX*, pp. 125-148. Dirigido por Juan de Sahagun Lucas (Hermeneia, 5). Salamanca: Ed. Siguema 1976. 277 p.

Marchant, Patricio. "Socrates o Sade: una apuesta filosofica." *Dialogos*, no. 22, 1972. [Mainly on Ricoeur's interpretation of Freud.]

Pintor-Ramos, Antonio. "Simbolo, hermeneutica y reflexíon in Paul Ricoeur." *Ciudad de Dios*, vol. 185, 1972, pp. 463-495.

_____. "Paul Ricoeur y el estruturalismo." *Pensamiento*, vol. 31, April-June 1975, pp. 95-123.

Santos, M. "La 'repeticion' filosofica del mito. Introduccion al pensamiento de Paul Ricoeur." *Stromata,* vol. 27, July-Dec 1971, pp. 495-513.

F) *Danish*

Krause-Jensen, Esbern. *Den franske strukturalisme: Pa sporet af en teori for de humane videnskaber.* Copenhagen: Berlingske Forlag, 1973.

G) *Dutch*

Bakker, R. *Het anonieme denken, Foucault en het structuralisme.* Baarn: Het Wereldvenster, 1973 (ch. 6: Jean-Paul Sartre and Ricoeur).

Groot, H. "Paul Ricoeur, Symbolen van het kwaad I & II." *Amersfoortse Stemmen,* Tweenvijftigste jaargang, no. 6, Nov. 1971, pp. 230-231.

Heering, H. J. "Paul Ricoeur," in *Filosofen van de 20e eeuw.* Onder redactie van C.P. Bertels en E. Petersma. Assen, Amsterdam, Van Gorcum; Amsterdam, Brussel, Intermediair, 1972, pp. 141-150.

_____. "Het denken van Paul Ricoeur." *Amersfoortse Stemmen,* Drieenvijftigste jaargang, no. 1, January 1972, pp. 31-33.

_____. "Paul Ricoeur—ter introductie." *Amersfoortse Stemmen,* Tweenvijftigste, no. 6, Nov. 1971, pp. 211-219.

_____. "Paul Ricoeur als godsdienst-wijsgeer." *Nederl. Theol. Tijdschr.,* vol. 25, 1971, pp. 437-453.

Van Bergen, J. "Het Symbool gleeft te denken. Een studie in Ricoeur." *Tijdschrift voor Theologie,* vol. 13, 1973, pp. 166-188. (Summary: A study of symbolism in Paul Ricoeur, pp. 188-189.)

Vandenbulcke, J. "Het taalbegrip van de strukturele linguistiek en zijn vooropstellingen." *Tijdschrift voor Filosofie,* vol. 32, no. 4, Dec. 1970, pp. 614-650.

Vansina, Dirk. Review of *Politick en gelof. Essays gekozen . . . door A. Peperzak* (1969). *Tijdschrift voor Filosofie,* vol. 31, 1969, pp. 162-164.

_____. "Schets, orientatie en betekenins van Paul Ricoeur's wijsgerige onderneming." *Tijdschrift voor Filosofie,* vol. 25, 1963, pp. 109-178. (Summary: Sketch, orientation and significance of Paul Ricoeur's philosophical enterprise." pp. 178-182.)

Wylleman, A. "Paul Ricoeur. Eindigheid en schuld: Die grenzen van een ethische wereldbeschouwung." *Tijdschrift voor Filosofia,* 1961, pp. 527-546.

Zuidema, S.U. "Oorspronkelite affirmatie en theologische eschatologie en Paul Ricoeur's denken, speciall in zyn *Histoire et vérité.*" *Philosophia Reformata,* vol. 31, 1965, pp. 113-136.

IV   *REVIEWS AND CRITICAL NOTICES*

A) *Karl Jaspers et la philosophie de l'existence* (M. Dufrenne & P. Ricoeur)
Wahl, Jean.— *Critique,* vol. 4, no. 25, 1948, 523-530.

B) *Gabriel Marcel et Karl Jaspers*
Dufrenne, Mikel—*Esprit,* 17e annee, no. 156, juin, 1949, 903-905

C) *Philosophie de la volonte,* I

Anonymous.—*Revue de Metaphysique et de Morale,* 1953, 441-443.

Anonymous.—"Un philosophe de la volonté: Paul Ricoeur." *Regards sur la philosophie contemporaine* (Paris-Tournal: Casterman, 1956). 147-151.

Brisbois, E.—*Nouvelle Revue Théologique,* 1952, 320-321.

Burgelin, Pierre.—*Revue de Theologie et de Philosophie,* 3e serie, tome XI, no. 11, 1961, 150-161.

Burloud, A.—*Revue Philosophique de la France et de l'Etranger,* 1954, 282-285.

Creegan, R.F.—*Philosophy and Phenomenological Research,* vol. 28, 1968, 608-610.

Daly, J.—*Philosophical Studies* (Maynooth), vol. 17, 1968, 325-328.

Ehman, R.R.—*Man and World,* vol. 2, 1969, 310-318.

Epstein, Fanny.—*Philosophy Today,* vol. 11, Spring 1967, 38-46.

Embree, L.—*Social Research,* vol. 35, 1968, 565-570.

Geiger, L.B.—*Revue des Sciences Philosophiques et Théologiques,* 1954, 296-297.

Kohak, E.V.—"The philosophy of Paul Ricoeur," translator's introduction *Freedom* and *Nature: The voluntary and the involuntary.* Evanston, Ill.: Northwestern University Press, 1966.

Kopper, J.—*Philosophische Literaturzeiger,* 1952, 79-84.

Lacroix, Jean.—"Philosophie de la volonté." *Christianisme Social* 59. Mars, 1951, 246-249.

Medina, A.—*New Scholasticism,* vol. 42, 1968, 155-159.

Mindan, M.—Revista de Filosofia (Madrid), 1954, 340-344.

Nedoncelle, Maurice.—*Revue des Sciences Religieuses,* 1951, 331-333.

Strasser, S.—*Annalen van het Genootschap voor Wetenschappelijke Philosophie,* 1951, 1952, 89-94.

Vander Gucht, R.—*La Revue Nouvelle,* 1961, 294-306.

Warnock, Mary.—*Philosophical Quarterly,* vol. 17, 1967, 279-280.

D) *Histoire et verité*

Anonymous.—*Revue de metaphysique et de Morale,* 1959, 245-246.

Boas, George.—*History and Theory,* vol. 6, 1967, 265-270.

Czarnecki, J.—"L'histoire et la vérité selon P. Ricoeur." *Foi et Vie,* vol. 53, no. 6, 1955, 548-555.

Dumas, J.L.—*Les Etudes Philosophiques,* 1955, 528-529.

Dupre, Louis.—*New Scholasticism,* vol. 45, 1971, 147-149.

Heering, H.J.—*Nederlands Theologisch Tijdschrift,* vol. 26, 1972, 108-111.

Kelbley, Charles A.—"Translator's introduction," *to History and Truth.* Evanston, Ill.: Northwestern University Press, 1965.

Taylor, Charles.—*Journal of Philosophy,* vol. 65, 1968, 401-403.

Tonnard, F.J.—*Revue des Etudes Augustiennes,* 1957, 499-501.

Widmer, G.—*Revue des Theologie et Philosophie,* 1956, 156-157.

E) *Philosophie de la volonté, II*

Czarnecki, Jan.—"Finitude et culpabilité d'après Paul Ricoeur." *Christianisme social* 70, Janvier-Février, 1962, 85-92.

D'Agostino, Fr.—*Rivista Internazionale de Filosofia del Diritto*, vol. 48, 1971, 396-397. [*Finitudine e colpa*]

Dreyfus, Dina.—*Mercure de France*. Vol. 341, Avril, 1961, 737-744.

Fisher, Alden L.—*The Modern Schoolman*, vol. 47, 1969-70, 142-143. [*The Symbolism of Evil*]

Hick, John.—*Theology Today*, vol. 24, no. 4, 1969, 5-6. [*The Symbolism of Evil*]

Keen, Sam.—*The Christian Century*, LXXXIV, no. 32, Aug. 9, 1967, 1023. [*The Symbolism of Evil*]

Poncelet, Albert.—*International Philosophical Quarterly* 1, 1961, 713-724.

Renzi, Emilio.—"Paul Ricoeur, Una Fenomenologia della finitezza e del male." *Il Pensiero* 5, 360-371.

Ruyssen, Theodore.—"La notion de culpabilité. A propos d'un livre récent." *Revue de la France et de l'étranger* 153, 1963, 85-100.

Ryan, Michael.—*Dialogue*, vol. ii, Dec. 1972, 666-668. [*The Symbolism of Evil*]

Rutsche, J.—*Philosophisches Jahrbuch*, vol. 80, 1973, 415-422. [Phenomenology der Schuld, I-II]

E.A.R.—*Review of Metaphysics*, vol. 22, 1968-69, 763-764.

Stack, George J.—*Man and World*, vol. 1, 1968, 626-635. [*The Symbolism of Evil*]

Stinnette, G.—*Journal of Religion*, vol. 46, 1966, 60-61. [*Fallible Man*]

Waelhens, Alphonse de.—"Pensée mythique et philosophie de mal." *Revue Philosophique de Louvain*, vol. 59, 1961, 315-347.

F) *De l'Interpretation. Essai sur Freud*

Beirnaert, Louis.—*Etudes*, no. 323, 1965, 49-52.

Bertherat, M.—*Esprit*, vol. 34, 1966, 466-479.

Bourke, Vernon J.—*The Modern Schoolman*, vol. 50, March 1973, 318-322.

Bres, Y.—*Revue Philosophique de la France et de l'Etranger*, vol. 94, 1969, 425-429.

Chazaud, J.—*Revue Francaise de Psychanalyse*, vol. 31, 1967, 499-500.

Ellenberger, Henri—*Dialogue*, vol. 5, no. 2, Sept. 1966, 256-266.

Gajano, Alberto.—"Psicanalisi e fenomenologia nel saggio su Freud di P. Ricoeur." *Giornale Critica della Filosofia Italiana*, vol. 49, 1970, 406-432.

Gargiulo, Gerald J.—"A modern dialogue with Freud." *The Psychoanalytic Review*, vol. 58, no. 2, Summer 1971, 295-302.

Grolnick, Simon A.—"Freud and philosophy." *The Psychoanalytic Quarterly*, vol. 41, no. 3, 1972, 435-443.

Ihde, Don.—*International Philosophical Quarterly*, vol. 12, March 1972, 138-139.

Ijsseling, Samuel—"Paul Ricoeur en Sigmund Freud." *Tijdschrift voor Filosofie*, vol. 30, Dec. 1966, 695-714.

Jervis, G.—"Note su alcuni libri di psicoanalisi." *Quarderni Piacentini*, vol. 28, Sept. 1966, 98-108.

Julien, Philippe.—*Archives de Philosophie*, vol. 29, 1966, 620-626.

Lang, H.—*Psyche* (Heidelberg), vol. 21, 1967, 468-470.

Lichetenstein, Heinz.—*Philosophy and Phenomenological Research,* vol. 32, March 1972, 412-413.

Llamzon, B.S.—*Thought,* vol. 46, 1971, 628-632.

Marchant, P.—*Dialogos,* no. 8, 1972, 107-137.

Moloney, Robert.—*Heythrop Journal,* vol. 13, Jan. 1972, 80-85.

Pettit, Philip.—*Philosophical Studies* (Maynooth), vol. 21, 1972, 236-243.

Pohier, J.M.—*Esprit,* vol. 34, no. 3, 1966, 480-500, and *Ibid.,* vol. 34, no. 4, 1966, 947-970.

Reider, Norman.—*Journal of the History of the Behavioral Sciences,* vol. 8, no. 1, Jan. 1972, 142-144.

Renzi, Emilio.—"Freud e Ricoeur." *Aut Aut,* no. 98, 1967, 7-51.

Ricardi, F.—"Una interpretazione di Freud." *Psicoterapia e Scienze Umane,* Jan.-March 1968, 8-13.

Rütsche, J.—*Philosophisches Jahrbuch,* vol. 78, 1971, 401-422.

Scherer, R.—*Critique,* vol. 21, 1965, 1052-1067.

———.—*Journal de Psychologie Normale et Pathologique,* vol. 63, 1966, 119-121.

Slaughter, John W.—*International Journal of Philosophy of Religion,* vol. 3, Spring 1972, 356-358.

Stack, George J.—*The Modern Schoolman,* vol. 50, 1972-1973, 318-322.

Valabrega, J.P.—*Critique,* vol. 22, 1966, 68-78.

Vivas, Eliseo.—*Journal of Value Inquiry,* vol. 5, Winter 1971, 310-314.

Waelhens, Alphonse de.—"La force du langage et le langage de la force." *Revue Philosophique de Louvain,* vol. 63, 1965, 591-612.

Warnock, Mary.—"Signs and symbols." *New Society,* vol. 16, no. 412, Aug., 20, 1970, 335-336.

G) *Husserl. An Analysis of his Phenomenology.*

Ballard, E.G. & Embree, L.E.—"Translators' Foreword" to *Husserl. An Analysis of his Phenomenology.* Evanston, Ill.: Northwestern University Press.

Daly, James.—*Philosophical Studies* (Maynooth), vol. 20, 1972, 310-312.

Dupré, Louis.—*New Scholasticism,* vol. 45, 1971, 149-152.

Edie, James M.—*Journal of Philosophy,* vol. 64, 1968, 403-409.

H) *Entretiens. P. Ricoeur et G. Marcel.*

F.-L.L.—*Dialogue,* vol. 7, 1968-69, 706.

Sales, Michel—*Archives de Philosophie,* vol. 32, Oct.-Dec. 1969, 692-694.

I) *The Religious Significance of Atheism. Ricoeur & MacIntyre.*

Flew, Antony.—*Inquiry,* vol. 12, Winter 1969, 469-473.

Phillips, D.Z.—*Philosophical Quarterly,* vol. 21, Jan. 1971, 93.

J) *Le Conflit des interprétations*

Bernard-Maitre, H.—*Revue des Sciences,* vol. 92, 1971, 105-106.

Brés, Y.— *Revue Philosophique de la France et de l'Etranger,* vol. 94, 1969, 425-429.

Capuzzi, Frank.— *Research in Phenomenology,* vol. 1, 1971, 157-161.

Clemens, Eric.— *Critique,* no. 277, Juin 1970, 546-555.

Corvez, Maurice— *Revue Thomiste,* vol. 70, 1970, 651-654.

Gisel, Pierre.— *Esprit,* vol. 38, no. 397, Nov. 1970, 776-784.

Hebert, R.— *Dialogue,* vol. 10, Mars 1971, 179-181.

Kuzminski, A.— *Salmagundi,* no. 36, Winter 1977, 124-132.

Lacroix, Jean.— *Le Monde* [*des Livres*], no. 7846, 5-6 Avril 1970, 15.

Lascault, Gilbert.— *Revue d'Esthétique,* vol. 23, Avril-Juin 1970, 216-218.

Levin, David M.— *Philosophical Review,* vol. 85, April 1976, 267-270.

Margolin, J.-C.— *Les Etudes Philosophiques,* no. 2, 1970, 247-248.

Riefstahl, H.— *Zeitschrift für Philosophische Forschung,* vol. 25, 1971, 631-663.

Tilliette, Xavier.— *Les Etudes,* Octobre 1970, 457.

Vincent, G.— *Revue d'Histoire et de Philosophie Religieuses,* 1971, vol. 51, 222-225.

Watté, Pierre.— *La Revue Nouvelle,* 26e année, LII, nos. 7-8, Juillet-Août 1970, 104-106.

K) *La Métaphore vive*

Brisson, Luc.— *Dialogue* (Canada) vol. 15, no. 1, Mar. 1976, 133-147.

Petit, Maria da Pena.— *Revue de Métaphysique et de Morale,* 81e année, no. 2, Avril-Juin 1976, 271-276.

Reagan, Charles.— *International Philosophical Quarterly,* vol. 16, no. 4, Dec. 1976, 359-362.

Steiner, George.— *Times Literary Supplement,* no. 38, August 1, 1975, p. 879.

V BIBLIOGRAPHY

of Ricoeur

Vansina, Frans Dirk. "Bibliographie de Paul Ricoeur." *Revue Philosophique de Louvain,* vol. 60, Aug. 1962, 394-414 and *Ibid.* vol. 66, Feb. 1968, 85-101 and *Ibid.* vol. 72, Feb., 1974, 156-181.

on Ricoeur

Lapointe, François H.—"A bibliography on Paul Ricoeur." *Philosophy Today,* vol. 16, no. 1, Spring 1972, 28-33; and *Ibid.,* vol. 17, no. 2, Summer 1973, 176-182.

XI

Frans Vansina

BIBLIOGRAPHY OF PAUL RICOEUR

This is a selective bibliography of Ricoeur's works, listing primarily his philosophical work in English or French and likely to be found in major U.S. libraries. Thus, articles issued in less widely known or not easily accessible periodicals are not listed here. Only English translations are included.

Frans D. Vansina is Lecturer in philosophy at the University of Louvain, Louvain, Belgium. He has previously published a virtually complete bibliography of Ricoeur's work (to 1972) in *Revue Philosophique du Louvain*. He is continuing to compile the bibliography.

Bibliography of Paul Ricoeur

Frans D. Vansina

This bibliography is selective, and only lists the main publications of Paul Ricoeur from the beginning through 1976. The aim is not to reproduce in English the quasi-exhaustive "Bibliographie de Paul Ricoeur" which I have already published in *Revue philosophique de Louvain* 60 (1962), August, 394-413; 66 (1968), February, 85-101; 72 (1974), February, 156-181. The point is only to offer a reasonably complete list of Ricoeur's writings which are likely to be available in larger U.S. libraries. Therefore, articles issued in less widely known or not easily accessible periodicals are not listed here. Only English translations of Ricoeur's publications are reported.

All entries are numbered and presented in chronological order. The title of a book is followed by the name of the collection to which it belongs. As for articles, the sequence of citations runs as follows: volume, year of publication, number of the issue, and pagination. Finally, the following abbreviations are used:

HT: History and Truth (1965)

H: Husserl. An Analysis of His Phenomenology (1967)

CI: The Conflict of Interpretations (1974)

PSE: Political and Social Essays (1974)

1947

1. DUFRENNE M. AND RICOEUR P., *Karl Jaspers et la philosophie de l'existence* (Esprit). Preface to K. JASPERS, Paris, Seuil, 1947, 399 p. (The pages from 173 through 393 represent the contribution of Paul Ricoeur.)
2. *Gabriel Marcel et Karl Jaspers. Philosophie du mystère et philosophie du paradoxe* (Artistes et écrivains du temps présent), Paris, Temps Présent, 1947, 455 p.

1948

3. *Pour un christianisme prophétique,* in "Les chrétiens et la politique (Dialogues)" Paris, Temps Présent, 1948, 79-100.
4. *Dimensions d'une recherche commune,* in "Esprit" 16 (1948), December, 837-846.
5. *La pensée engagée. M. Merleau-Ponty. Humanisme et terreur,* in "Esprit" 16 (1948), December, 911-916.

1949

6. *Le renouvellement du probleme de la philosophie chrétienne par les philosophies de l'existence,* in "Le problème de la philosophie chrétienne (Les Problèmes de la Pensèe Chrétienne)" Paris, Presses Universitaires de France, 1949, 43-67.

7. *Husserl et le sens de l'histoire,* in "Revue de métaphysique et de morale" 54 (1949). 280-316. July-October, 280-316. English translation in H.

8. *L'homme non violent et sa présence à l'histoire,* in "Esprit (Révision du pacifisme)" 17 (1949), February, 224-234. English translation in HT.

1950

9. *Philosophie de la volonté: I. Le volontaire et l'involontaire* (Philosophie de l'esprit), Paris, Aubier, 1950, 464 p. English translation by no. 111.

10. HUSSERL E., *Ideés directrices pour une phénoménologie*(Bibliothèque de philosophie). Translation of *Ideen I* with an introduction and notes by P. RICOEUR, Paris, Gallimard, 1950, XXXIX-567 p. The English translation of the introduction in H.

11. *Une philosophie personnalistè* [on E. MOUNIER], in "Esprit (Emmanuel Mounier)" 18 (1950), December, 860-887. English translation in HT.

1951

12. *L'unité de volontaire et de l'involontaire,* in "Bulletin de la Société française de Philosophie" 45 (1951), January-March, 3-22. English translation by no. 127.

13. *Analyses et problèmes dans Ideen II de Husserl,* in "Revue de métaphysique et de morale" 56 (1951), October-December, 357-394. English translation in H.

14. RICOEUR P. and DOMENACH J. M., *Masse et personne,* in "Esprit" 19 (1951), January, 9-18. English translation by no. 24.

15. *Pour une coexistence pacifique des civilisations,* in "Esprit (La paix possible)" 19 (1951), March, 408-419. English translation by no. 101.

16. *Réflexion sur "Le diable et le bon Dieu,"* in "Esprit" 19 (1951), November, 711-719. English translation by no. 44.

17. *Vérité et mensonge,* in "Esprit" 19 (1951), December, 753-778. English translation in HT.

18. *Le christianisme et la sens de l'histoire. Progrès, ambiguité, espérance,* in "Christianisme social" 59 (1951), April, 261-274. English translation by no. 25 and in HT.

1952

19. *Histoire de la philosophie et sociologie de la connaissance,* in "L'homme et l'histoire. Actes du VIe Congrés des Sociétés de philosophie de langue française" Paris, Presses Universitaires de France, 1952, 341-346. English translation in HT.

20. *Méthodes et tâches d'une phénoménologie de la volonté,* in "Problèmes actuels de la phénoménologie (Textes et écrits philosophiques)" edited by H.

L. VAN BREDA, Bruges-Paris, Desclée de Brouwer, 1952, 110-140. English translation in H.

21. *Analyses et problèmes dans Ideen II de Husserl*[continuation], in "Revue de métaphysique et de morale" 57 (1952), January-March, 1-16. English translation in H.

22. *Le temps de Jean-Baptiste et le temps de Galilée* [on P. MONTUCLARD, *Les événements et la foi*], in "Esprit" 20 (1952), May, 864-871.

23. *Propositions de compromis pour l'Allemagne*, in "Esprit (Misère de la psychiatrie)" 20 (1952) December, 1006-1011.

24. RICOEUR P. and DOMENACH J. M., *Mass and Person*, in "Cross Currents" 2 (1952), Winter, 59-66. English translation of no. 14.

25. *Christianity and the Meaning of History. Progress, Ambiguity, Hope*, in "Journal of Religion" 21 (1952), 242-253. English translation of no. 18 and reprinted in HT.

26. *L'homme de science et l'homme de foi*, in "Le Semeur" 50 (1952), November, 12-22. English translation in HT.

1953

27. *Analyses et problèmes dans Ideen II de Husserl*, in "Phénoménologie-Existence (Revue de métaphysique et de morale)" Paris, A. Colin, 1953, 23-76. English translation in H.

28. *Geschichte der Philosophie als kontinuierliche Schöpfung der Menschheit auf dem Wege der Kommunikation*, in "Offener Horizont (Festschrift für Karl Jaspers zum 70. Geburtstag)" edited by K. PIPER, Munich, 1953, 110-125. English translation in HT.

29. *Vraie et fausse angoisse*, in "L'angoisse du temps present et les devoirs de l'esprit (Recontres internationales de Genève 1953)" Neuchâtel, La Baconnière, 1953, 33-53. English translation in HT.

30. *Culpabilité tragique et culpabilité biblique*, in "Revue d'histoire et de philosophie religieuses" 33 (1953), no. 4, 285-307.

31. *Travail et parole,* in "Esprit (Esprit a vingt ans)" 21 (1953), January, 96-117. English translation in HT.

32. *Sur la phénoménologie. I* [on TRAN-DUC-THAO, *Phénoménologie et matérialisme dialectique*], in "Esprit" 21 (1953), December, 821-829. English translation by no. 208.

33. *L'homme de science et l'homme de foi*, in "Recherches et Débats (Pensée scientifique et foi chrétienne)" 2 (1953), no. 4, 77-88. Partial English translation in HT.

34. *Objectivité et subjectivité en histoire*, in "Revue de l'enseignement philosophique" 3 (1953), July-September, 28-40. English translation in HT.

1954

35. BREHIER E., *Histoire de la philosophie allemande* (Bibliothèque d'histoire de la philosophie). Third edition of *Histoire de la philosophie allemande* by E. BREHIER with an introduction and appendix devoted to some contemporary philosophers by P. RICOEUR, Paris, Vrin, 1954, 181-258. The English text of Ricoeur on Husserl is published in H.

36. *La relation à autrui. Le socius et le prochain*, in "L'amour du prochain (Cahiers de vie spirituelle)" Paris, Cerf, 1954, 293-310. English translation by no. 46 and in HT.

37. *Sympathie et respect. Phénoménologie et éthique de la seconde personne*, in "Revue de metaphysique et de morale" 59 (1954), 380-397.

38. *Etude sur les "Méditaitons Cartésiennes" de Husserl*, in "Revue philosophique de Louvain" 52 (1954), no. 1, 75-109. English translation in H.

39. *L'histoire de la philosophie et l'unité du vrai*, in "Revue internationale de philosophie" 8 (1954), no. 29, 266-282. English translation in HT.

40. *Kant et Husserl*, in "Kant-Studien" 46 (1954-1955), no. 1, 44-67. English translation in H and by no. 121.

41. *Philosophies de la personne. I. "L'existence d'autrui"* [de M. CHASTAING], in "Exprit" 22 (1954), February, 289-297.

42. *"Morale sans péché" ou péché sans morale?* [on A. HESNARD, *Morale sans péché*], in "Esprit" 22 (1954), August-September, 394-312. English translation by no. 52.

43. *Subjectivité et Objectivité en Histoire*, in "Les Amis de Sèvres. Bulletin d'information" 6 (1954), June, 5-21. English translation in HT.

44. *Sartre's Lucifer and the Lord*, in "Yale French Studies" 1954-55, no. 14, 85-93. English translation of no. 16.

1955

45. *Histoire et Vérité* (Esprit), Paris, Seuil, 1955, 289 p. English translation by HT.

46. *"Associate" and neighbour*, in "Love of our Neighbour" London, Blackfriars Publications, 1955, no. 8, 149-161. English translation of no. 36.

47. *La parole est mon royaume*, in "Esprit (Réforme de l'enseignement)" 23 (1955), February, 192-205.

48. *Sur la phénoménologie. II. Le "Problème de l'âme"* [by S. STRASSER], in "Esprit (Le monde des prisons)" 23 (1955), April, 721-726.

49. *Philosophie et Ontologie. Retour à Hegel* [on J. HYPPOLITE, *Logique et existence*. Essai sur la logique de Hegel], in "Esprit" 23 (1955), August, 1378-1391.

50. *Aux frontières de la philosophie. II. Philosophie et prophétisme* [on A. NEHER, *L'essence du prophétisme*], in "Esprit" 23 (1955), December, 1928-1939.

51. *Vraie et fausse paix,* in "Christianisme social" 63 (1955), September-October, 467-479.

52. *"Morality Without Sin" or Sin Without Moralism*, in "Cross Currents" 5 (1955), Fall, 339-352. English translation of no. 42.

53. *French Protestantism Today*, in "The Christian Century" 72 (1955), 26 October, 1236-1238.

1956

54. GUARDINI R., *La mort de Socrate*. Translation of *Der Tod des Sokrates* by P. RICOEUR, Paris, Seuil, 1956, 269 p.

55. *Négativité et affirmation originaire*, in "Aspects de la dialectique

(Recherches de philosophie)" Bruges-Paris, Desclée de Brouwer, 1956, 101-124. English translation in HT.

56. *Que signifie "humanisme"?*, in "Comprendre. Revue de la société européenne de culture (L'humanisme d'aujourd'hui)" 1956, no. 15, 84-92. English translation in PSE.

57. *Certitudes et incertitudes d'une révolution*, in "Esprit" 24 (1956), January, 5-28.

1957

58. *The State and Coercion*, Geneva, John Knox House, 1957, 16 p. Reproduced in HT.

59. *Phénoménologie existentielle*, in "Encyclopédie française XIX. Philosophie et religion" Paris, Larousse, 1957, 19.10-8 through 19.10-12.

60. *Renouveau de l'ontologie*, in "Encyclopédie française XIX. Philosophie et religion" Paris, Larousse, 1957, 19.16-15 through 19.18-3.

61. *The Relation of Jaspers' Philosophy to Religion*, in "The Philosophy of Karl Jaspers. A Critical Analysis and Evaluation (Library of Living Philosophers)" edited by P.A. SCHILPP, Stuttgart, Kohlhammer, 1957, 604-635.

62. *Un philosophe protestant. Pierre Thévenaz*, in "Esprit" 25 (1957), January, 40-53.

63. *Le "Traité de Métaphysique" de Jean Wahl*, in "Esprit" 25 (1957), March, 529-540.

64. *La paradoxe politique*, in "Esprit (Le temps de la réflexion)" 25 (1957), May, 721-745. English translation in HT.

65. *"L'essai sur le Mal" de Jean Nabert*, in "Esprit" 25 (1957), July-August, 124-135.

66. *La "philosophie politique" d'Eric Weil*, in "Esprit" 25 (1957), October, 412-429.

67. *Faith and Culture*, in "The Student World (The Greatness and Misery of the Intellectual)" 50 (1957), 246-251. Reprint in PSE.

1958

68. *Perplexités sur Israël*, in "Esprit" 26 (1958), June, 868-876.

69. *Les aventures de l'Etat et la tâche des chrétiens*, in "Christianisme social" 66 (1958), June-July, 452-463. English translation in PSE.

70. *Ye Art the Salt of the Earth*, in "The Ecumenical Review" 10 (1958), 264-276. Reprint in PSE.

1959

71. *Le sentiment*, in "Edmund Husserl 1859-1959. Recueil commémoratif (Phaenomenologica)" The Hague, Nijhoff, 1959, 260-274.

72. *"Le symbole donne à penser"*, in "Esprit" 27 (1959), July-August, 60-76. English translation by no. 76.

73. *De marxisme au communisme contemporain*, in "Christianisme social" 67 (1959), March, 151-159. English translation in PSE.

1960

74. *Philosophie de la volonté. Finitude et Culpabilité. I. L'homme faillible*
(Philosophie de l'esprit), Paris, Aubier, 1960, 164 p. English translation by
no. 104.

75. *Philosophie de la volonté. Finitude et Culpabilité. II. La symbolique du mal*
(Philosophie de l'esprit), Paris, Aubier, 1960, 323 p. English translation by
no. 123 and 147.

76. *The Symbol: Food for Thought*, in "Philosophy Today" 1960, Fall, 196-207.
English translation of no. 72.

77. *La sexualité. La merveille, l'errance, l'énigme*, in "Esprit (La sexualité)" 28
(1960), November, 1665-1676. English translation by no. 102.

78. *"L'image de Dieu" et l'épopée humaine*, in "Christianisme social" 68 (1960),
July-August, 493-514. English translation by no. 86 and in HT.

79. *Le "Péché Originel": étude de signification*, in "Eglise et Théologie. Bulletin
trimestriel de la Faculté de Théologie Protestante de Paris" 23 (1960),
December, 11-30. English translation in CI.

80. *L'antinomie de la réalité humaine et le problème de l'anthropologie
philosophique*, in "Il Pensiero" 5 (1960), no. 3, 273-290. English translation
by no. 128.

1961

81. *Histoire de la philosophie et historicité*, in "L'histoire et ses interprétations.
Entretiens autour de A. TOYNBEE (Congrès et Colloques. Centre culturel
international de Cerisy-la-Salle, 1958)" Paris-The Hague, Mouton, 214-227.
English translation in HT.

82. *Hermeneutique des symboles et reflexion philosophique*, in "Archivio di
Filosofia ((Il problema della Demitizzazione, Rome 1961)" 31 (1961), no. 1-
2, 51-73. English translation by no. 91 and in CI.

83. *Philosophie, sentiment et poésie. La notion d'a priori selon Mikel Dufrenne*,
in "Esprit" 29 (1961), March, 504-512. English translation by no. 113.

84. *Civilization universelle et cultures nationales*, in "Esprit" 29 (1961), October,
439-453. English translation in HT.

85. *Le socialisme aujourd'hui*, in "Christianisme social" 69 (1961), July-August,
450-460. English translation in PSE.

86. *"The Image of God" and the Epic of Man*, in "Cross Currents" 11 (1961),
Winter, 37-50. English translation of no. 78 and reproduced in HT.

1962

87. *Nature et liberté*, in "Existence et Nature. (Actes du XIe Congrès des Sociétes
de philosophie de langue française, 1961)" Paris, Presses Universitaires de
France, 1962, 125-137. English translation in PSE.

88. *Herméneutique et réflexion*, in "Archivio di Filosofia (Demitizzazione e
immagine, Rome 1962)" 32 (1962), no. 1-2, 19-34. English translation in CI.

89. *L'acte et le signe selon Jean Nabert*, in "Les études philosophiques (Jean
Nabert)" 17 (1962), July-September, 339-349. English translation in CI.

90. *L'Humanité de l'Homme. Contribution de la Philosophie Française
contemporaine"* in "Studium generale" 15 (1962), no. 5, 309-323.

91. *The Hermeneutics of Symbols and Philosophical Reflection*, in "International Philosophical Quarterly" 2 (1962), no. 2, 191-218. English translation of no. 82 and reproduced in CI.

1963

92. *Symbolique et temporalité*, in "Archivio di Filosofia (Ermeneutica e tradizione, Rome 1963)" no. 33 (1963), no. 1, 5-31. English translation in CI.
93. *Kierkegaard et le mal*, in "Revue de théologie et de philosophie" 13 (1963), no. 4, 292-302.
94. *Philosopher après Kierkegaard*, in "Revue de théologie et de philosophie" 13 (1963), no. 4, 303-316.
95. *Le conflit des herméneutiques: épistémologie des interprétations*, in "Cahiers internationaux de symbolisme" 1 (1963), no. 1, 152-184.
96. *Faith and Action: A Christian Point of View. A Christian must rely on his Jewish memory*, in "Criterion" 2 (1963), no. 3, 10-15.

1964

97. *Histoire et vérité* (Esprit). Second and enlarged edition, Paris, Seuil, 1964, 336 p. English translation by HT.
98. *Technique et non-technique dans l'interprétation*, in "Archivio di Filosofia (Tecnica e casistica, Rome 1964)" 34 (1964), no. 1, 23-27. English translation in CI.
99. *Le symbolisme et l'explication structurale*, in "Cahiers internationaux de Symbolisme" 2 (1964), no. 4, 81-96.
100. *Faire l'Université*, in "Esprit (Faire l'université)" 32 (1964), May-June, 1162-1172.
101. *The historical presence of non-violence*, in "Cross Currents" 14 (1964), Winter, 15-23. English translation of no. 15.
102. *The Dimensions of Sexuality*, in "Cross Currents (Sexuality in the Modern World)" 34, 14 (1964), Spring, 133-141. English translation of no. 77.

1965

103. *De l'interprétation. Essai sur Freud* (L'ordre philosophique), Paris, Seuil, 1965, 434 p. English translation by no. 158.
104. *Fallible Man*. Translation of *L'homme faillible* by CH. KELBLEY, Chicago, Henry Regnery, 1965, XXIX-224 p. English translation of no. 74.
105. *History and Truth* (Northwestern University Studies in Phenomenology and Existential Philosophy). Translation of *Histoire et vérité* with an introduction by CH. KELBLEY, Evanston (Illinois), Northwestern University Press, 1965, XXXIV-333 p. Abbreviation: HT. English translation of no. 45 and no. 97.
106. *La psychanalyse et le mouvement de la culture contemporaine*, in "Traité de psychanalyse. I. Histoire" Paris, Presses Universitaires de France" 1965, 79-109. English translation in CI.
107. *Existence et herméneutique*, in "Interpretation der Welt. Festschrift für

Romano Guardini zum achtzigsten Geburtstag" edited by H. KUHN, H. KAHLEFELD and K. FORSTER, Würzburg, Im Echter-Verlag, 1965, 32-51. English translation in CI.

108. *Démythiser l'accusation*, in "Archivio di Filosofia (Demitizzazione e morale)" 35 (1965), no. 1, 49-65. English translation in CI.

109. *Tâches de l'éducateur politique*, in "Esprit (Amérique latine et conscience chrétienne)" 33 (1965), July-August, 78-93. English translation by no. 193 and in PSE.

110. *De la nation à l'humanité: tâche des chrétiens*, in "Christianisme social" 73 (1965), September-December, 493-512. English translation in PSE.

1966

111. *Freedom and Nature. The Voluntary and the Involuntary* (Northwestern University Studies in Phenomenology and Existential Philosophy). English translation of *Le Volontaire et l'involontaire* by E. V. KOHAK, Evanston (Illinois), Northwestern University Press, 1966, XL-498 p. English translation of no. 9.

112. *Le conscient et l'inconscient*, in "L'Inconscient (VIe Colloque de Bonneval) (Bibliothèque Neuro-Psychiatrique de Langue Française) directed by H. EY, Paris, Desclée de Brouwer, 1966, 409-422. English translation in CI.

113. DUFRENNE M., *The Notion of A Priori* (Northwestern University Studies in Phenomenology and Existential Philosophy). Translation of *La notion a priori* by E. CASEY with a preface by P. RICOEUR, Evanston (Illinois), Northwestern University Press, 1966, IX-XVII. English translation of no. 83.

114. *L'université nouvelle*, in "L'éducation dans un Québec en évolution (Publications de la faculté des Sciences de l'Education de l'université de Laval)" Québec, Les Presses de l'université Laval, 1966, 231-245.

115. *Une interprétation philosophique de Freud*, in "Bulletin de la Société française de Philosophie" 60 (1966), no. 3, 73-89. English translation in CI.

116. *Le problème du "double"-sens comme problème herméneutique et comme problème sémantique*, in "Cahiers internationaux de symbolisme" 1966, no. 12, 59-71. English translation in CI and by no. 153.

117. *Le projet d'une morale sociale*, in "Christianisme social" 74 (1966), May-August, 285-295. English translation in PSE.

118. *L'Athéisme de la psychanalyse freudienne*, in "Concilium (Problèmes frontières)" 2 (1966) no. 16, 73-82. American and British edition by no. 119 and 120.

119. *The Atheism of Freudian Psychoanalysis*, in "Concilium (Is God dead?) 3 2 (1966), no. 16, 59-72. American edition of no. 118.

120. *The Atheism of Freudian Psychoanalysis*, in "Concilium (Church and World)" 2 (1966), no. 2, 31-37. British edition of no. 118.

121. *Kant and Husserl*, in "Philosophy Today" 10 (1966), no. 3/4, 147-168. English translation of no. 40 and reproduced in H.

122. *A Conversation* [with P. Ricoeur], in "The Bulletin of Philosophy" 1 (1966), no. 1, 1-8.

1967

123. *The Symbolism of Evil* (Religious Perspectives). Translation of *La symbolique du mal* by E. BUCHANAN, New York-Evanston-London, Harper and Row, 1967, XV-357 p. English translation of no. 75.

124. *Husserl. An Analysis of His Phenomenology* (Studies in Phenomenology and Existential Philosophy). Translation of several writings of P. RICOEUR with an introduction by E. G. BALLARD and L. E. EMBREE, Evanston (Illinois), Northwestern University Press, 1967, XXII-238 p. Abbreviation: H.

125. *Philosophy of Will and Action* [exposition followed by a discussion with F. KERSTEN, and others], in "Phenomenology of Will and Action (The Second Lexington Conference on Pure and Applied Phenomenology, 1964)" edited by E. W. STRAUS and R. M. GRIFFITH, Pittsburgh, Duquesne University Press, 1967, 7-33, 34-60.

126. *Husserl and Wittgenstein on Language*, in "Phenomenology and Existentialism" edited by E. N. LEE and M. MANDELBAUM, Baltimore, The Johns Hopkins University Press, 1967, 207-217.

127. *The Unity of the Voluntary and the Involuntary as a Limiting Idea*, in "Readings in Existential Phenomenology" edited by N. LAWRENCE and D. O'CONNOR, Englewood Cliffs (New Jersey), Prentice Hall, 1967, 93-112. English translation of no. 12.

128. *The Antinomy of Human Reality and the Problem of Philosophical Anthropology*, in "Readings in Existential Phenomenology" edited by N. LAWRENCE and D. O'CONNOR, Englewood Cliffs (New Jersey), Prentice Hall, 1967, 390-402. English translation of no. 80.

129. *Langage religieux. Mythe et symbole*, in "Le langage. II. Langages. (Actes du XIIIe Congrès des Sociétés de philosophie de langue française, 1966)" Neuchâtel, La Baconière, 1967, 129-145.

130. *Interprétation du mythe de la peine*, in "Archivio di Filosofia (Il mito della pena, Rome 1967)" 37 (1967), no. 2-3, 23-42. English translation in CI.

131. *La structure, le mot, l'événement*, in "Esprit (Structuralisme. Idéologie et méthode)" 35 (1967), May, 801-821. English translation by no. 144 and in CI.

132. *Violence et langage*, in "Recherches et Débats" 16 (1967), no. 59, 86-94. English translation in PSE.

133. *Urbanization et sécularization*, in "Christianisme social" 76 (1967), no. 5-8, 327-341. English translation in PSE.

134. *New Developments in Phenomenology in France: the Phenomenology of Language*, in "Social Research" 34 (1967), no. 1, 1-30. Reprinted in CI.

1968

135. RICOEUR P. and MARCEL G., *Entretiens Paul Ricoeur-Gabriel Marcel* (Présence et pensée), Paris, Aubier, 1968, 131 p. English translation by no. 184.

136. *Liberté: responsabilité et décision*, in "Actes du XIVe Congrès International de Philosophie" Vienna, Herder, 1968, 155-165.

137. *L'art et la systématique freudienne*, in "Entretiens sur l'art et la psychoanalyse (Décades du Centre culturel international de Cérisy-la-

Salle)" directed by A. BERGE, A. CLANCIER, P. RICOEUR et L. H. RUBINSTEIN, Paris-The Hague, Mouton, 1967, 24-36. English translation in CI.

138. *Aliénation*, in "Encyclopaedia universalis. I" Paris, Encyclopaedia Universalis France, 1968, 660-664.

139. *The Critique of Subjectivity and Cogito in the Philosophy of Heidegger*, in "Heidegger and the Quest for Truth" edited by M. S. FRINGS, Chicago, Quandrangle Books, 1968, 62-75. Reprinted in CI.

140. *Tasks of the Ecclesial Community in the Modern World*, in "Theology of Renewal. II. Renewal of Religious Structures" edited by L. K. SHOOK, New York, Herder and Herder, 1968, 242-254.

141. BULTMANN R., *Jésus. Mythologie et Démythologisation*. Preface by P. RICOEUR, Paris, Seuil, 1968, 9-27. English translation of the preface in CI.

142. *Approche philosophique du concept de liberté religieuse*, in "Archivio di Filosofia (L'ermeneutica della libertà religiosa)" 38 (1968), no. 2-3, 215-234. English translation in CI.

143. *Réforme et révolution dans l'Université*, in "Esprit (mai 68)" 36 (1968), June-July, 987-1002.

144. *Structure-Word-Event*, in "Philosophy Today" 12 (1968), no. 2/4, 114-129. English translation of no. 131. Reprinted in CI.

145. *The Father Image. From Phantasy to Symbol*, in "Criterion" (1968-1969), no. 1, 1-7. Reprinted in CI.

1969

146. *Le conflict des interprétations. Essais d'herméneutique* (L'ordre philosophique), Paris, Seuil, 1969, 506 p. English translation by no. 198.

147. *The Symbolism of Evil* (Religious Perspectives). Translation of *La symbolique du mal* by E. BUCHANAN, Boston, Beacon Press, 1969, 357 p. [paperback]. English translation of no. 75.

148. *Philosophie et langage*, in "Contemporary Philosophy. A Survey. III. Metaphysics, Phenomenology, Language and Structure" edited by R. KLIBANSKY, Firenze, La Nuova Italia Editrice, 1969, 272-295.

149. *Le philosophe et la politique devant la question de la liberté*, in "La liberté et l'ordre social (Rencontres internationales de Genève 1969)" Neuchâtel, La Baconnière, 1969. 41-65.

150. *Prospective du monde et perspective chrétienne*, in "L'Eglise vers l'avenir" Paris, Cerf, 1969, 127-146.

151. *Pour une prédication au monde*, in "L'Eglise vers l'avenir" Paris, Cerf, 1969, 147-156.

152. *Croyance*, in "Encyclopaedia universalis. V." Paris, Encyclopaedia Universalis France, 1969, 171-176.

153. *The Problem of the Double-sense as Hermeneutic Problem and as Semantic Problem*, in "Myths and Symbols. Studies in Honor of Mircea Eliade" edited by J. M. KITIGAWA and CH. H. LONG, Chicago-London, University of Chicago Press, 1969, 63-79. English translation of no. 116 and reprinted in CI.

154. *Religion, Atheism, and Faith*, in "The Religious Significance of Atheism"

edited by A. MACINTYRE and P. RICOEUR, New York-London, Columbia University Press, 58-98. Reprinted in CI.

155. *Guilt, Ethics and Religion*, in "Talk of God (Royal Institute of Philosophy Lectures. II. 1967-1968)" London-Melbourne-Toronto-New York, Macmillan-St. Martin's Press, 1969, 100-117. Reprinted in CI.

156. NABERT J., *Elements for an Ethic* (Northwestern University Studies in Phenomenology and Existential Philosophy). Translation of *Eléments pour une éthique* by W. J. PETREK and prefaced by P. RICOEUR, Evanston (Illinois), Northwestern University Press, 1969, XVII-XXVIII.

157. *La paternité: du fantasme au symbole*, in "Archivio di Filosofia (L'analisi del linguaggio teologico. Il nome di Dio, Rome 1969)" 39 (1969), no. 2-3, 221-246. English translation in CI.

1970

158. *Freud and Philosophy. An Essay on Interpretation*. Translation of *De l'interprétation* by D. SAVAGE, New Haven-London, Yale University Press, 1970, 573 p. English translation of no. 103.

159. *Psychanalyse et culture*, in "Critique sociologique et critique psychanalytique (Etudes de sociologie de la littérature)" Brussels, Editions de l'Institut de Sociologie' 1970, 179-185.

160. *Qu'est-ce qu'un texte? Expliquer et Comprendre*, in "Hermeneutik und Dialektik. Aufsätze II. Sprache und Logik. Theorie der Auslegung und Probleme der Einzelwissenschaften" edited by R. BUBNER, K. CRAMER and R. WIEHL, Tübingen, J. C. B. Mohr, 1970, 181-200. English translation by no. 173.

161. *The Problem of Will and Philosophical Discourse*, in "Patterns of Life-World" edited by J. M. EDIE, F. H. PARKER and C. O. SCHRAG, Evanston, Northwestern University Press, 1970.

162. *Hope and the Structure of Philosophical Systems*, in "Proceedings of the American Catholic Philosophical Association (San Francisco) (Philosophy and Christian Theology)" edited by G. P. McLEAN and P. DOUGHERTY, Washington, The Catholic University of America, 1970, 55-69.

163. *Guilt, Ethics and Religion*, in "Concilium (Moral Evil under Challenge)" 1970, no. 56, 11-27. Reprint of no. 155.

1971

164. *Langage (Philosophie)*, in "Encyclopaedia universalis. IX." Paris, Encyclopaedia Universalis France, 1971, 771-781.

165. *Liberté*, in "Encyclopaedia universalis. IX." Paris, Encyclopaedia Universalis France, 1971, 979-985. English translation by no. 217.

166. *Mythe 3. L'interprétation philosophique*, in "Encyclopaedia universalis. XI." Encyclopaedia Universalis France, 1971, 530-537.

167. *Du conflict à la convergence des méthodes en exégèse biblique*, in Exégèse et herméneutique (Parole de Dieu)" Paris, Seuil, 1971, 35-53.

168. *Sur l'exégèse de Genèse 1, 1-2, 4a*, in "Exégèse et herméneutique (Parole de Dieu)" Paris, Seuil, 1971, 67-84.

169. *Esquisse de conclusion*, in "Exégèse et herméneutique (Parole de Dieu)" Paris, Seuil, 1971, 285-295.

170. *Contribution d'une réflexion sur le langage à une théologie de la parole*, in "Exégèse et herméneutique (Parole de Dieu)" Paris, Seuil, 1971, 301-319.

171. *Le Philosophe*, in "Bilan de la France 1954-1970 (Colloque de l'Association de la presse étrangère)" Paris, Plon, 1971, 47-59.

172. *L'avenir de l'université*, in "L'enseignement supérieur: Bilans et prospective" Montréal, Les Presses de l'Université de Montréal, 1971, 61-78.

173. *What is a Text? Explanation and Interpretation*, in "Mythic-Symbolic Language and Philosophical Anthropology" by D. M. RASMUSSEN, The Hague, M. Nijhoff, 1971, 135-150. English translation of no. 160.

174. *The Symbol Gives Rise to Thought*, in "Literature and Religion (Forum Books)" edited by G. B. GUNN, London, SCM Press, 1971, 211-220. Slightly abbreviated version of the conclusion of book no. 123.

175. IHDE D., *Hermeneutic Phenomenology. The Philosophy of Paul Ricoeur* (Studies in Phenomenology and Existential Philosophy). Preface by P. RICOEUR, Evanston (Illinois), Northwestern University Press, 1971, XX-192 p.

176. *Evénement et sens*, in "Archivio de Filosofia (Rivelatione e Storia, Rome 1971)" 41 (1971), no. 2, 15-34.

177. *The Model of the Text: Meaningful Action Considered as a Text*, in "Social Research" 38 (1971), no. 3, 529-562. Reproduced by no. 188.

178. *From Existentialism to the Philosophy of Language*, in "Criterion" 10 (1971), Spring, 14-18.

1972

179. *Ontologie*, in "Encyclopaedia universalis. XII." Paris, Encyclopaedia Universalis France, 1972, 94-102.

180. *Signe et sens*, in "Encyclopaedia universalis. XIV." Paris, Encyclopaedia Universalis France, 1972, 100, 1011-1015.

181. *Remarques sur la Communication de Karl Löwith*, in "Truth and Historicity. Vérité et historicité (Entretiens de Heidelberg 1969)" edited by H.-G. GADAMER, The Hague, M. Nijhoff, 1972, 22-28.

182. *L'herméneutique du témoignage*, in "Archivio de Filosofia (La Testimonianza, Rome 1972)" 42 (1972), no. 1-2, 35-61.

183. *La métaphore et le problème central de l'herméneutique* [followed by a summary]. in "Revue philosophique de Louvain" 70 (1972), February, 93-112, 115. English translation by no. 197 and no. 206.

1973

184. MARCEL G. and RICOEUR P., *Tragic Wisdom and Beyond. Including Conversations between Paul Ricoeur and Gabriel Marcel* (Studies in Phenomenology and Existential Philosophy). Translation of *Pour une sagesse tragique* by G. MARCEL and of *Entretiens Paul Ricoeur-Gabriel Marcel* by ST. JOLIN and P. McCORMICK, Evanston (Illinois), Northwestern University Press, 1973, XXIX-256 p. English translation of no. 135.

185. *Discours et communication*, in "La communication (Actes du XVe Congrès des Sociétés de Philosophie de langue française 1971) II" Montréal, Montmorency, 1973, 23-48.

186. *Volonté*, in "Encyclopaedia universalis. XVI." Paris, Encyclopaedia Universalis France, 1973, 943-948.

187. *Herméneutique et critique des idéologies*, in "Archivio di Filosofia (Demitizzazione e ideologia, Rome 1973)" 43 (1973), no. 2-3, 25-61.

188. *Human Sciences and Hermeneutical Method: Meaningful Action Considered as a Text*, in "Explorations in Phenomenology (Selected Studies in Phenomenology and Existential Philosophy)" edited by D. CARR and E. S. CASEY, The Hague, M. Nijhoff, 1973, 13-46. Reproduced in "New Literary History" 5 (1973), 91-117 and reprint of no. 177.

189. *A Philosophical Journey. From Existentialism to the Philosophy of Language*, in "Philosophy Today" 17 (1973), Summer, 88-96.

190. *Creativity in Language. Word, Polysemy, Metaphor*, in "Philosophy Today" 17 (1973), Summer, 97-11.

191. *The Task of Hermeneutics*, in "Philosophy Today" 17 (1973), Summer, 112-128. English translation of no. 210.

192. *The Hermeneutical Function of Distanciation*, in "Philosophy Today" 17 (1973), Summer, 129-141. English translation of no. 211.

193. *The Tasks of the Political Educator*, in "Philosophy Today" 17 (1973), Summer, 142-152. English translation of no. 109. Reprinted in PSE.

194. *Ethics and Culture. Habermas and Gadamer in Dialogue*, in "Philosophy Today" 17 (1973), Summer, 153-165. Reprinted in PSE.

195. *A Critique of B. F. Skinner's Beyond Freedom and Dignity*, in "Philosophy Today" 17 (1973), Summer, 166-175. Reprinted in PSE.

196. *Critique of Religion and the Language of Faith*, in "Union Seminary Quarterly Review" 28 (1973), Spring, 203-224.

197. *Metaphor and the Central Problem of Hermeneutics*, in "Graduate Faculty Philosophical Journal (New School for Social Research)" 3 (1973), no. 1; 42-58. English translation—with notes and commentary of article no. 183. Reproduced by no. 206.

                                    1974

198. *The Conflict of Interpretations: Essays in Hermeneutics* (Northwestern University Studies in Phenomenology and Existential Philosophy). Translation of *Le conflit des interprétations* edited with an introduction by DON IHDE, Evanston (Illinois), Northwestern University Press, 1974, XXV-512 p. Abbreviation: CI, English translation of no. 146.

199. *Political and Social Essays*. Translation of several essays prefaced by P. RICOEUR and introduced by the editors D. STEWART and J. BIEN, Athens, Ohio University Press, 1974, IX-293 p. Abbreviation: PSE.

200. *Science et idéologie* [followed by a summary], in "Revue philosophique de Louvain (Vérité et Praxis)" 72 (1974), May, 329-355, 355-356.

201. *Manifestation et Proclamation*, in "Archivio de Filosofia (Il Sacro. Studie e Richerche, Rome 1974)" 44 (1974), no. 2-3, 57-76.

202. *Hegel aujourd'hui*, in "Etudes théologiques et religieuses" 49 (1974), no. 3, 335-355.

203. *Conclusions* [of the colloquium], in "Vérité et vérification. Wahrheit und Verification (Actes du quatrième Colloque international de Phénoménologie, Schwabisch Hall, 1969)" The Hague, M. Nijhoff, 1974, 190-209.

204. *Phénoménologie et herméneutique*, in "Man and World" 7 (1974), no. 3, 223-253. Reprint by no. 213 and partial English translation by no. 224.

205. *Philosophy and Religious Language*, in "The Journal of Religion" 54 (1974), no. 3, 71-85. French text by no. 220.

206. *Metaphor and the Main Problem of Hermeneutics*, in "New Literary History (On Metaphor)" 6 (1974), no. 1, 95-110. English translation of no. 183 and reprint of 197.

207. *Listening To The Parables. Once More Astonished. Text: Matthew 13:31-32 and 45-46* [Sermon], in "Criterion" 13 (1974), Spring, 18-22. Reproduced by no. 226.

208. *Phenomenology*, in "The Southwestern Journal of Philosophy (Husserl Issue)" 5 (1974), no. 3, 149-168. English translation of no. 32.

1975

209. *La Métaphore vive* (L'ordre philosophique), Paris, Seuil, 1975, 414 p.

210. *La tâche de l'herméneutique*, in "Exegesis. Problèmes de méthode et exercices de lecture" edited by F. BOVON and G. ROUILLER, Neuchâtel, Delachaux et Niestlé, 1975, 179-200. French version of no. 191.

211. *La fonction herméneutique de la distanciation*, in "Exegesis. Problèmes de méthode et exercices de lecture" edited by F. BOVON and G. ROUILLER, Neuchâtel, Delachaux et Niestlé, 1975, 201-215. French text of no. 192.

212. *Herméneutique philosophique et herméneutique biblique*, in "Exegesis. Problèmes de méthode et exercices de lecture" edited by F. BOVON and G. ROUILLER, Neuchâtel, Delachaux et Niestlé, 1975, 216-228. English translation by 225.

213. *Phénoménologie et herméneutique* [with a German summary], in "Phänomenologie Heute. Grundlagen- und Methodenprobleme (Phänomenologische Forschungen. Phenomenological Studies)" Freiburg-Munich, Verlag Karl Alber, 1975, 31-75, 76-77. French reprint of no. 204 and English translation by no. 224.

214. *Au carrefour des cultures. Les cultures et le temps. Etudes préparées pour l'UNESCO* (Bibliothèque scientifique). Introduction by P. RICOEUR, Paris, Payot/UNESCO, 1975. 19-41.

215. *Le "lieu" de la dialectique*, in "Dialectics" edited by CH. PERELMAN, The Hague, M. Nijhoff, 1975, 92-108.

216. *Analogie et intersubjectivité chez Husserl*, in "Enige facetten over opvoeding en onderwijs (Festschrift Stephan Strasser)" Den Bosch, Malmberg, 1975, 163-169.

217. *Phenomenology of Freedom*, in "Phenomenology and Philosophical Understanding" edited by E. PIVCEVIC, Cambridge, University Press, 1975, 173-194. English translation of no. 165.

218. *Objectivation et Aliénation dans l'expérience historique*, in "Archivio di Filosofia (Temporalità et alienazione, Rome 1975)" 45 (1975), no. 2-3, 27-38.

219. *Parole et symbole*, in "Revue des sciences religieuses" 49 (1975), no. 1-2, 142-161.

220. *La philosophie et la spécificité du langage religieux*, in "Revue d'histoire et de philosophie religieuses" 55 (1975), no. 2, 13-26. French text of no. 205.

221. *Le probleme du fondement de la morale*, in "Sapienza (Problema della fondzione della morale)" 28 (1975), no. 3, 313-337.

222. *Le Dieu crucifié de Jürgen Moltmann*, in "Les quatres fleuves. Cahiers de recherche et de réflexion religieuses (Le Christ, visage de Dieu)" 1975, no. 4, 109-114.

223. *Biblical Hermeneutics: the Parables of Jesus*, in "Semeia. An experimental Journal for Biblical Criticism" 1975, no. 4, 27-148.

224. *Phenomenology and Hermeneutics*, in "Nous" 9 (1975), no. 1, 85-102. Partial English translation of no. 204 and no. 213.

225. *Philosophical Hermeneutics and Theological Hermeneutics*, in "Studies in Religion. Sciences religieuses" 5 (1975), no. 1, 14-33. English translation of no. 212.

226. *Listening to the Parables. Once More Astonished. Text: Matthew 13: 31-32 and 45-46* [sermon], in "Christianity and Crisis" 34 (1975), January, 304-308. Reprint of no. 207.

227. *Puissance de la parole: science et poésie*, in "La philosophie et les savoirs (L'Univers de la Philosophie)" Montreal-Paris-Tournai, Bellarmin-Desclée, 1975, 159-177.

1976

228. GADAMER H.-G. *Vérité et méthode. Les grandes lignes d'une herméneutique philosophique* (L'ordre philosophique). Translation of *Wahrheit und Methode* by E. SACRE et P. RICOEUR, Paris, Seuil, 1976, 346 p.

229. *L'imagination dans le discours et dans l'action*, in "Savoir, faire, espérer: les limites de la raison. I. (Publications des Facultés Universitaires Saint-Louis)" Brussels, Facultés Universitaires Saint-Louis, 1976, 207-228.

230. *Entre Gabriel Marcel et Jean Wahl*, in "Jean Wahl et Gabriel Marcel (Bibliothèque des Archives de Philosophie)" presented by J. HERSCH, Paris, Beauchesne, 1976, 57-87.

231. *Gabriel Marcel et la phénoménologie* [exposition followed by a discussion], in "Entretiens autour de Gabriel Marcel (Langages) (Colloque Cerisy-la-Salle, 1973)" Neuchâtel, La Baconnière, 1976, 53-74, 75-95.

232. *L'herméneutique de la sécularisation. Foi, Idéologie, Utopie*, in "Archivio di Filosofia (Ermeneutica della Secolarizzazione, Rome 1976)" 46 (1976), no. 2-3, 49-68.

233. *Psychoanalysis and the Work of Art*, in "Psychiatry and the Humanities. I." edited by J. H. SMITH, New Haven, Yale University Press, 1976.

234. *Interpretation Theory: Discourse and the Surplus of Meaning*, Foth Worth, The Texas Christian University Press, 1976, 107 p.